The BELL
and the RIVER

January 1, 2006

This is the third printing of The Bell and the River, and it gives me great pleasure that the Washington/Montana Region of The Providence System is sponsoring this 150th anniversary edition in honor of the arrival of the Sisters of Providence in the West.

As Sister Barbara Schamber wrote in the introduction of the 1986 edition, "Mother Joseph was a woman of faith and of compassion reliant always on the Providence of God to guide her in servings others. Today the faith and vision of Mothered Joseph lives on in the works she established in the West as Sisters of Providence and their lay collaborators continue to bring a mission of healing the sick education and caring for children and protecting the homeless. Her life and spirit are an inspiration to all of us."

As we read this history, let us be reminded of the legacy that has been left to us by Mother Joseph and the other pioneer Sisters of Providence. Let us be as courageous and determined to bring about the social good that will transform our communities as Mother Joseph so bravely demonstrated. Let us never get discouraged with the barriers set before us. Let our faith and hope in God be strong.

John V. Fletcher

John Fletcher, Chief Executive
Washington/Montana Region
Providence Health and Services

Mother Joseph of the Sacred Heart

The BELL
and the RIVER

By Sister Mary of the
Blessed Sacrament McCrosson

In collaboration with
Sister Mary Leopoldine
and
Sister Maria Theresa

NIHIL OBSTAT
Joannes McCorkle, S.S.
Censor Librorum

IMPRIMATUR
Thomas A. Connolly, D.D., J.C.D.
✠ Archiepiscopus Seattlensis

DECEMBER 7, 1956
SEPTEMBER 30, 1986
JANUARY 6, 2006

Foreword

The Sisters of Charity of Providence, Servants of the Poor, have published this biography of Mother Joseph of the Sacred Heart, to commemorate the, centennial observance of the establishment Of their first Mission in the Northwest. Indeed, they have every reason to memorialize that historic and auspicious event. For this year of jubilee marks a century of unselfish, personal and devoted service to the infirm, the poor, the aged and the children of this entire region.

It is an interesting and engaging narrative for it constitutes a record of the courageous and completely successful efforts of a small band of Religious, three Sisters and two Postulants, to extend the frontiers of the Kingdom of Christ and to pioneer the spiritual and corporal works of mercy in a veritable wilderness. It is a valuable contribution to the history of this favored portion of the Master's Vineyard because it affords the reader the opportunity of studying in detail the somewhat bewildering panorama of events connected with the gradual settlement and development of the wild and rugged Oregon Territory of one hundred years ago.

When Mother Joseph and her companions arrived in Vancouver, Washington, on December 8, 1856, after a perilous journey from the Motherhouse in Montreal by sea and across the Isthmus of Panama, the Diocese of Nesqually (Seattle) had been in operation for six years. Under ordinary, circumstances a diocese is erected to promote a more direct and efficient administration of the Church's temporalities and to encourage and advance the propagation of the faith and the cause of religion in a given area. A diocese, properly speaking, consists of a number of established parishes and ecclesiastical institutions, staffed by priests and religious, and' has from its" beginning a certain recognizable stability that forecasts some appreciable growth and continued development. In the formation of the Diocese of Nesqually, however, the reverse was true. When Bishop Augustine Blanchet took possession of his newly established diocese, he had few priests, no religious and, apart from the small settlements at Vancouver, Nesqually, Cowlitz and Whidbey Island, cities, towns and even hamlets were practically nonexistent.

This was the scene that greeted these valiant and intrepid missionaries when they arrived at the small settlement that was to be the base of Mother Joseph's charitable operations for almost a half century. A woman of indefatigable zeal and indomitable courage and energy, Mother Joseph immediately set about her task of founding an asylum for the poor and a school for children. Within the short space of a few years, she and her companions were operating a boarding and day school, a lunatic asylum, a hospital, and separate orphanages for boys and girls together with, a small home for the aged and chronically infirm.

That no work of religion or charity was foreign to the Sisters of Charity of Providence is evident almost from the earliest years of their foundation. It is openly manifested in the life of Mother Joseph and her many accomplishments in the face of tremendous and frightening odds. A cold recital of facts and figures enumerating the increase in institutions under her energetic and resourceful leadership would tell little of the sacrifices, struggles, disappointments and hardships that went into, their establishment. She led a life of complete dedication to her apostolate. Despite the fact that she was a perfectionist and that she possessed a certain intolerance of the weakness of others, her first concern was for the comfort and the wellbeing of her companions.

The growth of the Community kept pace with the rapidly expanding fields of its labors and the fact that these works of Charity and education which she inaugurated not only survived but prospered, is proof of the enduring influence of this consecrated woman who valued charity above all, things. Through them one can easily trace the noble heritage of the Sisters of

Charity of Providence back to their saintly Foundress, Mother Gamelin, whose life was fashioned and directed by God to bring comfort, consolation and knowledge to the infirm, the poor and the unlettered. The spirit which inspired Mother Joseph and her vigorous and purposeful Community of a century ago still lives on in the quiet lives of the Sisters of Charity of Providence who are conducting our hospitals and schools and homes for the aged.

It is all beautifully and accurately set down in these pages by the co-authors who have approached the subject with a willing, albeit, sympathetic understanding. It is an interesting and fascinating, tale in which the Hand of God is apparent on every page.

Most Reverend Thomas A. Connolly
Archbishop of Seattle

December, 1956

Introduction

"On January 24, 1848, three men walked toward the discharging tailrace of the Sutter sawmill on the American fork of the Sacramento River. Charles Bennett suddenly stopped, picked a small object from the water at a depth of a few inches . . . and handed it to Sawmill Superintendent James W. Marshall, remarking simply, 'I calculate this is gold. . . .' "

"Gold was first found on Thompson River (tributary of the Fraser) by an Indian, in 1857, a quarter of a mile below Nicomen. The Indian was taking a drink out of the river and having no vessel he was quaffing from the stream, when he perceived a shining pebble, which he picked up, and it proved to be gold. . . ."

The coming of five Sisters of Charity of Providence to the Oregon Country of 1856 was a modest incident in the latter years of a tumultuous decade in the region's early history. Ile first effect of the California gold discovery had been to reduce the manpower of the new Oregon Territory—which reached from Vancouver Island Colony to California and from the North Pacific coast to South Pass in the Rocky Mountains. Hundreds of cabins in clearings of new farms were left empty; trappers, traders, boatmen and laborers quit the forces of the ruling Hudson's Bay Company; sailors abandoned ships, soldiers deserted the new U. S. Army command at Fort Vancouver; and in the settlements pioneering young business men shut up shop and sailed in pursuit of fortune.

The Spanish-American dream of a "Kingdom of Quivira," a realm of fabulous wealth, had come true in California. Gold was king there. The simple fact was a royal call that rang around the world.

By 1850 California had a population of a hundred thousand and more. Shelter was at a premium in the gold-rush port of

San Francisco. Oregon lumber sold at the dock for as much as $500 per thousand board feet. Repeated fires swept the flimsy structures of the booming city. Many ships that arrived from around the Horn and from Panama sailed on to Puget Sound and the Columbia River for cargos of lumber. At the end of 1853 there were fourteen new saw-mills at work around Puget Sound, and as many more on the banks of the Columbia, making lumber for the California market.

The Fraser River gold discoveries of 1857-1859 brought a hundred thousand into the Northwest, and then gold rushes up the Clearwater to the Bitter Roots and eastward on the Lewis and Clark trails of 1804-1806 caused the division of Washington Territory-itself hewn from Oregon Territory in 1853–into the Territories of Idaho and Montana.

At the end of the 1850s Captain John Mullan of the U.S. Army Engineers built a freighting road from the head of navigation on the Columbia River to the head of navigation on the Missouri. At the same time Sir James Douglas, Governor of the Colonies of Vancouver Island and British Columbia, completed a road up the Fraser River.

The United States Army, with headquarters at Fort Vancouver fought and labored through the 1850s to "pacify" the freedomloving Indian tribes of the Northwest, and to confine them on reservations. In 1859 the Army reopened the country east of the Cascade Mountains to agricultural settlement.

Other governmental and economic forces were powerfully at work in California and the Northwest territories during the 1850s. Pacific commerce was given magnificent new opportunities through the trade treaty that was negotiated with Japan in February, 1854, by Yankee Commodore Matthew Calbraith Perry.

The next year saw the conclusion of the Crimean War. A new promise of European peace dawned in the Treaty of Paris, agreed to in March 1856. This peace held forth fresh hope for extension of the Roman Catholic missions in the Northwest wilderness-the Prince Rupert Land of Canada and the Louisiana Purchase and Oregon Country of the United States. The source of the hope was in two hundred years of history.

Priests had toiled westward with the *voyageurs* and hunters of the fur trade–with the French, the Scots and the Iroquois of the Montreal *Companie du Nord* and the French and English of the Hudson's Bay Company (of which Pierre Esprit Radisson and Medart Chouart, sieur des Groseilliers, were the frontier founders).

John Greenleaf Whittier, the Quaker poet, came to write his immensely popular ballad, "The Red River Voyageur," singing in this spirit of the Canadain frontier:

"The *voyageur* smiles as he listens
To the sound that grows apace;
Well he knows the vesper ringing
    of the bells of St. Boniface.

"The bells -of the Roman mission,
That call from their turrets twain,
To the boatmen on the river,
To the hunter on the plain.

"Even so in our mortal journey
The bitter north winds blow,
And thus upon life's Red River
Our hearts, as oarsmen, row. . . "

This spirit and its lesson, were essentials of continued life and growth for the individual, the family and the community in all areas of settlement throughout the Pacific Northwest-the old Oregon Country. The faithful of France and Belgium gave this work continuing financial support.

Sir George Simpson, Dr. John McLoughlin, Sir James Douglas, and other principals of the Hudson's Bay Company who dictated the early governing policies of white settlement and enterprise in Western Canada and the Oregon Country, were vitally awake to the essentiality of Christian values, practices, teaching and service in the whole development of civilization in the region. Simpson, McLoughlin and Douglas, like the pietistic David Thompson who preceded them in command of the Columbia River District, prohibited the use of whiskey as trade goods with the Indians. It was the business judgment of these frontier chieftans, as well as their moral convictions, that called for the offices and the works of the Christian Church in behalf of the family and the community at each post of the Northwest fur trade. So, from 1838 onward, the Hudson's Bay Company fostered the work of the Roman Catholic Church at Forts Vancouver, Walla Walla, Nesqually and Victoria, and in the territory south of the Columbia. The Company's hospitality was equally extended to Protestant missionaries.,

Priests had sailed from Mexico with the Captains Perez, Heceta and Quadra in 1774-1775, up the North Pacific coast, to the discovery of Nootka Sound on the western shore of today's Vancouver Island.

Sir George Simpson made visits to California before it was possessed by the United States. His views of the missionaries who were continuing the labors of Junipero Serra and his fellow Franciscan priests of 1770, agreed with the observations of the great botanical explorer of the North Pacific, David Douglas. Douglas wrote of his own California visit in a letter dated October 26, 1832, to Joseph Sabine of the Royal Horticultural Society of London:

"I lived almost exclusively with the fathers who without exception afforded me the most essential assistance, hospitality to excess, with a thousand little courtesies which we feel and cannot express. I had no bickerings . . . no attempts at conversion or the like . . . indeed so much to the contrary, that on no occasion was an uncharitable word directed to me. When there I was under no restraint; my time was entirely my own, feast day and fast day, all the same, the good men of God gave me always a good bed, and plenty to eat and drink of the best of the land. A more upright and highly honorable class of men I never knew. They are well educated. I had no difficulty from the beginning with them, for saving one or two exceptions, they all talk Latin fluently, and though there be a great difference in pronunciation between one from Auld Reekie, and (one from) Madrid, yet it gave us little trouble. They know and love the sciences too well to think it curious to see one go so far in quest of grass. . . ."

This spirit prevailed in the country to the north as French Canadian priests began their Oregon work in 1838, while joint occupation of the region by the Americans and the British was still in effect. When the treaty of 1846 awarded the United States possession of the Oregon Country areas between California and the 49th northern degree of latitude, there was no diminishing of the good will of the vast majority of Americans in their new territory for the priests from Montreal and Red River. All families of American, British and French origins alike, Catholic and Protestant together were unified by the over-all need for schools, hospitals, and other institutions of the kind that were essential to civilized community growth.

The more populous Columbia River, Willamette Valley and Puget Sound regions prospered with California trade after 1848, due mostly to demand for lumber, shingles, piling, and salt salmon, potatoes and flour. California gold installed new sawmills and fisheries and ships, and, with these industries, new towns. Families built homes. More babies were born, month by month. So there was more sickness, too in all seasons, despite the healthful climate. There were injuries-too many of them maiming the victims for life because no skilled surgical service and nursing care were available.

There were old people without relatives or homes who lived on and on, even after they were unable to apply their hands and bodies to useful work. They needed a common refuge and dwelling place. There were the hopelessly ill-consumptives and helpless victims of other diseases that were incurable in those days. Mental illness was in this category. It called for asylums. And then the cry of orphaned children was heard in the new Christian communities, counties, and territories-the new Northwest Corner territories of the United States and the new Southwest Corner of the coming Confederation of Canada, Vancouver Island Colony.

Five Montreal Sisters of Charity of Providence had waited, prayed and labored, preparing themselves through years for the call that eventually brought them from the St. Lawrence to the Columbia, all in the spirit of these lines:

> "'Whoever thou art whose need is great
> In the name of God, the Compassionate
> And   Merciful One, for thee I wait. . . .'"

Indian attacks on the Oregon Trail emigration and its stations came to a tragic climax in the Whitman Massacre of November, 1847. The Indian uprisings continued, even after the arrival of U. S. Army forces in the region.

It was a bad time for all in the Oregon Country. Early in 1857 a financial depression blanketed both Canada and the United States. Many of the jobless and bankrupt struck out for the Fraser-then for Idaho and Montana, as gold finds there sent aloft another magnetic pole of romance and adventure. Many of the young men in the new tide of Northwest immigration arrived in hunger and need. Many more left the gold fields in poverty and despair. They asked for jobs of plain labor and "took up" land claims. A notable example was Samuel Benn, founder of Aberdeen, or Grays Harbor. Thousands were added to the populations of the established sawmill settlements.

In 1850 the population of all Oregon Territory was numbered at 13,294. The Census listed twenty-nine "denominational" and other private schools and three public schools. By 1860 the settled population of the region (divided into two territories) numbered 64,059. In 1870 the population figure had doubled, and by 1880 it had grown to 270,673.

Public education grew slowly and painfully through these years of political change, economic development and social adjustments. Medical service and nursing care evolved even more slowly from its frontier condition of makeshift infirmary and casual surgeon. It was not until November 4, 1861, that a permanent public school system was opened in Seattle. This was in the new territorial "university" building, with one college student and thirty pupils of the lower grades. The young president of the university, Asa Shinn Mercer, resigned his post to make two voyages to the East Coast, in the midst of the Civil War, to recruit single young ladies of good education to teach school-and mayhap to marry-in the sawmill village of Seattle. So the romantic history of "the Mercer Girls" began. Eleven came to the Northwest on the first voyage, forty-six on the second.. All but one married fine young men.

The need was great indeed for schools. The need for care of the forlorn aged, the poor, the widow, the orphan, the sick and the forlorn aged, the poor, the widow, the orphan, the sick and the maimed, was increasing everywhere-and in every place "the need was great." And the appeals came in greater strength, year after year, to the Sisters of Charity of Providence at Vancouver. They were prepared to respond, first at Fort Vancouver itself, then at Portland, Seattle, Spokane, Yakima, and other seedbeds of Christian civilization in the vast wilderness in the Pacific Northwest.

The response was magnificent, it endures, and it increases. Therefore, the story that is told in this book is a vital and glorious chapter of the whole history of the Pacific Northwest.

JAMES STEVENS

Acknowledgments

Saying "Thank You" is always a pleasure and a privilege; but in presenting "The Bell and the River," I feel that this is a special occasion. However, had it not been for the magnanimous unselfishness and superb cooperation of the friends of Sister Mary of the Blessed Sacrament, it would have been impossible for this biography of Mother Joseph of the Sacred Heart to be completed.

The very sudden death of Sister Mary of the Blessed Sacrament seemed unfortunate. Eighteen' of the planned twenty-five chapters were written. Thanks to the capable generosity of Sister Maria Theresa who finished the work; to Mother Berenice, our gracious Superior General, for opening the archives of the Community to the authors; to the indefatigable efforts and almost interminable research of Sister Mary Leopoldine for collecting and assembling the data; to Sister Francis for hours of typing the manuscript; to Sister Catherine Mary for checking and re-checking the copies; to Sister Cecilia Mary who "carried on" for Sister Mary of the Blessed Sacrament and dedicated her labors to negotiations for publishing this volume; to Reverend Vincent Conway, S.J., Head of the History Department of the Seattle University; to Edith L. Bristol and Mrs. John Brooke of Portland, both of whom helped in countless ways in the early part of this work; to E. B. MacNaughton, chairman of the First National Bank of Portland, Oregon, who graciously made and gave the pencil sketch of Providence Academy for this book; to these and to many personal friends, I wish to voice the most sincere gratitude of all the Sisters of Charity of Providence, daughters of our Mother Joseph of the Sacred Heart.

MOTHER MARY PHILOTHEA, *Provincial Superior*
Province of the Sacred Heart
Seattle, Washington

CHAPTER 1

Athin, chill wind swirled grey November mists in the halflight of early morning, as the bishop's carriage led the way from the Providence Asile to the Saint Lambert ferry. High above the cobbled street the cross-surmounted dome was poised against the semi-darkness of the city. Behind the travelers lay the world they knew: Montreal, the Ville-Marie; Montreal, the city of churches; Montreal, the bastion of the faith, built two hundred years ago by their sturdy forefathers from Normandy and Brittany and Ile de France, and by that gallant chevalier, Paul de Chomedy, Sieur de Maisonneuve.

Before them lay the Saint Lawrence, and beyond the river that strange, indeterminate world over which they had yearned as the object of their Christian zeal, a world now suddenly monstrous and obscure in the morning fog and as frightening as the vast finality of death. While the little procession moved south and west toward the pier, a sense of bereavement as acute and engrossing as that accompanying the loss of a loved one possessed the thoughts of each of the new missionaries. Grief held them silent. The carriages rolled on to the waiting ferry in the cold dawn. All time seemed to be caught up and bound to the dark, unchanging current of the river, carrying them farther away and forever away from the ordered and pleasant land of their birth.

In the first carriage Augustine Magloire Alexander Blanchet, Bishop of Nisqually, sat erect and solemn near Father John B. Drapeau, the chaplain of the Longue Pointe Foundation. His

1

Lordship's face was a pale blue and his sturdy shoulders showed an unaccustomed tendency to slump, the result of his recent illness; but neither physical weakness nor fatigue was more than momentarily successful against the spirit of the apostle.

That the little company was thus setting out in late fall instead of in September was due to His Lordship's health. A year ago, in 1855, he had gone to Europe. What a grand tour that had been! Up and down the highways of the continent he had traveled, begging in Rome and Venice, in Vienna and Prague, in Munich and Ghent-begging for the very money being spent this day for himself and the nuns in the carriages behind him. He, Magloire, son of Pierre and Rosalie Blanchet, of Riviere-du-Sud, had knelt in the presence of the great pontiff, Piux IX, spiritual lord of the universal Church. He had described for the Pope his erstwhile Diocese of Walla Walla.

But even if there had been time, how does one man acquaint another with the changing reality of the Palouse country, its barren outcroppings of volcanic rock, softened by expanses of grey sage, suddenly dipping into rolling, green valleys, and as suddenly rising again to wooded uplands shadowed by blue mountains? How make him know the tribes who lived there, the Cayuses, the Chinooks, the Nez Percés, the Yakimas, with their varied traits and endowments?

Of his present diocese of Nisqually, with its see in the old Hudson's Bay fort of Vancouver on the Colum bia, more could have been said, though to speak of missions there was to use a figure of speech. There were no missions in reality, though there were missionaries now and had been since his brother Francis had gone there in 1838 by way of the Red River country. Since 1846 Francis Norbert Blanchet had been wearing the pallium as Archbishop of Oregon City, it was true; but as a vineyard of the Lord, Oregon City fared no better 'than Vancouver. What both sees needed was the establishment of institutions to give permanence and stability. This fact His Holiness had grasped easily. He had understood the urgency for more priests; he had seen, too, the need for sisters to aid them. Sisters would help by teaching the children and, aiding the unfortunate; they would above all give an example of the Christian virtues and of orderly living. Pius IX had been very kind and had listened with interest and sympathy, so that when he, Magloire, had knelt to kiss the Fisher man's Ring, he had the Pope's beneficent approval on his European begging tour.

In 1855 the Church in Europe was having its own struggle— not with the dark superstitions of the Klickitat nor the treachery, of the Wailatpu, nor the indolence of the Nez Percé; but with principalities and powers in high places who were quick to use the Church for their own aggrandizement, and with that noon-day devil which led rank-and-file Catholics to indifference, worldliness, and skepticism.

Here now on the ferry in the grey dawn, the Bishop of Nisqually felt some comfort as he remembered their Lordships of Austria that day last April when he had appealed to them for funds. At first he had thought them cold and uninterested. Before their studied brilliance and aloof splendor, he had been conscious of his own lowly Canadian origins and of his personal lack of suavity. Then suddenly he had sensed that they envied him his wilderness. There the attack on evil was forthright, and the weapons were the good, sound ones of faith, hope, and charity. But what did one use against an encroaching state which would bind the Church hand and foot to its own political and economic ambitions? How did one combat the lies and ribald insolence of an empty, atheistic intellectualism? How did one surmount selfishness and arrogance within the Church itself?

Well, bless God for the Oregon country! The Lords spiritual of the Church in Austria had contributed generously in money, but they had also made him realize the advantageous location of his apostolate. He had not minded the hardships of the subsequent months nor the toll which the sea voyage had exacted of him. It was sufficient that he had left Paris with enough money for the nuns and himself and young Father Louis Rossi.

The nuns . . . The Bishop of Nisqually thought of them now with satisfaction. That they were on the way at all was an achievement of no mean proportions. Every argument that human prudence could muster had been used to counter his request for nuns for the Oregon foundation. The Providence was still a young community, they said, having been founded only thirteen years earlier. The demands made on it had outrun its personnel, and there were those who whispered that Monseigneur Bourget had lost his senses in even considering the sisters for a savage country that had already swallowed up two groups of religious. Why send nuns so far away from Montreal when Montreal itself was clamoring for the ministrations of their healing hands?

The Bishop of Nisqually relaxed peacefully as he remembered the largeness of spirit of the man, Ignace Bourget, Bishop of Montreal. For him it was as if the critics had never existed, so intent was he on the care of souls in that vast land extending even to the distant Pacific, confided to Canada by the Holy See. In spite of a brace of over-cautious vicar-generals, Monseigneur had moved quickly to come to the aid of his brother bishop. If there were not Sisters of Providence available elsewhere then he would forego the services of those sisters who cared for his own Bishopric. That would release five sisters for the West and for Nisqually. If the other attempts at establishing sisters there had failed, that was due to the amplitude of God's design which wanted them in California and Chile, however much the shepherds in Oregon City and Vancouver had been grieved at their going.

The knife still turned in the heart of the Bishop of Nisqually as he remembered arriving in Vancouver in 1852 to find the sisters not there. He had gone to great pains and expense to arrange for the coming of the Sisters of Providence to his poor diocese. They had made the long, perilous journey. And then in a moment of confusion, all his precious plans had come to naught. He had been delayed in Mexico and his instructions had not been understood.

Unsure of the geography of the territory, the sisters had taken refuge in Oregon City with his brother and the Sisters of Notre-Dame-de-Namur. Then, beset by uncertainty, fear, and injudicious advice, they had left the Oregon country before he could make provision for them in Vancouver.

But though he felt himself to have been sorely tried, he knew that there is no finality in human affairs, and since the cause was good, he had proceeded doggedly to have recourse once more to the Sisters of Providence and their great-hearted founder, Bishop Ignace Bourget. Neither had failed him.

As the ferry shuddered and creaked to the south bank, he was jolted from his musing. The carriages moved up the incline, then through Longueuil and beyond, south-west to Saint Lambert. A wave of suppressed excitement carried the little group out of their carriages and toward the train which was waiting for them at the Saint Lambert station.

In the growing light of day, each person lost the anonymity with which the semi-darkness had clothed him. The clerics, Father Drapeau and young Father Rossi, walked sedately to the right and left of the bishop; the nuns eddied around Mother Caron, the Superior General, who with Sister Wilson was accompanying the five missionaries as far as New York. To add to the strangeness of the scene, the nuns were clad in secular garb, and were scarcely recognizable.

Among the five, neither the Bishop of Nisqually nor any other spectator would have had difficulty in singling out Sister Joseph, the lately named superior of the new Providence-to-be in Vancouver. She moved now with vigor and purpose toward the railway carriage, managing the progress of the whole group with dignity and dispatch.

Quietly each of her sisters was accounted for-Sister Praxedes of Providence, former superior of Saint John of God; Sister Blandine of the Holy Angels, her three-months-old vows resting seriously on her eighteen years; Sister Adelaide Theriault, postulant, with the willing, capable hands; Sister Mary Ellen Norton, postulant, the glow of her youthful beauty dimmed for the moment by the strain of the last hours of parting-and herself, no longer Sister Joseph, but now Sister Joseph of the Sacred Heart. The new name sounded through her thoughts like a summons and a benediction. Bishop Bourget, that venerable man of God, had renamed her with this title of predilection when he had laid on her the obedience of superior. Neither pleadings nor tears had been able to shake his decision that she should be the religious superior, the Sister Servant; so with the new name she bent her will to accept the burden he had confided to her, to her–Esther Pariseau that was.

A welter of baggage was stowed aboard from the wooden station platform, as the engine panted and wheezed in preparation. The passengers mounted the railway carriages and settled themselves into the meager comfort of the closely packed seats, grateful for the little current of warmth that touched their chilled bodies. The train gave a mighty lurch, then picked up momentum, and the little village passed before their eyes. The noise of the shrill whistle mingled with the solemn sound of church bells high in the twin towers of the parish church of Saint Lambert summoning the devout to Mass for All Souls.

To Sister Joseph the deep and somber tone of the bells recalled the words of this day's Epistle.

> The trumpet shall sound, and the dead shall rise incorruptible and we shall be changed. For this corruptible body must put on incorruption and this mortal body must put on immortality. . . .Death is swallowed up in victory! O Death, where is thy victory? O Death, where is thy sting?

The human sickness which had crowded her heart and benumbed her faculties shifted now with the remembrance. The cold misery which had gripped her spirit was eased. As dawn grew into the light of day, as the world outside the train took on familiar color and pattern, and the motion of the train became an accustomed though intricate rhythm, the darkness and turmoil of her soul were exorcised by the light of faith. If Death itself would be swallowed up in victory, the sting of every death-like parting would also be mitigated and healed.

Looking up, she caught the reflective glance of the Bishop of Nisqually lingering thoughtfully upon her. Here was a watchful shepherd, wielding crook and staff to protect and guide her. He had traveled the long way to Oregon before her; he had hewn out of the wilderness the rudimentary beginnings of a great spiritual empire which would one day rise up to bless the Heart of Christ. This she firmly believed. In the spread of that empire, she herself wanted a full and generous part; no present fears nor doubts must ever cast a shadow on that aim.

"Although I walk in a darksome valley, I shall fear no evil, for Thou art with me."

Looking steadily at His Lordship, she repeated the words she had so lately said at the Asile to Sister Martin, the beloved Julie of childhood days.

"Let us rejoice on this day which the Lord has made."

Quietly her thoughts slipped along the accustomed pathways of the world of faith.

This world of faith, she reflected, need not obscure the abode that God has provided for men to live in. In reality, the keener the faith the more the mind can divine the mysterious order and beauty which govern nature. . . .

To the travelers of that day in mid-fall 1856, the scene outside their coach window was familiar in contour and color; only this unaccustomed journey and their own inner bereavement had made it seem alien. The railway route cut across the rich,, dark land of Chambly and Iberville counties which lie between the Saint Lawrence and the Richelieu, a route which not only had seen history but had also made it and determined the destiny of a continent.

The Richelieu had once been called Riviere-des-Iroquois, and as such had marked off that central ground which had soaked in the blood of so many gallant Frenchmen. Down this valley had come the valiant Samuel de Champlain, the dauntless Isaac Jogues, and the intrepid Count de Frontenac, each intent on his own type of conquest for the King of France or the King of Heaven, or both. Here had been built the outposts of an empire. At Chambly to their left, below the baleful rapids, the crumbling palisades of old Fort Saint Louis were still to be seen.

But of more interest to the missionaries, at Saint Jean they reached a busy little metropolis whose railway center had already seen twenty years of existence. This was the terminal of Canada's first railroad, and through it their foundress, Madame Emmelie Gamelin, had gone thirteen years earlier on her first trip to the United States. It was already five years since Mother Gamelin had been laid to rest under the altar of Saint Vincent de Paul at the Asile, but the name of Saint Jean, of which she had so frequently spoken, evoked her memory.

To Sister Joseph there came the remembrance of that strong, controlled woman whom she had loved and understood so well. In the eight years they had been together she had fathomed somewhat of how God had dealt with His dear servant. He had deigned to trust Emmelie Gamelin with a share in the passion of His own Son, so that she had known pain and rejection and the last bitter ignominy of horrible death. But she had also known God's love and mercy and had re-enacted them in her own heart. Well, thanks be to God, Mother Gamelin was long since in eternity. Sister Joseph felt her presence now approving and blessing this trip to Oregon.

"Monseigneur," she had said to His Lordship on September 23, "it seems to me that I hear our Mother urging us to take up again our mission in Oregon."

"And did you hear her well?" His Lordship had asked in reply.

Here in Saint Jean d'Iberville, Sister Joseph realized the compulsion with which the thought of Oregon had pursued her. Surely their Mother had spoken, and this time they had heard her well, God be praised. This spirited little town was another wayside shrine on their long pilgrimage.

The Sister Servant found herself torn in mind between the impulse to forge ahead toward that distant country of her adoption, and the desire to gaze backward at all the pleasant associations of the dear land of her birth.

Oregon had always beckoned. When the question of founding a house there had first arisen in April 1852, she had felt a renewed attraction for the work of the missions. How often in the old days had she and Mother Gamelin spoken on that subject dear to both of them. It had been their shared delight to make with meticulous care a small supply of altar linens for His Lordship's new diocese in the Oregon Territory when he had been soliciting contributions throughout Montreal ten years ago.

She well remembered His Lordship as he was in those days. In fact, since there was hardly a time in her religious life in which he had not figured, she could recall the progressive stages in his career as a churchman. The will of God had ordered each successive step for him toward a destiny in Oregon, and now it seemed that He had also arranged that His Lordship's life and her own would converge in a concerted enterprise.

Seeing him now seated there ahead of her in the coach, she could look back at the brisk, youthful abbé who had been Bishop Bourget's right hand as Canon of the Cathedral a decade ago. He had served as their chaplain at the Asile in those days, and she had come to know him well. They had all been acquainted with his history and his lineage. There were any number of Blanchets in the Province of Quebec, and many were distinguished members of the clergy and of the laity who had done outstanding service for the Church. It was common knowledge that the young Abbé had been an impassioned and fiery patriot and had suffered a brief imprisonment at the hands of the authorities during the troubles of 1837. Now the fires were banked and controlled, but they were still there, thank God. Only a man of stamina could have endured that first vicariate in the Oregon country. It had been this self-same Abbé Blanchet to whom Emmelie Gamelin had turned for confirmation and assurance with regard to her religious vocation. The Sister Servant smiled as she remembered that brief encounter.

"You a religious!" he had exclaimed. "You are no more meant to be a religious than I am to be a bishop."
But he had come to respect the vocation of Madame Gamelin and none had been more sincerely grieved at the news of her sudden going in 1851. To Sister Joseph all that seemed only yesterday, so fresh was her memory and so keen remained the sense of loss of her beloved one.

As the midmorning light poured in at the windows, His Lordship had taken up his breviary, and the other priests had quietly followed suit. How easily he seemed to bear the episcopal burden of authority! With what vigor he wore the pectoral cross and its precious relic of man's salvation.

She had seen that cross laid upon him when Bishop Bourget had consecrated him bishop before the magnificence of the high

altar at Saint James Cathedral in Montreal ten years ago. Before
they had worn the amethyst those hands had held another book
and turned it, too, easily and caressingly—the book of Rules of
Saint Vincent de Paul.

It had been brought by Madame Gamelin from the Sisters at
Emmitsburg, Maryland. Bishop Bourget had entrusted him with
the priceless little volume so that it might be copied for the use of
the newly founded community of Providence, for his own Daughters of Charity, his Servants of the Poor. That Sister Joseph could
carry her copy with her now was thanks to His Lordship's service
to her young community. Silently she saluted the man of God
who had been given authority over her life; silently too she spoke
to God of the good friend and monitor who would guide her to
that perfection of her vocation of which her rule spoke. The rule
was but the means; the end was always God and His creative life
within her own soul.

Suddenly they were at Rouse's Point. Sister Joseph, Esther Pariseau that was, realized with a tightening of her heart, that they had
passed the Canadian boundary and that she was for the first time
in a foreign land. There was no reason to find this country different from the valley of the Richelieu, from County Chambly or
Chateaugay or her own native Laval. Here was the same November landscape of brown earth and quiet sky, of groves of leafless
maples and willows against the deep green of hemlock and spruce.
But the heart has its own reasons for knowing. Sister Joseph of
the Sacred Heart looked briefly to the north, then turned with
decision to the business at hand.

Again there was the flurry of activity as the passengers transferred from train to depot and made their way to the dock at the
head of the lake. Here there awaited them the Champlain steamer
which would carry them south to the Hudson Valley. Yankee ingenuity had surpassed itself in designing and building the lake and
river boats of the era, and the steam packet on which the Oregon
missionaries embarked was a craft of elegance and luxury.

With Bishop Magloire Blanchet again in the lead, the missionaries moved aboard.

To most of them so much magnificence was disconcerting. Yet

the Sister Servant looked about her with unabashed and observant eye, noting the lavish furnishings and the orderly comfort of this floating palace which for the remainder of the day would carry them southward to Whitehall. She observed the richness of the highly polished furniture, the gleaming mirrors, the heavy carpets. Her practical mind assayed the compact arrangement of decks and cabins, of dining room and services. She had a deep respect for well-turned woodwork.

Twenty years ago in the carriage shop she herself had stood at her father's elbow and had learned from him how to handle tools. The capable, blunt-fingered hands of Joseph Pariseau had taught her craftsmanship in the selection and use of wood and had trained her own hands to work with discernment and skill. In the thirteen years since he had brought her from Ile Jesus to the Providence, she had not looked back. For that matter she had been much too busy with the works of the Providence to spend time in reminiscence or in keeping alive her natural yearning for her father and her family. But to the core of her being she knew herself to be the child of Joseph and Françoise Pariseau. They had set the mark of their heritage upon her, their third child. . . .

CHAPTER 2

O<small>N THE</small> I<small>LE</small> J<small>ÉSUS,</small> the year had turned the long corner. After a lingering winter, April had sent the snow plunging down over the eaves and had melted the ice on the rivers. Up beyond Riviedes-Mille-Iles in Terrebonne, the Laurentians were cold and white, but in the foothills patches of snow were now interspersed with patches of brown soil. Clumps of alders and willows stirred along the banks of La Prairie River to the south, and were of a sudden clothed in a thin, gold radiance. The year was 1823, and the calendar on the kitchen wall was circled at April 16; but on the Ile Jésus it was earth's time and God's time—a time of awakening and renewal, of birth and growth.

Within the stone farmhouse of Joseph and Françoise Pariseau at Saint Elzear a protesting and querulous cry marked the arrival of a newborn child. This was their third, the girl Esther. There were no signs and portents to accompany her birth, nor any fevered preparations or harrowed emotions. The French Canadian world into which she was born looked on life and birth with great simplicity. Here was another child whom God had sent for the waiting cradle. That same cradle had been occupied five years ago by small Joseph and two years later by small Luce. If the Lord continued His blessings, there would be many more.

But if he accepted the fact of existence simply, the French Canadian did not view it lightly. To the core of his being he reverenced the dignity of human life. The very texture of his thinking was Catholic, and though he might be poor in worldly goods, though

12

he might be subject to the most abysmal of human frailties, he was by his faith the son of God. This was the heritage of his blood and of his race.

The Ile Jésus and the adjacent island of Montreal were not so much the heart of French Canada as was the rock-like fortress city of Quebec farther down the Saint Lawrence. Yet the two great cities together and their environs formed a compact little world within a world which was complete and vigorously alive. Viewed from one angle it was more French than France, conserving and distilling the Gallic spirit to its very essence. Here were Frenchmen who were faithful sons and daughters of that great nation of the "ancien régime," holding tenaciously to its customs, its language, and its religion as given them in the almost legendary era of New France in the seventeenth century. They had meager understanding and little patience with the France of the nineteenth century. That latter-day France did not seem to be properly repentant for the horror it had unleashed upon the world some thirty years ago— a horror of blood and violence which had engulfed their poor, slow-witted king and his beautiful queen, and had aimed not only at toppling the throne of the Bourbons but at upsetting the altars of the Church as well. The lilies of France were elevated again, it is true, but they were bruised and blemished. The French Canadian was shocked at the spectacle of the eldest daughter of the Church turned now into a Rahablike creature bargaining at the crossroads of the world.

Besides all this, he was wounded in his loyalties. He could not forget that in 1763 all of New France had been dismissed as a negligible loss, had been made the pawn in a shoddy game between the inglorious sons of Saint Louis and the English milords. The same delirious voice which had cried shrewishly, *"Ecrasez l'infame,"* at the Rock of Rome had belittled the land of Champlain and Frontenac as "a few acres of snow."

Snow there was and plenty of it in the long Canadian winters. But under the snow was the good earth, and along the river and beyond it lay a whole continent which refused to be dismissed by the snobbery and shortsightedness of the continental French. These latter had been unkind and fatuous enough to criticize the French Canadian for his country speech, for his simple piety, for his uncouth manners. Did they not realize that he had been betrayed, that he was so intent on clinging to his very existence that he had had to sacrifice all but the barest essentials for survival? Survive he did, and would. God would not forsake him because he had not forsaken God.

At Saint Elzear the newest occupant of the Pariseau cradle, a ruddy little creature with black hair and well-defined features, rested quietly for a day within the warm stone cottage. Then on April 17, she was bundled securely against the raw spring weather for the three-mile ride to the parish house of Saint Martin de Laval. The roads were rutted with thick, brown mud, but the long line of poplars which bordered the way were bursting with shining, russet buds. Above all, the pale Laurentian sky dwarfed the whole of man's handiwork—the cultivated fields awaiting the plow, the stone walls marking the boundaries of each small holding, the clustered farmhouses. Remote and cool, it set the mood of the whole landscape—a mood of infinite detachment. Across the fields the bells from the church spires sent their cascade of heavenly harmony in welcome to the child being borne this day so triumphantly to the portals of Holy Mother Church.

"Esther, what do you ask of the church of God?" asked the Abbé Brunet in the magnificent lines of liturgy.

"Faith," replied the child by the voice of Restitue Dufresne, her godmother.

"What will faith bring you?"

"Life everlasting."

. . . .

Within the child's world, the years moved slowly. In the underlying rhythm of seasonal change, the swinging pendulum, of time seemed to lose motion during the long winters. From November until April the snow lay in heavy drifts obscuring fence posts and landmarks. Only the tireless efforts of the men of the household kept the paths to the house and barn clear and passable.

On some days the scene beyond the frosted windows was of grey skies and grey-white fields merged and shrouded beyond recognition. On others when the air was clear and snapping cold, one could see the mountains. Far to the north across the frozen river, they gleamed in somber, glacial majesty. Against them was the limitless mystery of the forest crowding down toward the farms in Terrebonne.

The child Esther learned how God made provision for the Pariseaux. It is true He did not build the fire in the hearth; her father or Joseph did that. But He provided the fragrant cedar and the resinous pine which gives a quick, hot flame, the red spruce which burns more steadily and slowly, and finally, the birch and the maple which left glowing red embers lasting even through the night. Her mother said that He had given them pine wood to make the kettle boil and white birch for baking bread. Had He also built the fire, her mother said, it would not have been good for either Joseph or her father. They might forget that we are here in this world to lay up treasure for heaven, our true country. Only by work, hard work, could one become strong and enduring for that task. There on the wall was the sacred symbol of what the Son of God had endured for us. With a fire on the hearth and the crucifix on the wall, all was peace within the stone cottage.

But if the long snow was always to be reckoned with and provided against, it was also the source of much gaiety. On Sundays, what fun to be bundled warmly into the sleigh her father had made with his own hands, to sit with her parents and Joseph and Luce, and later with Julie and Stanislaus and the baby. When the horses tossed their heads' there was no melody on earth so merry as that of the tinkling sleigh bells. In no time at all their light, pleasant music was joined by the heavy tones of Great Bourdon in Saint Martin's spire booming out across the white world the hour of Mass. Tenor and bass, her father called the song of sleigh bells and church bells.

Once within the holy precinct that fantasy of speed and sound was dwarfed into insignificance beside the mystery of faith. It was not merely the lighted candles, nor the searing plain chant ascending with the incense. It was a secret thing of the good God. She was conscious of an adoration shared with those around her—

with great, strong men like her father, and profoundly wise women like her mother, all kneeling now in the presence of the Blessed Sacrament. And when for a still moment, the Abbé Brunet bent above the altar, knelt briefly, and then raised the Sacred Host for all to see' she knew that with her own eyes she was seeing God. Even had her mother not told her she would have known. The holy angels there with bowed heads and motionless wings she did not see, but she could imagine how they looked. She thought they must look as Joseph and Luce and Julie and Stanislaus looked when their father had first let them all see the baby when it came.

. . . .

While the farm waited out the months for the snow and the frost to pass, activity within the carriage shop took precedence over cultivation of the land. M. Pariseau did a brisk business in supplying the neighboring villages with vehicles and carriage parts. He was regarded as a skilled workman at that highly specialized trade. Designer, wheelwright, body–maker, blocksmith, carver, and painter-he combined the inherited lore of the coach-maker with a native dexterity in fashioning wood and metal. To the Pari-seau children, the shop and the adjacent sheds were the abode of enchantment and enterprise.

Esther joined the little groups that stood about to see the timber unloaded. She watched the quietly wise men, old acquaintances of her father from nearby villages, as they carted the timber into the yard and unloaded it. Sometimes it was a matter which called for some ingenuity; there was an exchange of keen glances and a quick direction, but always there was a sense of understanding and good temper among them. With the horses and the timber, they seemed to bring the scent of the lonely woodlands, the vista Of far-off roads, into the Saint Elzear farmyard.

In the winter the timber was sawed. It was cold work for the men, and one could not stand still in watching them. But there was a fascination which held both workers and onlookers attentive to the task. Now M. Pariseau's judgment in choosing and buying these trees would be put to the test, though the final verdict could be given only years later on the workman's bench.

Beyond this practical consideration, there was the awe one felt at fir st viewing the heart of oak or elm or ash. The eye of God alone had seen this mystery, and only He knew beforehand the years this tree had stood in the forest. How beautiful was the pattern which the saw revealed of the pale ash, the golden, closeknit oak, the butter-colored elm! Sometimes from the ash there came the penetrating odor of wood burning—not a good sign always, because that might mean the tree was black-hearted and not trustworthy as wood. The scent of the oak was unmistakable and at the same time nameless; it had the fresh smell of the forest and brought with it the long memory of mid-summer days, full of sun and drowsy heat. Esther learned not only to recognize the hardwoods but also to hazard an appraisal of them as they were carefully stored for seasoning. They must wait "a year for each inch of thickness," her father had told her.

Nothing but the best could be used for carriages. Wood for the body was of toughest ash, taken from locations carefully chosen. A tree was like a man, her father said. It became strong and supple enough to endure the strains put upon it by being exposed to the blustering storms which roared down from the northeast. It struck deep roots and bent to the winds, but it did not break. No white ash which had stood sheltered from the raw northern weather would ever make a good carriage. And no man who had not learned from his youth to bear hardship and pain could have the tough fiber of the true Christian. One had only to look on the Calvaire at the Saint Martin crossroad to know what winds were likely to beat against the spirit of man. So said her father.

Since the wheels were the most important part of the carriage, the greatest care was taken in the selection of wood for them. There was elm for the hub, ash for the felloes, oak for the spokes. The pale brown elmwood was smooth and slightly fragrant. Strange, Esther thought, that this tough hardwood which resisted' the axe should come from the lady-like tree that stood so gracefully against the sky—a tree that attracted deer and quail and rabbits and other shy creatures. The grey squirrel was happiest, it is true, with the white oak. Those busy little creatures gave service for service, eating the acorns or storing them so deeply that many of them became seedlings. From the oak, spokes were made, and they were sure to outlast the carriage.

All this and much more Esther had learned by the time she was ten. By the time she was twelve she knew the name and purpose of each of her father's tools; moreover, her hands knew the feel of them. Sometimes he permitted her to put them carefully in place for him in the meticulous order which is the mark of the craftsman. Very early he taught her how to grasp the hickory-handled hammer to best advantage. She loved the power that came to her with its sturdy strength, and she liked to keep it with her, hooked over her belt when not in use. She also learned to use the knife, the saw, the chisel, the draw-knife, the spikeshave, the bit brace, the plane, the square. She watched iron become white-hot in the forge and shower sparks as it was shaped and hammered on the anvil. Sometimes, even, she was allowed to take Joseph's place with the bellows. She was not only fascinated and awed as something serviceable and practical emerged from her father's workmanship; she was also kindled to emulate his creative achievements.

There was the winter she made the sewing box. Zoë was four; Elodie was two, and the baby again. Little Eulalie had occupied the cradle so short a time before returning to the Lord that it seemed to Esther she had never really been a member of the Pariseau household at all. Her mother sang less that winter, and there were fewer dancing lights in her eyes, Esther thought. So since Julie was now ten and able to help Luce with the work inside the stone cottage, Esther decided she would make the box. There was the piece of red maple which her father had put aside as too soft for the dash board of the sleigh he was finishing. She would use that and with it the ash and sugar maple that she had stored away in the shop.

A smile again reached the eyes of Françoise Pariseau as she held Esther's gift and ran her fingertips lightly over the smooth work on the lid. It was good that her daughter's handiwork was strong and serviceable as well as beautiful, she said. Moreover, she was particularly pleased that Esther had done so well with the inside. Sometimes she thought that her capable daughter leaned too much toward the work in the shop and on the farm, and not enough toward the household tasks which were a woman's domain. The sewing box would be a symbol and remain with the Pariseaux for many, many years. Now that the youngest was two, perhaps there might be leisure to make something delicate and lovely with the needle.

Esther could not remember a time when she had not been able to sew. Her mother's ceaseless industry in the care of the household continued from before dawn until hours after the lamps were lit in the evening. The long workday was sometimes punctuated by less active periods when she gathered the girls around her to put the family wardrobe in order. These were times of quiet companionship and agreeable talk. Luce and Esther and Julie each presided over some allotted share of the general task under the watchful eye of Madame Pariseau. To the nimble fingers of Luce were confided the more intricate assignments, while young Julie did the simpler things. But eventually each of the girls took her turn at the various kinds of sewing and mending. Each learned, too, to card the wool, to spin, and finally to weave the sturdy, homespun fabrics which clothed the family.

Françoise Pariseau used this precious time to its full advantage. There were the truths of the faith to discuss along with the sewing. There were the Bible narratives to tell and explain-how the little Jesus was born of the Virgin and was protected by strong Saint Joseph, how He lived in Nazareth and and grew up a fine obedient Son, and how He taught the world goodness by His speech and His example. There were His miracles and His stories. There was the mystery of His death. As their needles dipped in and out of the material of Joseph's linen shirt or Stanislaus' brown trousers or the softness which was the baby's dress, they were stitching together into one seamless robe the practical duties of their everyday life and their share in the loving-kindness of God. It is true that God could at times be very severe, but He was never remote. And the saints—well certainly, Esther reflected, good Saint Anne was as near as one's godmother, Madame Dufresne, who lived two farms away, and she was much more powerful.

Sometimes they sang as they sat together in the comfortable cheer of the stone cottage—old hymns which had been sung by Grandmother Rousseau, their mother said. But there was one afternoon on which Esther could not keep her mind on either the melody or the words of the hymn. That was the time her mother first told the story of the Rich Young Man.

CHAPTER 3

WITH THE RETREAT of winter, the world of Saint Elzear took on a luminous quality. Spring came slowly in the Province of Quebec. When it did finally arrive, it had an intensity and sweetness which suffused every living, growing thing. One day the fields and woodland paths were expanses of mud across which one moved painstakingly, pulling up first one well-shod foot and then the other; then a day or so later it seemed one had to walk carefully to avoid crushing the arbutus, the blue hepaticas, and the starlike celadine. From that time on, things moved with an accelerated pace and an enrichment of color. Near the barn, by some miracle the crab apple tree which had been bereft of all signs of life these many months suddenly burst into a thing of enchantment. The children pulled down masses of the patterned pink and white blossoms and thrust them gaily into the widemouthed crockery jar before the picture of Our Lady, until Esther remonstrated that at that rate there would be no fruit for their mother's jellies. In no time at all the orchard on the northern slope was in full bloom—apple, cherry, plum—all in precise and perfect timing.

Their father and Joseph were busy in the fields, plowing and planting and harrowing. Monsieur Pariseau kept a vigilant eye on the weather which was likely to turn to the treachery of frost or hail, and there was need to invoke the saints and Our Lady and even the Lord Himself that all would go well. The brown furrowed land needed every protection and blessing. But then with all their prayers they knew that God understood these things, and after a few weeks of right weather, all the fields around Saint Elzear were tinged with a faint green. The Pariseau farm was good land, and their father was a man of industry and wisdom, and the rest could safely be left to Providence which never failed them.

The garden nearer the stone cottage was left mostly to Madame Pariseau and the girls and Stanislaus. Esther's strong fingers loved the touch of the rich soil, and she liked the challenge of quick and delicate work which the earth demanded of her hands. This, too, was creative labor, as that in the carriage shop had been in the winter. She disliked slovenly work in either place, and she had small patience with the fumbler or the laggard. Only the perceptive and authoritative spirit of Madame Pariseau kept her second daughter from being sometimes overbearing and imperious in her greater skill and accomplishment. Hers was the sturdier back, her mother reminded her; for that she had God to thank. Others with greater good will and the asset of her health and strength might have grown even larger and redder tomatoes. Who knows? Patience and humility were the flower and fruit most desired of her by our Lord when He visited her heart in Holy Communion. Did she think that the second beatitude which the Abbé Brunet had taught her in preparation for her First Communion that unforgettable day three years ago was an empty phrase?

Of the earth and its tenancy, God had spoken through His Son—"Blessed are the meek, for they shall possess the land." The land referred to by our Lord could sometimes be measured in acres, but it was always something more than a patch of ground enclosed by a hedge and a rail fence. Of much more value to the holder, there was such a possession as a quiet heart. Only the meek had that, and only they would sometime inherit that true country of God, that homeland of our Heavenly Father, for only the meek and humble could feel at ease in the company of the meek and humble Jesus.

It was well to reflect on these things as one planted and watered and weeded here at Saint Elzear. It gave one a right sense of values. Eventually one's mind arrived at the truth that all human goodness is possible only through the grace of God, for by some unfathomable mystery of His generosity He gives us whatever goodness we ask of Him, even that great good thing offered the young man in the Gospel, if we want it.

. . . .

Esther afterwards remembered her fourteenth spring and summer for two reasons: one for events within the Pariseau household, and the other because of the tide of affairs which swept in on Saint Elzear from the whole Province of Quebec.

That spring Françoise Pariseau worked neither in the garden nor in the kitchen. After the New Year, Esther noticed her mother's firm step become slow and heavy as her body thickened with her tenth child. It was only by supreme and exhaustive effort that she was able to attend Mass with them on Easter. From that day in late March, Madame Pariseau waited out her time in declining strength. The quiet, dark oldest daughter, Luce, took over the management of the house itself, while Esther supervised the outside chores and the garden. Sometimes the exuberant activity of the gardeners spilled over to the inside, but it was soon muted and stilled at the couch of their mother.

The child Salomie was born the first week of May and barely lived through her baptism. That their mother almost followed the child through the dark gateway of death struck cold fear into all their hearts. Esther was conscious of that month of Our Lady 1837 as a period of intolerable waiting. She watched her father become gray and old, and realized for the first time that her parents were people who had another life apart from the lives of their children, however completely they let themselves be absorbed by their family. But when June came in with a flood of hot sunshine, and the broom billowed against the hills like low-lying yellow clouds, and one could see the northern mountain again in the clear air, Françoise Pariseau grew a little stronger. It seemed evident that God had heard their prayer and would allow their mother to stay with them in their need. She was able to go with them to Saint Martin de Laval for the feast of Saint Jean Baptiste. Joseph had curried the horses until their coats fairly shone and their harness glinted in the sun. The new carriage which their father had made looked very fine. When with the dust of the road there was mingled the scent of the briar rose blooming in profusion along their route, the world was beautiful and complete again, and happiness flowed around them and through them like the rich, deep tones of Great Bourdon. The coming of that summer, however, had marked the end of the childhood of Esther Pariseau.

· · · · · · · · ·

For as long as Esther could remember there had been a name spoken among the people on the Ile Jésus. The children had heard their father deep in conversation with other Canadian Frenchmen on the subject of Monsieur Louis Joseph Papineau. There were cautious questions and guarded answers, followed by long deliberations on the man and his principles. There was, too, much weighty consideration of how his policies would affect their own lives. Of late there had been fiery words and bitter argument on the subject, and the result was that now her father sometimes failed to greet or even see certain men in the parish, a strange and puzzling situation among people who had grown up together. It was "Papineau, Papineau, Papineau," blown along on the hot wind of a controversy which lashed not only Saint Elzear, but the whole province of Quebec, and finally buffeted the towers of empire in Westminster itself.

The trouble had been a long time growing and its roots went deep into the very nature of Canadian life. It was small wonder that those who were caught up in the dissension and violence of those years found the whole situation full of bitterness and contradiction.

Esther had heard how Great-grandfather Martin Pariseau had come here from Lorraine in 1756. He and his family had cleared the farm in the Saint-Laurent district across La Prairie River and had clung to the land during the perilous years of change when the white flag with the lilies had been hauled down and the red ensign had been run up in Montreal's Place d'Armes. Those were times spoken of by one's elders in quiet tones; as they spoke their eyes were seeing some vision never touched by the words on their lips. Ah well, they said, those days were past, and they had not fared so badly on the resources left to them. They still had their religion, their language, and their laws, and they meant to keep them. The British, on the whole, had made some effort at fairness after those first cruel years. In Grandfather Joseph Pariseau's time, they had reached what they had hoped was a final settlement and the assurance that the French Canadians would survive as a people.

What they wanted most was to be left alone. For two hundred years these French Canadians had borne the burden of this continent. They had explored it to the far reaches of the western seas and the frozen lands to the north. They had laid the basis of the great empire of the fur trade, pushing up fierce, swift rivers and crossing a thousand miles of lake water; they had portaged over wilderness paths known only to savage Indian guides; they had returned after months and years loaded with the stinking pelts which meant fortunes to the great ones in the cities beyond the seas. All this their people had done, besides fighting a hundred years of warfare against heavy odds. For themselves they were not and never had been interested in conquest. They wanted to live in peace within the confines of their parish; they wanted never to move again beyond the sound of their church bells, and they wanted their land.

About the time they had convinced themselves that the British meant their fair promises to respect their customs and their race, they began to discern that there were, in the main, two breeds of Englishmen. There were those near the King in England who had garnered some slight wisdom about dealing with the loyalties and the sensibilities of other men who were not English. Perhaps, the Canadian said wryly, the men of Boston had helped them to learn wisdom, though of those *Bostanais* the less said, the better. The fault of those in England was that they allowed their good intentions to lag behind the needed remedies. In the interval it was the second group of English who took over. Of them it could be said that they had learned nothing and forgotten nothing. If they were stupid in London, they were malicious in Quebec. These were the men of the "Chateau clique," bent. on becoming rich and powerful at the expense of the men of the soil and the simple workers. It was on the wave of frustration which their self-ishness and arrogance set in motion that Louis Joseph Papineau came to the fore in the Province of Quebec, and it was he and his followers, the *Patriotes,* who in 1837 planned to meet the high-handed and arbitrary suppression of the assembly's rights with violence.

All during the time of their mother's illness Joseph Pariseau had been frequently abstracted and withdrawn in spite of the fact that he had been Françoise Pariseau's eldest and dearest. At first, the others had paid little attention to him because he was given to holding himself apart from the rest of them. It was a relief not to have his whims and his demands to contend with along with their other anxiety. But around him and related to him, there was uneasiness in the air and a sudden, dark word that could stir up echoes out of nowhere.

Their father, too, was likely to return from the village in a mood of silence. Talk they had heard, of course, that Monsieur Papineau was rumored to have said this and Monsieur le Curé had certainly said that. There were smouldering resentments and an occasional half-sentence hanging in the air which sent a prickle of fear through their hearts, but behind all this unnamed confusion of thought and feeling was a stubborn reliance on God to see them through whatever it was that lay ahead.

In July it was learned that the old king, William IV, had died and was succeeded by a mere chit of a girl, Alexandra Victoria. For a while there was a ray of hope that things might improve, because the young queen was a daughter to Prince Edward of Kent, that personable young man who had spent a long idyllic interval in Canada. He had lived at Montmorency at his pleasant country house there, the friend of a beautiful, well-bred lady of their own ancestral land. Surely the new queen would have some inbred sympathy, some natural social grace which would heal the rift between *les Anglais* and the French Canadians. But it was soon evident, gossip said, that the new little queen was not much more than a pawn herself in the game for power. So they shrugged their shoulders and then squared them to await the event.

It came almost as a relief one day in early summer to have ten year-old Stanislaus come flying home from the village with the news about Joseph. "The Mayor," he burst out, "had called up all those sixteen and over to form a *patriote* militia and Joseph Pariseau was to be captain of the Saint Elzear company." Things moved rapidly after that beyond the Ile Jésus, not only rapidly, but tragically.

There was a short, joyous interim before October when the countryside was wild with hope and seething activity. The young Pariseaux were caught up into the prevailing spirit of ardour and high purpose not only to defend their ancient liberties but to win new ones.

At first Joseph was a hero, that same Joseph at whom they had grumbled when their mother insisted they wait up in the evening and put the carriage and horses away after he had gone calling on the little La Fleche girl. Joseph himself wore his new role arrogantly. Not only was he curt with his younger brothers and sisters, but also he assumed the air of field-marshal for the whole village.

It was Esther who undertook to correct that situation and whittle Joseph to his proper size. Whatever he could do, the rest of them would do. *Sons of Liberty?* Well, then why not Younger Sons and Daughters of Liberty as a home guard militia? That way the honors as well as the responsibility for reserve units would be shared. The idea was worked out with Julie, the beloved comrade of every enterprise, and with Stanislaus, the reliable. Then it was submitted for approval first to their father and finally to the curé, Monsieur Mercier.

The result was that some forty Saint Elzear and Saint Martin boys from ten to fourteen years of age were rigorously marched and countermarched under Captain Stanislaus Pariseau, who in turn took orders from Esther. Occasionally Stanislaus' command was set aside, and Esther herself took over. Under the approving eyes of the villagers, she could be seen with hair flying and arms gesticulating peremptorily as she led the *Younger Sons of Liberty* in the more intricate military maneuvers.

It turned out to be no mean company. Each young militiaman carried his own weapon, thanks to Esther and Julie who themselves designed wooden guns- and turned them out in the carriage shop. Moreover, the company was sharply reminded that smart appearance and sound morale are concomitants. The nimble fingers of Esther and Julie made jaunty homespun caps, complete with blue, red, and white pompons. A true son of liberty wore his cap with an air of distinction at the same time that he marched with precision to the rhythm of the drum.

By September, Captain Stanislaus Pariseau and his men were carrying off all the parish prizes for being the best drilled, best dressed, best disciplined unit in Saint Elzear. That was good, Esther thought, for two reasons. First, it gave the boys a share in the world of their elders; secondly, it gave the important Joseph, some healthy competition.

It was on a Sunday morning that the whole parish of Saint Martin de Laval was rocked back on its heels over the question of Monsieur Papineau and the Patriotes. Monsieur le Curé read the Gospel in such an ordinary voice that Esther could never afterwards remember what it had been about; and then after fumbling briefly with some papers he held, and before they were well seated for the sermon, he began in a voice. as solemn as Great Bourdon itself: "Jean Jacques Lartigue, by the grace of God and the Holy apostolic See, Bishop of Montreal, to the clergy and the laity of the diocese of Montreal, greetings and benedictions in Our Lord Jesus Christ. . . . It has seemed to us . . ."

At first, Esther merely supposed that His Lordship's letter could not mean what she thought it was saying; she was simply not hearing correctly, or she was not grasping the significance of the words. But when she saw the Mayor sitting bolt upright in his pew down front, his face suffused with a purple flush, and when turning she saw her own father's face expressionless and deathly still, she knew she was not misunderstanding. His Lordship, the Bishop of Montreal, that gentle, kindly prelate at whose hands the Holy Spirit had come to her in the holy sacrament of Confirmation was now commanding the people of the parish of Saint Martin de Laval along with those of every other parish in his diocese to respect the civil authority now ruling them and to desist from every act and word of violence under pain of grievous sin!

Thinking of the blue, red, and white cockades, Esther wished that the floor beneath would open and swallow her. Every word was certainly being aimed at her. How could all of them have been so wrong? A red turmoil arose convulsively in her heart and threatened to engulf her. Gradually the shame passed to be followed by a hollow, unthinking obstinacy. This simply could not be happening to her.

Somehow the Mass went on and the Pariseaux were with the rest of the congregation on the way out of the church. Today, however, they did not linger on the church steps but without a word were ushered by their parents into the carriage. When Esther would have spoken of M. Papineau, her father forestalled her.

"Monseigneur, His Lordship of Montreal, speaks for Holy Mother Church. Therefore, his voice is the voice of God speaking. It is for good children to listen and obey."

At her father's words the turbulence within her died. She knew that he felt as strongly as she did about those selfish and powerful ones in Quebec who were bent on restricting their people in the exercise of their language, their customs, their faith. She let her hurt pride be soothed by the knowledge that he would never be weak or slack in the face of danger; he would take positive and suitable action in defense of what he held right and dear. This must be the way of prudence. The Church had had eighteen hundred years of learning forbearance. Who was she to say otherwise?

The sun overhead was warm, and the horses were moving toward home at a good brisk pace, their polished harness tinkling pleasantly. Esther had the smell of dust in her nostrils, and the taste of it in her mouth; but some new wisdom helped her to see the splendor of the autumn woods, and along the road, the goldenrod. . . .

The most painful thing which followed at Saint Elzear, in Esther's eyes, was the disbanding of Captain Stanislaus Pariseau's corps. But after the snow lay deep across the fields there came really tragic news of *patriote* groups to the south—and how on the road between Longueuil and Chambly they had briefly stood their ground against the British regulars only to be routed later at Saint Denis and Saint Charles and Saint Eustache. Monsieur Papineau fled to the United States for safety, but before the trouble was over, there were a thousand French Canadians in the prisons at Montreal and Quebec. After a year twelve of them were executed, and a score were exiled to the Bermudas and Australia. Out of the welter of heartache and bloodshed there would eventually grow a nation which would honor the principle for which the men of 1837 and 1838 had striven with more zeal than competence. But that day was not yet.

In Montreal, there was one who had mitigated the misery of the time by visiting the imprisoned *Patriotes*. She was a great lady who herself had known grievous sorrow and out of her personal loss had set before her, insofar as she was able, the task of binding up the wounds of society. Because of her loving kindness in those years she was afterwards called "The Angel of the Prisons." Into the world of Esther Pariseau there had not yet entered the name of Emmelie Gamelin, but imperceptibly that world was being made ready.

Before another year was out the little new Queen proved to be worth something after all when on the occasion of her solemn coronation a general amnesty opened the prisons to all but the most active of the *Patriotes*. It was at least a step on the long road in which two peoples must travel if they wish to survive; they would need to learn that each has something to give the other, even so simple and Christian a thing as forgiveness. To be equal, in the new Canada which must emerge, it would not be necessary to be identical.

. . . .

In the fall of 1840 Mademoiselle Elizabeth Bruyère came to Saint Martin de Laval to open a boarding school. Ile event had been heralded by the Cure, Monsieur Arthur Caron, during the previous summer. Mademoiselle Bruyère had been a pupil of the Sisters of the Congregation of Notre Dame and was able to impart to the young ladies who came to her those finer points in education which their homes had not been able to give them. There was no village school in the parish of Saint Martin de

Laval; hence this was an opportunity not to be neglected by any girl whose future might take her beyond the Ile Jésus.

Madame Pariseau herself had been a pupil of the Sisters of Notre Dame in Montreal and along with her other duties had taught her children to read and write. She was eager to have her work strengthened and supplemented for the second daughter whose lively and incisive mind needed the curb of a balanced intellectuality. So when Esther in a glow of enthusiasm presented the idea to her father, she found an ardent advocate in her mother.

The additional expense could easily be met, Françoise Pariseau argued, for both the carriage shop and the farm were prospering. With Joseph married and Luce about to be, there would be help enough with the other children. Julie could manage the household under her direction; Stanislaus at thirteen was capable and steady, and the younger children were now able to care for themselves and share the chores. There were times when she, Françoise, discerned in Esther a disposition of heart and mind which sought something beyond the ordinary bonds of family. For whatever it was that God would call her, she must be made ready. It was their duty as Christian parents to see to it. Monsieur Pariseau allowed himself to be easily persuaded, though he would miss Esther's companionship and ready assistance.

So it was that Esther became a pupil at the school of Mademoiselle Bruyère in the late fall of 1840. At the 'age of seventeen she had nothing of the immature school girl about her. Behind her was a happy, active childhood spent within the warm, secure confines of her own family. But though those years at Saint Elzear had been happy, they had been tempered by their measure of heartache and anxiety. The natural vigor of her character had been disciplined and sobered not only by exacting work but also by the give-and-take of living with other able and strongwilled Pariseaux. Peace among them had been purchased at the price of self-control and constant generosity of spirit; moreover, peace had been the only condition which would have been tolerated by their parents, who ruled them lovingly–but ruled none the less firmly for all their love.

In many ways, Esther was an amazing pupil. There was almost nothing in the way of practical living that she had not done. She was adept at spinning wheel, loom, and needle, at kitchen stove and oven. She could launder, scrub, and make candles. She could grow vegetables and flowers. She could adapt designs used in the carriage shop to articles of household use and she could invent traps for animals and snares for birds—to the amazement and delight of her younger brothers and sisters. She had learned to care for her ailing mother, and acted as nurse for the younger children when they were ill. She knew the simple songs and hymns of her people and sang them unfalteringly in a clear, strong voice. She had a natural genius for organization and command, and these qualities were borne out by a physical dignity and presence.

By the time she was seventeen she was well above medium height, erect and decisive of carriage, with strong, well-marked features and direct grey eyes. It might be expected that Esther would prove a formidable pupil to the young school mistress at Saint Martin's. But the quick and enduring friendship which sprang up between them attests the contrary fact.

That Mademoiselle was a true gentlewoman the girl recognized at once. She was accomplished at arts with which she, Esther, was ill at ease and diffident—the art, for example, of the written or spoken word. And Mademoiselle had refinement of spirit as well as of speech. She was full of gentle encouragement for the practical hands which found the pen a clumsy instrument until gradually Esther found herself able to produce the fine, careful penmanship which was the mark of the educated woman. As for improvement in the mode of expression, that came much more slowly. Her simple directness of thought led her to a style which not only lacked rhetoric but bordered on bluntness. However, she had a great respect for those who could not only preceive beauty but could express it in words, and under Mademoiselle's careful and patient tutelage she labored to improve her own use of language.

It came as no surprise to Esther early in 1843 when Mademoiselle Bruyère announced that her work as school mistress was being taken over by Mademoiselle Gravel. After well-nigh two years with her, Esther knew what was in her teacher's mind before she was told. They had often spoken of the great Canadian heroines of earlier times—among others, of Jeanne Mance and Marguerite Bourgeoys, of Mother Marie of the Ursulines and Madame D'Youville. Of late the conversations had been more and more of Madame D'Youville and her spiritual daughters, the Grey Nuns. Along with the talk, there had been intervals of prayer. How does God make His will known in so important a decision, Esther wondered. It was soon apparent that He had made His wishes known to Mademoiselle, no matter what the manner of the manifestation. For her it was to be the novitiate of the Grey Nuns, and that immediately.

Esther finished out the year of study under Mademoiselle Gravel, knowing as she did so that this was a period of waiting for herself. She was comfortingly aware of the fact that her family was waiting with her. Whatever took place after this, it would be a Pariseau affair.

CHAPTER 4

A PARISEAU affair? Since every major event in her life had been so until now, Esther had reason to believe that her vocation would be something arranged with her family. She would turn the matter over in her mind and appraise the future, and then with much deliberation they would all help her to reach a decision. They would ask God to bless their plans. During her last months at school Esther redoubled her prayers that she and they would choose wisely.

It was comforting to commit the problem to God while in the presence of the Eucharist at Saint Martin de Laval. She found herself visiting the church with mounting frequency in the last weeks at Mademoiselle Gravel's. A brisk walk through the village, followed by the withdrawn and muted serenity within the parish church, cleared her mind of trivialities. She would begin with a torrent of words and petitions to Our Lord, to His Virgin Mother, to the parish patron, Saint Martin, him of the divided cloak whose statue stood over the high altar. Then gradually the flood of her exuberant supplications would recede, and she would remain in simple and receptive quiet, barely conscious of the passage of time. From childhood she had always felt at home in church. Because of the patrimony of faith received from her people, God and His saints were regarded as dear and companionable members of the celestial branch of her own family. Now there grew in her a deeper sense of intimacy, a more mature spiritual awareness. There were times when no words at all were needed between herself and God.

It was in one such time that she knew suddenly and clearly that God wanted her to be a religious. It was a matter beyond either her planning or her careful deliberation. She was not choosing Him; He was choosing her. Her whole mind was possessed by the thought of God's personal love for her and of His Will disposing all things gently and sweetly that she might give herself entirely to Him. Life apart from His immediate service would for her be no life at all. He wanted her to feed His hungry ones and shelter His homeless ones, to instruct those who were ignorant of His goodness as well as to comfort His sorrowing children. Above all He was asking her, Esther Pariseau, to make room in her mind and in her heart for the action of His grace. "If you will be perfect, come follow Me."

She remembered with perfect clarity Luce and Julie and herself as they had bent over their sewing that afternoon when her mother had told them of the gospel incident of the Rich Young Man. Here in the church the simple and comfortable warmth of her home seemed almost palpable; yet without a moment's hesitation her will accepted a vocation which would completely divest her of that loving solicitude which was hers in her father's home. So complete was her joy in knowing that she had been singled out by God as His own that from that moment on the thought of anything less than religious life would have been misery. To seek Christ, to see Him waiting for her in every least event of her day, to follow in the way of faith–this would be her life under the sweet yoke of the vows of poverty, chastity, and obedience.

Her good news was received with awe by her family. In calling Esther to religion the good God was conferring a great honor on them all, her mother reminded them. This distinction they must receive in humility and thankfulness. God had spoken; it remained for them to carry out His wishes. The manner of their doing so was yet to be decided upon. A vocation was a heavenly thing, but it must put down earthly roots in some one of the religious orders. The question now was which order. Each of these was considered and discussed at length with Abbé Caron. Hotel Dieu, Congregation of Notre Dame, Ursulines, Grey Nuns–all were carefully pondered and assayed from the view of

Esther and her aptitudes. Remembering Mademoiselle Bruyère, Esther herself looked lingeringly toward the Grey Nuns and their myriad activities in the relief of human ills. Madame Pariseau favored the Congregation though she doubted that her daughter's training fitted her for the Notre Dame nuns. Monsieur Pariseau was quick to assert that any order should be glad to have their daughter with her keen native ability and her sound background and training. In any case, there was time to choose carefully because Esther was young.

It was at this juncture that Abbé Caron brought them word that they were soon to be visited by His Excellency, Monseigneur Ignace Bourget, the good bishop of Montreal. According to his mandate of November 11, 1842, which was read from the altar on the following Sunday, Monseigneur was undertaking the visit of every family in his vast diocese.

The duty of a shepherd being above all to know his sheep and to enter as much as possible into all their needs, we undertake the general visitation . . . with the full confidence that the Lord will make it useful for the salvation of each member of our flock. As we are under obligation to all . . . we shall visit all without distinction, calling to mind the example of the Sovereign Pastor of whom it is written that *He did not regard the person of men.*

It seemed, moreover, that Monseigneur had embarked upon a project of no mean proportions for the furtherance of good works among his people, and he had set himself the task of conducting a begging tour throughout Montreal and its environs. To each of his faithful he was addressing the words of Scripture: "If you have much, give abundantly; if you have little, give little, but with a good heart."

The much and the little would be devoted in particular to making ready for the Daughters of Charity of Saint Vincent de Paul from France who had been promised to Monseigneur Bourget for works which at the present time were being taken care of by Madame Emmelie Gamelin and a group of women known as the Association of Charity. The core of the works in question was known as the "Providence Asile," an asylum or refuge to be built for the care of aged and infirm women. The Asile was to be the fulfillment of long years of unselfish devotion on the part of Madame Gamelin, who some fourteen years before as a young widow of twenty-eight had undertaken to fill the void in her life by a more intimate service to Christ and His poor. Her work had grown to such proportions that her own comfortable fortune had been used up, and her physical strength and time were insufficient to meet the demands made on them by the many in need. She had not had the heart to deny food, clothing, and shelter to some twenty to thirty aged guests whom she had cared for first in her own home on Saint Philippe Street and then later in the more commodious building on Saint Catherine and Saint Christopher streets which had been donated to her by Monsieur Olivier Bertholet, a generous Montreal merchant.

This second refuge had become famous as the "Yellow House." All Montreal looked on while those of the aged women who were able to work helped card, spin, weave, and sew under the direction of Madame Gamelin and her assistant, Mademoiselle Madeleine Durand. Here were made the highly prized arrow-stitch sashes, *les ceintures fiechées*, worn by every *bourgeois* and *coureur du bois* who could afford one. Here too were woven other commodities much sought after in the city, rag carpets, table covers, figured rugs, as well as lacelike straw fabric used by the better milliners. To the Yellow House came troupes of children to view the smiling Jesus, a waxen image of the Infant Christ, displayed for veneration in the oratory.

In an effort to stabilize her work at the Yellow House and to widen its scope Madame Gamelin had come to rely upon a group of her relatives and friends for both donations and services. In the tradition of Monsieur Vincent at the court of Anne of Austria these women became known as the Ladies of Charity, and were eventually legally set up as the Association. It was this unselfish circle of benefactors to whose work Monseigneur Bourget wished to give continuity by confiding it to the Daughters of Charity of Saint Vincent de Paul. A religious community once successfully planted in Montreal would endure long after Emmelie Gamelin had passed on to the reward of her charity and benevolence. As its part, the diocese of Montreal, the Ville Marie, was building the new Asile at the cost of some 2,500 gold louis.

And so it was that Monseigneur came `Saint Elzear early in 1843, begging for the new foundation. Snow was piled high across the fields and had drifted over against the lower branches of the fir and spruce on the island. Saint Elzear was cold, but Terrebonne, to the north, across the level stretch of frozen water looked colder, and they had heard that His Lordship had been there.

When he came into the Pariseau home off the heavy roads that mid-winter day, he brought a glowing warmth with him despite the fact that the natural pallor of his fine aristocratic face was heightened by the blue lines of cold. Esther was startled that a bishop should look so young. There was authority on the broad brow and quick fire in the eyes, but there was also a gentleness about the mouth which made the gesture of kneeling to kiss his ring not a mere propriety but an act of reverence. As her lips touched the cold stone, her mind leaped in recognition of God's plan for her. She could not speak of it now, for savoring the sweetness of her knowledge; but she could listen when a little later, after they had made Monseigneur comfortable, he spoke with quiet urgency of the work of the new Asile and of those who would serve and be served there.

. . . .

As it turned out, the time to speak was delayed by her mother's health. Madame Pariseau had lost three children in ten years. Three small plots outside Saint Martin de Laval and three names that echoed like a single line of poetry remained. Eulalie, Salomie, and Seraphine were, of course, with God. The advent of the twelfth child was a matter of grave concern for them all, and the whole household adjusted the rhythm of its activity to the coming of the child. Again the days stretched on endlessly, as they waited to see if their mother was to survive with the baby. Spring came, and summer, and finally September touching the trees once more with molten gold and blazing scarlet. On the day following the feast of the Nativity of Our Lady the last of the Pariseaux arrived and was given the name of Moyse. Their mother was never to be completely well again, but in the late fall she was able to help them reach a decision about Esther.

Abbé Caron had kept them informed of events in Montreal. It was learned from Paris that the Sisters of Charity had been requested by the Holy Father for a foundation in Rome, and by the French government for another in Algeria; in the face of these heavy commitments they had had to cancel their agreement with Monseigneur. The whole future of the Asile seemed to be jeopardized by this circumstance. The new building on Saint Hubert Street was almost ready for occupancy and the tide of enthusiasm for the relief of the aged and the poor was running high throughout the city. The women of the Association of Charity had been active, and people in all ranks of life and of all ages were eager to promote sales and bazaars and collections toward this work, which had not only merited episcopal approval but had also caught the public fancy. The spring of 1843 was no time for delay, and Monseigneur knew it. In an agony of indecision he had recourse to prayer for enlightenment on the best possible course out of his dilemma. The time when Heaven listened to his prayer and enlightened him on the matter proved that he was not only a great churchman but also a man of God whose faith matched his high purpose.

To the Pariseaux Abbé Caron read the laconic account carried by the diocesan paper, the *Melanges Religieux* of March 28.

Saturday last, feast of the Annunciation, Monseigneur opened the novitiate of the Sisters of Charity and gave the Holy Habit to the seven novices forming the beginning of this useful establishment. Everyone knows that since last fall, the Sisters of Charity, expected from Paris, were destined to have a foundation of their Order in Montreal. At the beginning of winter, the Reverend Father Timon, Lazarist, and delegate of the house in Paris for the foundation of the Order in this city, wrote to Monseigneur that, the French government having asked and obtained a colony of twenty-five Sisters for Algeria, and the Sovereign Pontiff having asked another colony for Rome, this double establishment created a scarcity of Sisters, and that for the present, it was impossible for the Community of Paris to respond to the needs of Montreal. In this trying circumstance, Monseigneur felt that we should not recoil before difficulties, or renounce a work already begun, impatiently expected, and considered a veritable necessity for this city and for the entire country. He again appealed to Paris for at least two Sisters to form the Canadian novices. Uncertain as to his success in securing them, and owing to the urgent need of the institution, he has recently made the choice of seven respectable girls to whom he has given the Habit and Rules of St. Vincent de Paul. He relies for the success of this enterprise on the protection of God and on the prayers of the faithful.

And thus there was born a new community, called by Monseigneur the "Daughters of Charity, Servants of the Poor." But so closely were they associated in the public mind with the Providence Asile, that they became known quite simply as the "Sisters of Providence."

There was frequent mention of affairs at the Asile in the *Melanges Religieux*. The editor of the paper, Canon Jean Charles Prince, became the spiritual director of the new community, and his dual role enabled him to work zealously to maintain public interest in the relief of the poor at the same time that he labored to inculcate stern virtue and religious spirit in the new novices.

Madame Gamelin remained in charge of the work of the Asile, but it was generally presumed that once the new community was under way, she would step aside and allow the work she had begun single-handed to be absorbed by the sisters. What the public did not know was that Madame Gamelin herself had a strong attraction to religious life, and was deterred from joining the novices only by the opposition of Canon Prince who had not yet been convinced that she should become a religious. But in September Monseigneur himself listened to her plea and gave permission for her entry into the novitiate.

Since she was the natural leader of the enterprise which she had inaugurated, Monseigneur Bourget counseled her to visit similar works in the United States before she became a novice. With three other ladies of the Association, she went to Boston, where her letters mention having gone to confession to Bishop Benedict Fenwick, her friend of earlier years—to New York, where she received Holy Communion at Saint Peter's on Barclay Street-to Emmitsburg, Maryland, where she remained for some time with Mother Xavier Clark and her sisters, absorbing as much of their spirit as she possibly could, and bringing away with her the precious copy of Saint Vincent de Paul's *Rules for the Sisters of Charity.*

By October 6, 1843, she and her companions were back in Montreal, and two days later the following inscription was written in the registry of admissions at the Asile:

On this, the eighteenth day of October, eighteen hundred and for-tythree, at six o'clock in the morning, we, the undersigned, specially commissioned by His Lordship, the Bishop of Montreal, went to the House of Providence to give the Holy Habit to Madame Emmelie Gamelin, widow, daughter of Antoine Tavernier and Marie Josephte Maurice, born at Montreal, February 19, 1800; the ceremony was performed with the chanting of the Veni Creator, an instruction, an act of consecration to the Blessed Virgin Mary, and the celebration of the Holy Sacrifice of the Mass, during which the said novice received Holy Communion.
Made and passed at the House of Providence the day and year above given.

J. C. PRINCE, *Canon, Secretary.*

With Madame Gamelin's position now defined and assured, Providence emerged from the uncertain and nebulous state of its development, and took on character and momentum as a way of life for interior souls at the same time that it -gave its human energies to the relief of the poor. As always 'for anyone who would feed the hungry Christ, shelter the homeless Christ, or visit Him sick or imprisoned, it was a way of abnegation and denial; so it remained almost exclusively until hand and heart were disciplined to their task, and the eye was clear to see by faith the Son of Man walking His earth along the city streets or the country roads. There were times in those early days, as there have been since to others who have come after, when the poverty and the work would have been not renunciation and discipline but a monstrous slavery, were it not that they, looking up, saw no one but only Jesus. But look up they did, and the peace of Christ which passes all understanding was in their eyes for all the world to see.

Esther came to the Asile with her father on December 26, 1843. The new building rising three stories above the busy Saint Laurent suburb was the object of much interest and admiration on the part of most sightseers. Monsieur Pariseau and his daughter were impressed but they were not awed; this was their world, too, as much as was the comfortable stone cottage now half-buried in the winter snow at Saint Elzear.

When the door of the Asile opened, Esther stepped briskly over the threshold, only partially aware that in doing so she had crossed a boundary into a new life. The hidden sweetness that her heart had known in the village church of Saint Martin and again when she had kissed Monseigneur's ring was in abeyance now by these strange surroundings. She was conscious of a new sickness somewhere within her—a sickness that had to do with Julie and Stanislaus, her mother and baby Moyse, and all the rest of them there at home as well as with her father here asking the portress so gravely for the Mother Superior. Out of her memories there came to her suddenly his own parable of the ash tree which put down deep roots and was able to bend before the wind without breaking—a white ash whose pale heart was sound and tough and strong because it had grown up under buffetings from stiff northcm gales. What a sturdy oak of a man he was himself, standing now with his grizzled head bent in deference to the Mother Superior, his strong face alert and proud as he acknowledged her quiet greetings!

Joseph Pariseau was quick to recognize greatness when he saw it. This Mother Superior, this Sister Gamelin, had a great mind and a great heart. He could speak to her. To Esther's amazement, she heard him say to the grave, quiet woman before him:

"Madame, I bring you my daughter Esther, who wishes to dedicate herself to the religious life. She is twenty years old, and for some time she has prayed with her family for enlightenment. Her mother and I have talked about her future with her as well as with Monsieur le Cur& It is a great sacrifice for me to part with Esther, but if you will accept her into your company, you will find her able to give you valuable assistance. She has had what education her mother and I could give her at home and at school.

She can read and write and figure accurately. She can cook and sew and spin and do all manner of housework well. She has learned carpentry from me and can handle tools as well as I can. Moreover, she can plan and supervise the work of others, and I assure you, Madame, she will some day make a very good superior."

As all these words were poured out in a Gallic torrent, Esther was torn between embarrassment and laughter. Finally she was overwhelmed into protest by his climax.

"Father! For the love of the good God! Must you tell all my abilities and accomplishments—all that my mother has taught me?"

"Let your father speak, my dear," came the quiet interruption of Sister Gamelin. "What he says interests me very much."

"Esther is healthy and strong," her father continued. "She has been eager to serve God in the Providence ever since Monseigneur Bourget visited us and appealed for helpers."

"And you, Monsieur Pariseau," asked Sister Gamelin, "are you quite willing to give up your daughter?"

"Certainly, Madame," came the prompt reply. "This is our Christmas gift to the Divine Child."

. . . .

Later, he had learned that another girl, Mademoiselle Hermengilde Choquet, of Saint Mathias' Parish, had been admitted to the Providence novitiate that same morning. That would make his daughter the thirteenth in the new family. He arranged with Sister Gamelin for Esther's dowry, and spoke of the vows which she would take. . . . Afterward he had seen her garbed in the simple habit of the postulant and had held her briefly in his strong arms; then had gone. Sister Pariseau remembered the sound of a wind rising.

CHAPTER 5

T HERE had been no luxury at Saint Elzear, but there had been an air of familiar comfort and warmth in the Pariseau home. The new Asile had been occupied for only a few months, and it was, besides, barren and impersonal, especially to eyes seeing it for the first time. The furnishings of the novitiate room were austere and strictly utilitarian, and no effort had been made to soften the barracks-like appearance. Sister Pariseau found satisfaction in its scrupulous cleanliness, while at the same time she wondered if human beings actually were expected to live here. Certainly, with the exception of a table and a few benches, there were few signs of present occupancy. About the place there was an awful emptiness. In the first dreadful hours of blind homesickness, while she was building up her outward composure by an intense attention to the business of each individual moment, she lashed out at that other Esther Pariseau, that soft creature of the fine intentions, and asked her what she had expected. Had she entered religion for a life of ease and comfort? But there came a time, before the week was out, when neither her carefully built exterior poise nor her self-opprobrium was enough. The bitter, rising tide of complete abjection and misery swept in and engulfed her spirit. Of herself, she had no defenses left, no courage with which to bear this pain that clawed its way through her mind and even over into the realm of her usually healthy body.

In the chapel on her knees before the Blessed Sacrament,

the storm had its way with her; and there in the semi-darkness she learned that it was not enough to be a Pariseau. She was helplessly swallowed up by wave after wave of pure anguish. Some grace, some habit of prayer, made her cry out in the face of this new knowledge of her own inadequacy. Gradually she again became conscious of time and of some abatement of her desolation. "Lord, save me." After a while she was given enough strength to rise from her knees and make her way to the little dormitory which awaited her in cold comfort. Surprisingly she slept–a sleep of utter exhaustion which liberated her heart and cleansed her mind of all self-pity and self-reliance.

At Mass next morning she smiled ruefully at that Esther of the exuberant audacity to whom to propose to do a thing was to do it. She knew now that what she had undertaken was a task beyond either her present understanding or her ability to accomplish. Unless the Lord build this house of her religious life, it would indeed never be built. She could only hope that the timber she had brought in for His building had been a good selection. Whatever strength and soundness it had–that too was His doing and He alone knew what was there. Then the bell rang at the Elevation of the Host and she raised her eyes to Him; there was no need for words.

During the day from time to time she thought she saw the eyes of Sister Gamelin resting quizzically upon her. But nothing was said to her, and since there were still too many sore spots for her to be comfortable about the experience, she did not speak to either Sister Gamelin or Canon Prince about any of it until. much later. In the meantime she found it easier to be patient with Sister Choquet as the two of them worked together in the kitchen and the women's wards. There was plenty of work for them to do, and it was well that they learned to share it between them as they replaced the novices at the various household tasks. Gradually the strangeness passed, and the ache in her heart was eased as she found herself caught up into the tempo of affairs at the Asile. But no matter how much she loved her vocation nor how much natural enjoyment she subsequently found accompanying it, she never forgot that for its fulfillment she was utterly dependent on the grace of God. It was a treasure she never afterwards took for granted.

In the next few weeks, Sister Pariseau plunged with youthful vivacity and strength into the round of duties which filled her waking moments. The Asile was a busy place, with much coming and going through its portals. Rich folk and poor, great ecclesiastics and prominent laymen were often seen in the corridors and in the simple reception rooms. There was an air of expectancy and high purpose in the very atmosphere which made itself felt even as far as the kitchen. This was God's house–the house of His Providence, and almost anything was likely to happen.

One knew, of course, that the reserves in the pantry were scant for the more than three-score people to be fed here daily, not to mention those others who found their way to the back doors. What one could have done with a few seeds and an acre or so in which to plant them! But if this were not Saint Elzear, there were other resources, and one learned to live by faith from meal to meal. God was not remote in His Heaven, unmindful of His children here on Saint Catherine Street. Like the good father He is, He had a way of making a timely arrival with what was needed. The hotel servants who came with the left-overs, or the ladies of charity and their attendants who brought contributions in food might be anything but godlike in aspect or demeanor–but the two postulants were sure, for all that, that only God could know what they had lacked to make a. good nourishing soup or a thick succulent stew. He knew each essential ingredient even to the onion. Sister Choquet and Sister Pariseau were never sure how much of what happened was miracle and how much was natural contingency.

Long afterwards in speaking of these days, one of them would tell the community historian:

The provisions had failed. The dispenser notified the treasurer, the treasurer informed Mother Gamelin, and Mother Gamelin sent one of the aged women to the chapel to tell Our Lord. Invariably alms fitting the circumstance came to replenish either the purse or the pantry. At other times when our venerated Mother was notified of the lack of food for the next meal, she would go to advise the cook or give her a helping hand; then, as always, there would be plenty for the "guests of Providence."

Those were years of scarcity that challenged the austerity and self-restraint of the new community which was in the process of being formed, which called for the ingenuity of the cooks. The food might be frugal, but with the traditional French talent for a satisfactory cuisine it became edible and sustaining. Sister Pariseau learned to deal with an economy of privation as formerly at Saint Elzear she had learned to manage an economy of plenty. She kept her respect for quality, but she became wise in the use of substitution and alteration; she learned the art of adaptation; above all, she learned to make the best of what was committed to her care. But it was not a painless experience, and occasionally she wondered how the great lady who was now known simply as Sister Gamelin could be so imperturbable and restrained in the face of his never-ending process of making something out of nothing.

As Sister Gamelin joined them in the kitchen one day in late February, Sister Pariseau was reminded of her own mother. The two were nearly the same age, and both had about them a quiet, inward quality which one fancied was deep rather than profuse. Both had a composure which could only have been tempered by profound sorrow. Neither was given to many words, nor to easy confidences, but both could appraise with a glance and lift one's heart with a phrase. As she remembered her mother's grief over the death of those small Pariseaux—Eulalie, Salomie, and Seraphine, her heart turned in quick pity and understanding to the woman now beside her. Françoise Pariseau had lived most of her life in a remote country district, whereas Emmelie Gamelin had been a part of the great world of Montreal and Quebec—a world of fashion and comfort and power. Yet fundamentally there was the same timbre of womanhood indelibly hurt by woman's deepest sorrow. No wonder that Sister Gamelin's greatest devotion was to Our Lady of Sorrows, that Mother who held in her arms the body of her Divine Son dead from the sins of men. Like that holy mother, she had recognized God's purposes and had turned from her own desolation to the ministry of charity. In place of her own children she had put others—ven those dear, eccentric old creatures upstairs for whom this asile had been built. How good He was to allow her to work beside Sister Gamelin, even in so humble a place as this kitchen! Into the cherished company of those she loved—her parents, Julie, Stanislaus, the other Pariseaux, and Elizabeth Bruyère—she now admitted another named Emmelie Gamelin. It was a friendship she would cling to up to the dark portals of death, and beyond.

There was little opportunity in the spring of 1844 for the quiet enjoyment of this friendship. Sister Gamelin was much absorbed in the general management of I affairs at the Asile, and besides, she was a novice. Canon Prince came daily to preside at the spiritual exercises of the novices, and Monseigneur Bourget himself was frequently at the Asile to give them conferences. Sister Choquet and Sister Pariseau sometimes speculated between themselves about what happened on such occasions, and they looked ahead with longing to the time when they too would be admitted to the holy of holies.

With the approach of the Feast of the Annunciation their yearning was intensified by the general atmosphere of anticipation which pervaded the whole house. Monseigneur had announced that, after the brief months of preparation, the seven were to be allowed to take their vows on the feast of Our Lady of Seven Dolors. The feast that year fell on March 29, and the novena for the Annunciation had just ended when the three-day retreat preceding the profession of vows began.

For those who made the retreat, the time of high tension which preceded it slipped over without event into the unvexed solitude of silence and prayer; for the three other novices and the two postulants, there was left the dual task of seeing that the retreatants were undisturbed, and of carrying on the work of the house as best they could. It was for the latter a fatiguing time. Fortunately, the Ladies of Charity came to their aid , and either came themselves to do the work in the kitchen and in the old people's quarters or sent their servants to help.

In the midst of things, Sister Gamelin fell ill. Of late years her health had been none too robust for the tremendous exactions laid upon it. The mental and physical stress of the last few weeks finally took its toll, and briefly threatened to incapacitate her for March 29. A wave of anxiety and unease surged through the Asile. Promptly Sister Pariseau assumed a place near Sister Gamelin and cared for her as best she could without interrupting the course of the retreat. To the great relief of all, the illness proved neither serious nor prolonged.

Preparations for the feast moved ahead. Again the Ladies of Charity were on hand to help. They had been given permission to make whatever contribution they desired as a memorial gift, and they used this authority to the full.

The Ladies defrayed the expense of decorating the chapel, the walls and altars of which were still unfinished. They had the Blessed Virgin's altar, the main altar, and all the woodwork painted. Unknown to the retreatants, eight wooden candlesticks beautifully decorated, five bouquets of artificial flowers for the main altar, eight for the small. altars, and four potted plants were put in place. They bought flowers and ribbon to decorate the waxen tapers for the professed. They made garlands for the sanctuary and wreaths for the seven little girls who were to represent the orphans at the profession ceremony. The vestments, linens and laces were made by Mademoiselle Burroughs and one of the novices.

Delighting in this unwonted munificence and desiring above all that this first profession in their little community should have a beautiful setting, the younger novices and the two postulants spent the entire night before the ceremony in preparing the chapel. When the fitful candlelight paled with the coming of the cool dawn, every bit of altar linen was smoothed into place, every flower was arranged in balanced and delicate beauty, every new vestment was laid out in elegant precision. It seemed then to Sister Pariseau, as she knelt briefly to ask Our Lord to take care of all the rest, that the city beyond their walls was already stirring. Even before she finished her prayer, she heard the sound of voices, and looking out on the street below she saw lines of people beginning to form. Where had they all come from at this hour? In the half-light she discerned some familiar faces—Madame

Cuvillier, Madame Nowland, and young Madame Fabre, all relatives of Sister Gamelin, here with Madame LaCroix, Madame Gerwin, Madame Delorme, and Mademoiselle Berthelet to take part in the ceremony. Behind them were scores of others, all of Montreal it seemed , pressing forward to make sure of a place in the chapel. The doors were soon opened, and the crowd surged in. Within an hour they had filled the chapel, now brilliant with the light of many candles.

It seemed to Sister Pariseau that there were a dozen places she should be at once. Certainly there were two places she would choose to be—one, at the side of Sister Gamelin, to be reassured that all was well with her as she waited with the others in the room across from the chapel—secondly, with Our Lord, who was king and center of all, on His Eucharistic throne. Thinking on Him and what this day must mean to Him, she felt again that sudden, expansive joy in her vocation swirl through her heart so that she could scarcely breathe for the happiness in her. The fatigue of the night hours dropped away, and she felt refreshed and strong. If she could only stop long enough to fix this exultation in her mind for all time! But there were these hundreds of people to find place for, and there was no longer any room. She did the next best thing—she consoled them with places outside in the halls and on the street, and assured them that Monseigneur would give them his blessing and that they should also see the new Sisters of Providence in good time. On one of her expeditions back and forth she caught a glimpse of the seven who had been joined by their attendants—the little girls carrying the symbolic new habits, the Ladies of Charity, the aged women. All were waiting in repressed quiet.

Shortly after six there was a flurry of movement, and the crowd parted to allow passageway for Monseigneur Bourget, Canon Prince, and Abbé Caron. Sister Pariseau thought she had never seen so magnificent a figure as Monseigneur in his bishop's purple and fine lace rochet, the silken elegance of his mozzetta enhancing the patrician dignity of his head and shoulders. As he made his way to the sanctuary, a sigh of eagerness went through the chapel, and there was the last-minute stir in the choir; then time was held suspended as he vested leisurely, in sight of them all, receiving each sacred vestment from the waiting hands of Abbé Caron or young Joseph Richard, the acolyte. Sister Pariseau was startled out of a nebulous dream-world by the Monseigneur's voice, clear and strong, intoning the *Veni Creator Spiritus.* Everything was suddenly under way with the choir's taking up the hymn, and the whole world was drenched with sound, color, and fragrance. The Mass was begun and moved ahead until the Gradual, when Abbé Caron left the sanctuary and advanced toward the seven waiting beyond the entrance of the chapel for the blessed invitation which now was given.

"Prudentes virgines, aptate vestras lampades, ecce sponsus venit, exite obviam ei."

The voice was that of Abbé Caron, broken with emotion, but actually it was only God who could make that request. Looking at the pale, illumined face of Sister Gamelin as she and the others followed Abbé Caron and Canon Prince into the chapel, Sister Pariseau humbly prayed that she too might have those words in her own ears and heart to treasure for all eternity. She prayed, too, for those now walking so solemnly down the aisle each accompanied by an aged lady of the Asile on her right, and a Lady of Charity on her left, and following a flower-crowned child in white. Let them walk always in the way of holiness so that the Kingdom of the Heart of Christ may grow! Because of them let many others be drawn to follow in their footsteps! Surely this spectacle of youth and age, of wealth and poverty, of simplicity and splendour should cause many to ponder a similar vocation. When Monseigneur turned for the official interrogation, her prayer took on a quality of greater immediacy.

"Daughters, is it really Jesus Christ whom you have come to serve in this holy house?"

If only their voices will not stick in their throats, she thought. The answer was one she wanted the whole world to hear. And when it came she was satisfied.

"Yes, my Lord, it is He whom we wish to serve in the person of the poor, and, with the help of His grace, it is He whom we wish to follow by consecrating ourselves today to the religious life."

The ceremony moved along; the new community was officially erected by Monseigneur, the vows were said, the Mass completed, and the final *Te Deum sung.*

The procession formed again, and the *Ecce Quam Bonum* was intoned.

Behold how good and how pleasant when brothers dwell in unity. Gracious as balm poured on the head. It is as if dew like the dews of Hermon were falling on this hill of Sion; here, where the Lord has promised to grant benediction and life everlasting.

It *was* good to dwell in this holy house of the Asile, and she meant to see to it that there was perfect unity between herself and Sister Choquet, though, of course, that was something that needed watching; as her mother had told her long ago, she herself was likely on occasion to be imperious.

In another month the two of them were on retreat in preparation for the reception of the Holy Habit. For three days Canon Prince instructed them, counseled them' and prayed with all the uncompromising devotion of his ascetic soul. Sister Pariseau found herself at one period stricken with consternation at the sight of so much to be done within her own soul, and then again rapt out of herself at the prospect of all that God had promised those who love Him. On Sunday, April 28, 1844, they were clothed with the grey habit and white cape of the novice according to the simple ritual of the newly introduced ceremonial. Monseigneur officiated and preached the sermon, using as his text the parable of the Ten Virgins. During the formal interrogation of intention when Monseigneur had asked them if they sincerely wished to dedicate themselves to Christ and if they felt equal to what they were undertaking, Sister Pariseau hoped in spite of the candle which trembled in her hand that her reply was loud enough to be heard not only by the good prelate before her but by all the heavenly court as well:

We believe that we are called to be servants of the poor, and we rely upon the grace of God to fulfil faithfully until death the arduous duties which are laid upon us by this glorious title.

Coming back into the novitiate arrayed in the new habit with the full panoply of the crisp white cape, she heard the choir sing the "Non nobis, Domine" of the psalm. Not to us, Lord, of course, not to us but to the glory of Your name! And then remembering the earlier verses of the same psalm, she had trouble restraining a smile at the plight of the Psalmist,

> When Israel came out of Egypt . . .
> The sea beheld and fled,
> Jordan turned backward.
> The mountains skipped like rams
> And the hills like little lambs.
> What ails thee, O sea, that thou fleest?
> O Jordan, what drove thee back?
> Ye mountains, why leap like rams,
> And hills, like little lambs?
> Tremble, O earth, at the Lord's presence.

It would be so easy to skip with the mountains. The Psalmist must have been a very old man no longer to understand that joy puts wings on one's feet.

. . . .

Time moved along making each day memorable at the Asile with its blend of the ordinary and the extraordinary. It was an era of beginnings, so that no day was casual. On May 1, Sister Thibodeau, later to be called Mother Mary of the Immaculate Conception, took up the duties to which she was elected as mistress of novices.

On the same day, twelve orphans were turned over to the Sisters' care, thus inaugurating that type of charitable work at the Providence.

Toward the end of the same month, on Pentecost Sunday, Monseigneur Bourget, with much pomp and circumstance, solemnly blessed "Marie Elizabeth Genevieve," the great bell donated to the Asile by Monsieur and Madame Louis de la Grave. Sponsors for the bell were the former Mayor of Montreal, the Honorable Jacques Viger, and the wife of the President of the Council Madame Amable-Forestier Viger. The bell had been cast in London and attuned to the note *la*, the *Melange Religieux* informed the public. It had to await the building of a belfry which was completed only in the fall. When Sister Pariseau first heard its silver tones announcing the lay retreat on September 18, she remembered the dusty road on the way to Saint Martin de Laval and Great Bourdon booming out a welcome to all the Pariseaux riding so proudly in the fine new carriage. How far away those days, and yet how remarkably near. She had no regrets for having left them, but she missed her family. It had been for her a long journey from December 26, 1843, to September 18, 1844. She was conscious of a new maturity within her own soul, a spiritual and intellectual growth which had come principally from living under the same roof with the gentle Lord of the Holy Eucharist. Perhaps, she thought, some of this growing wisdom was due to the proddings of Canon Prince who was not one to tolerate shabby, half-hearted efforts at the life of perfection. It was all or nothing with him, and it quickly became all or nothing with those he directed. Indeed, she mused, to be a Pariseau was not enough, but it was an excellent beginning. She would be guilty of denying God's gifts were she ever to disavow what her family meant to her. The bells of all the world would remind her always of Great Bourdon pouring out its rich harmony across the fields and meadows of home, across the buckwheat bobbing in the warm sun, across the bright wheat fields, through the orchards and over the pasture lands. Here in Montreal at Notre Dame Church there was another Bourdon, larger, it is true, than that of her native parish. So large it was, in fact, that it was rung only on special occasions. Its heavy bass was so deep as to crowd out all other sound. She herself preferred the more mellow and flexible tones of the Saint Martin Bourdon. In any case, she hoped that some day, when her Lord Himself would go with her through the dark portal, there would be the sound of bells. In the meantime she had better learn how to handle "Marie Elizabeth Genevieve" to the satisfaction of her Mother Mistress and Canon Prince -to the satisfaction of all Montreal, she supposed. For rising, there must be good brisk doubles for the space of a *Pater* and *Ave*; for the Angelus, three groups of three singles, spaced by an *Ave*, and then doubles; for the Community Mass, doubles during two *Paters* followed by thirty singles; for the *De Profundis*, three, four, five singles separated by an *Ave*, and then one single; for

retiring, nine slow singles spaced by an *Ave*; for the departing soul, the knell or nine tolls for a man and six for a woman
rung thrice, and the slow doubles through five minutes; for the
funeral—or that she had better go by the book. There had been
no funeral as yet.

That fall there were other things to be learned than the management of "Marie Elizabeth Genevieve." Minor elections on
October 2 included even Sister Pariseau's status. She was made
community chandler. Candlemaking she had been taught by her
mother, but here at the Asile she learned to deal with quantity.
Within a year the personnel had doubled, and the demands on
her department as on every other had seen a proportionate increase. Besides, some of the parish churches purchased candles
from the sisters thus enabling the latter to increase their slender
income. Moreover, she was no mere worker in wax and tallow.
She was working toward a constant remembrance of God and
His holy presence within and around her. So as she molded and
dipped she tried, in true recollection of spirit, to think of Christ,
the light of the world; Christ, as the Holy Child, held in His
mother's arms; Christ, the Son of Man, dispelling the bitter darkness from the hidden comers of men's hearts; Christ, the Son of
God, putting light into the eyes of the blind; Christ, the Jesus on
Tabor so shining and beautiful that even the brash Peter could
not look at Him. Sometimes she faltered in either the candlemaking or the recollection, so engrossed she was in the one at the
expense of the other. But God would accept her good will in lieu
of perfection in either undertaking. What Canon Prince would
accept was another story.

When she was not making candles, there were other tasks. She
and Sister Marchessault, a senior novice, were assigned to help
Mother Caron in her combined offices of treasurer, economist,
and apothecary. The economist's job entailed the supervision
and care of the kitchen, the bakery, the garden, the shoeshop,
the poultry yard, and the carpenter shop, as well as the weaving and dyeing of cloth, the making of soap, and the laundry.
As Sister Pariseau shuttled from one assignment to another,
she learned to deal not only with things but with people of all

ages and conditions, of all ranks and occupations. She learned
her way about the city, along streets whose names were like a
long litany of the saints. She frequently walked along Saint
Paul Street to the Bon Secours Market, where necessity taught
her to drive a close bargain for the poor folk at the Asile. As
she walked, she caught glimpses of life far beyond anything she
had dreamed of at Saint Elzear. There was the busy river front
with its tallmasted sailing ships and steamboats plying a traffic
which took them to every corner of the globe. Near the market place, high above the church of Notre Dame de Bonsecours
was the statue of Our Lady blessing the mariner outward bound,
and afterwards guiding him safely home from his voyage. Sometimes, accompanying Mother Gamelin or Mother Caron down
Saint James Street, she saw the great ones of the world of wealth
and fashion and accosted them with regard to the business of
the Providence. Now and then on the way back to Saint Catherine Street, it would have been pleasant to loiter under the shade
trees along the Saint Martin River near Viger Market. But the
rule was most explicit about that. The Sister of Providence had a
double vocation: she lived and worked in the world, but she was
nonetheless bound to keep her mind and heart cloistered. Again
and again the rule warned her of the difficulty of the situation:

> Their monastery at times, is but the homes of the sick; their chapel,
> the parish church; their cloister the city streets or the hospital wards;
> their enclosure, obedience; their grate, the fear of God; and saintly
> modesty, their only veil.

The novices were startled by Monseigneur Bourget's announcement on November 10 that Canon Prince would not be their
director any longer, though it had been evident that the worthy
canon was being groomed for ecclesiastical advancement. For
eighteen months he had guided the young community and per-
fected the details for which Monseigneur had lacked time. He
was an austere man and at times a severe one, to whom weakness was an abomination. However, neither Sister Pariseau nor
the other members of the community resented his occasional
harshness or held anything but grateful respect for his sincere and

careful training of them. They knew him to be affable and courteous as well as unvaryingly on hand when they needed him. It was
Canon Prince who urged that the sisters be sent to Hotel Dieu to
learn the care of the sick, and to the Congregation of Notre Dame
to learn how to make church vestments and other allied arts. It
was Canon Prince who insisted on competence and economy in
the various works of the Institute, and it was he who taught them
to keep records and accounts. He remained a true friend of Providence and never failed to return to the Asile whenever possible.
In fact, in October, 1845, after he had been raised to the episco-
pate, he was named the ecclesiastical superior of the Sisters of
Providence and remained so for two terms. There would come a
day, not too distant, when he would hasten to the Asile to stand
by the sisters in their darkest hour. No tie could bind him more
irrevocably to them than the comfort he had given them. In the
meantime, Canon Frederic Alexis Truteau was named chaplain
of the Motherhouse and became adviser and confessor for the
sisters.

The year 1844 merged into 1845, with its blessed promise of
profession day in mid-summer. The chronicles of the new year record an expansion of the works at the Providence, the coming and
going of dignitaries and benefactors, a new building program, and
also an account of the long retreat given by Monseigneur Bourget
himself to the members of the novitiate. Beyond the Asile, the
city lived its teeming life, electing a new mayor, organizing a new
medical school, building sprawling new suburbs; beyond the city,
the province waged its relentless warfare against an unfortunate
governor; to the south an aggressive young neighbor was reaching
out an imperialist hand to clutch more land in Texas and Oregon.
Some echoes of all this were heard on Saint Catherine Street, but
not many. Sister Pariseau's ear was bent to hear one voice that
spring and summer, and it was a voice which spoke in stillness.
So she waited until He should speak His acceptance through her
superiors. How much of life is spent in waiting!

Speak He did, in His good time . . .

"Marie Elizabeth Genevieve" was never so beautiful as on

July 21, 1845, when the doubles rang out high and clear summoning the ten Sisters of Providence to the community Mass and to the profession of the three who would be numbers eleven, twelve, and thirteen in their ranks; summoning, too, the Sénés from Pointe aux Tremble and Montreal, the Choquets from Saint Mathias, and the Pariseaux from Saint Elzear, to witness the simple ceremony of the vows.

Sister Pariseau found herself kneeling at the altar rail, found herself answering the protective kindness which was Monseigneur's voice, found herself conscious of listening to the other two:

"I, Emelie Sené, in religion Sister Emelie . . . Elizabeth Choquet, in religion Sister Elizabeth . . ."

Then she heard her own voice in the fragrant and golden silence, speaking to Christ:

In the name of the Father, and of the Son, and of the Holy Ghost, I, Esther Pariseau, in religion Sister Joseph, freely promise and willingly make to the Divine Majesty the vows of poverty, chastity, and obedience; to serve the poor for the rest of my life, according to the rules and constitutions of this house, under the authority of His Lordship, the Bishop, to whom I submit for the fulfillment as well as for the dispensation of these present vows.

I most humbly supplicate the divine mercy, through the infinite merits of Our Lord Jesus Christ, the intercession of His glorious Mother, and the prayers of the holy patrons of this community, to graciously accept these present engagements and to grant me the grace of being faithful until death. Amen.

The "Joseph" was for her father. That would make him happy.

CHAPTER 6

Aвве Augustine Magloire Alexander Blanchet had been afrequent visitor at both the Yellow House and the Asile. Ascanon of the Cathedral, he was often seen busy on official errands for Monseigneur Bourget, and Sister Joseph had come to expect that his influence in ecclesiastical affairs would some day tower above their little world on Saint Catherine Street.

The Abbé Francis Norbert Blanchet, his brother, had returned to Montreal after six grueling years in the Oregon country, to be raised to the espiscopate along with Canon Prince. The account of Bishop-Elect Blanchet's six-months' voyage from some remote spot called the Willamette was on everybody's lips in the summer of 1845, and all the world turned out to see this dour missionary from the wild West consecrated Bishop of Draza on July 25. The *Melange Religieux* reported that never before had such religious solemnity been seen in Canada.

Canada was interested in the Oregon country, as was the Holy See-and with good reason. By 1825 with the building of Fort Vancouver, the Hudson's Bay Company had pushed its empire to the banks of the Columbia and to the Pacific Coast area. Great Britain then had a reputable though unconfirmed claim to the Oregon territory on the basis of both explorations and settlement. There was a sharp contest on between the British lion and the American eagle for the land west of the Rockies which lay within the forty-second and the fifty-fourth parallels, and in the early forties the eagle was being uncomfortably shrill over the issue of "manifest destiny" and "fifty-four forty or fight." The question involved the fur traffic in the Northwest, the opening and settlement of new lands, as well as the Orient trade of China, the Philippines, the Sandwich Islands, and Russian America.

The French Canadian was not interested in empire. But both he and his religious leaders were concerned with Oregon for reasons connected with the faith. In the vanguard of Hudson's Bay were the men of the forest—the trappers, the traders, the *voyageurs*. No river was too furious for their long Indian canoes and cedar paddles, no forest too impenetrable for the light step of their moccasined feet. There were few families of Quebec who had not boasted at one time or another a *Jean, a Jacques*, or a *François* in the employ of the Honorable Company, as their ancestors before them had been in the service of the old French *Companie du Nord*. In times, many of them found occupation in the subsidiary interests of the company, sometimes at Cowlitz Farm or Nisqually Farm or French Prairie where rich farmland offered the comparative comfort of a settled existence after the untrammeled freedom of life among the portages. The more serious among them longed for the ministrations of the Church to regularize their family alliances and to help them establish a more ordered society. In this they were seconded by the Hudson's Bay Company which was interested in anything which would stabilize its widespread holdings. Moreover, their chief factor for the Columbia District, Doctor John McLoughlin, who was allied by blood and early association to the French Canadians of the Northwest, if not by practical Catholicism, was sympathetic toward their desire for priests among them.

So it was that in 1836 the region was added to the vicariate of Bishop Provencher of Manitoba, who himself was an auxiliary of the Bishop of Quebec, and in 1838 the Abbé Francis Norbert Blanchet of the Montreal diocese and young Abbé Modeste Demers from the Red River country were sent West. They traveled overland with the Hudson's Bay spring brigade to Fort Vancouver, which they reached after six arduous months over some 5,325 miles. On November 24 they were welcomed by Mr. James Douglas, the company commandant at Vancouver, who was the first authority during Dr. McLoughlin's absence in Europe. Mass was said at the fort school on the next day, Sunday. Holy Mother Church had come once more to her own.

The waters of baptism flowed freely during the next few months at Fort Vancouver and Cowlitz, at Willamette Mission and Fort Nisqually, on the heads of Pambruns, Proulx, and Gervaises, on Plomondons, Luciers, and LaFramboises. But the ministrations of the missionaries were not limited to those bearing French names; the old registers have their sprinkling of Kittsons and McDonalds and McCartys and Ogdens and McTavishes. Marriages between company servants and Nancy "Okanogan," Marie "Tchehilis," or Steni "Tchinouk" were blessed, with company officials looking on as approving witnesses. Over and over again the names of John McLoughlin, Forbes Barclay, James Douglas, Francis Ermatinger, William Frazer Tolmie, Thomas McKay were appended to the records in attestation of their concurrence. The motto of Hudson's Bay was the grimly realistic *Pro pelle cutum,* "a skin for a skin"; but the leaders of the Honorable Company were men of sufficient foresight to respect the Church in its role of civilizer. If these wild charges of theirs, whites as well as Indians, were ever to set up a good society, then they needed the blessings of God and the help of that ancient Mother Church who in an earlier era had patiently tamed the Celts and the Goths, the Saxons and the Normans, the Huns and the Slavs. It was this Church which found place in Fort Vancouver and Saint Paul in the person of Abbé Francis Norbert Blanchet.

But neither Father Blanchet nor his assistant, Father Demers, could begin to cover the vast territory assigned to their care. It extended from the Cayuse Indian country and the Bitterroot area in the east Oregon territory to the Quinault-Chehalis-Cowlitz land along the Pacific Coast, from Vancouver Island and the Kootenai in the north, to California on the south. They were joined in 1840 by Father Pierre jean DeSmet, the intrepid Belgian Jesuit, coming out from Saint Louis, Missouri, and working mostly among the Coeur d'Alenes and the Flatheads. Though they succeeded in building missions at Saint Paul, Vancouver, and

Cowlitz, they spent their time chiefly in endless journeying—by bateau and river boat, on horseback and afoot, to Fort Nisqually and Fort Victoria, to Fort Okanogan and Fort Colville, to Fort Boise and Fort Nez Percé, on and on interminably. Help came again in the fall of 1842 when Father Antoine Langlois and Father Zacharie Bolduc were sent from Canada, and in August 1844 when Father DeSmet arrived at Saint Paul's, Oregon, with five European Jesuits and Six Sisters of Notre Dame de Namur. The whole program of missionary activity was quickened and intensified.

To the great satisfaction of all those concerned it was learned that Rome itself was deeply interested in this new field and had shown its benign approval of the prodigious labors of the missionaries there. As early as December 1, 1843, Oregon was erected into a vicariate apostolic, and Father Francis Norbert Blanchet was created its bishop, though it was only on November 4, 1844, that word of his new dignity and responsibility reached him in Oregon. He set out for Montreal on December 5, 1844, and, after a voyage which took him to Honolulu, Cape Horn, London, and Boston, arrived in Montreal the following June. He was consecrated by Monseigneur Bourget at Saint James Cathedral.

Canon Augustine Magloire Alexander Blanchet looked on from his privileged place in the sanctuary; and young Sister Joseph, from the sisters' comer on the epistle side of the nave, was able to catch an occasional glimpse of the celebrities of that day's ritual. As the magnificent service moved on both were occupied not only with the solemn rite whereby this man was made a successor to the apostles but also with the thought of his vicariate.

The name Oregon sent echoes through the mind—thoughts that quickened and died and lived again to raise uncomfortable and teasing implications. There was the importunate remembrance of those other sheep outside the fold who were going shepherdless for no reason of their own making, poor unfortunate souls to whom no one brought the saving name of Jesus. Sister Joseph moved uneasily, suddenly conscious of the spiritual largess which had been showered upon her. None of it had been because of her deserts, surely. To him that has much, much is given, indeed, but to what purpose? She wondered about her own responsibilities, about the obligations imposed by God's generosity to her. He Himself must show the way to meet these obligations; that way might mean Oregon and work with those poor, savage inhabitants. In the midst of the richness of this present scene–the music, the spirals of incense, the rustle of silken vestments, the measured Latin of versicle and response–the thought seemed incongruous. She busied herself with her prayers and put Oregon aside as a distraction. Yet abruptly she knew that this was no distraction. The insistent voice speaking of Oregon was her Lord's and she bent her heart to listen to whatever He would say. That was not clear yet, but she did not doubt that He would make Himself understood in good time. Beyond, there in the sanctuary, she saw Canon Magloire Blanchet's face, pale now and a little tired, but it had a hidden look as if he too were waiting. As the ceremony burst into a thunderous finale, with the church bells pealing out overhead and the long line of the processional forming in jumbled order and then moving in leisurely and punctilious dignity down the center of the church, it seemed to Sister Joseph that the episcopal consecration was not to be the only business of this day. The Asile, when she reached it in company with the other sisters of Providence, had grown incredibly dearer.

. . . .

She was not surprised, the following summer, to learn that Canon Magloire Blanchet had been elevated to the episcopacy on July 28. His new diocese was that of Walla Walla in the Oregon territory. In the months that followed his consecration on September 27, 1846, Sister Joseph assisted Mother Gamelin in preparing linens and vestments for the new bishop. As they sewed they spoke often of that distant country and of the poor Indians who lived there without the knowledge of the God who made them. These conversations and the half-spoken aspirations to serve God in Oregon were other bonds between them.

. . . .

On November 2, 1846, Julie Pariseau came from Ile Jésus to join Sister Joseph at the Asile. For three years she had remained in her beloved Esther's place at Saint Elzear; but now that Stanislaus had reached a sturdy maturity and Zoë and Elodie were able to care for the household and help with Moyse, Monsieur and Madame Pariseau were willing that Julie, too, should follow her vocation to religion. The snow was not yet heavy on the roads when her father came down to Montreal a second time to give a daughter to God. The wintry years had, however, silvered his dark head and weighted his shoulders. He moved slowly, Sister Joseph noted. But there was still the strong, proud glance, and power as well as tenderness in his embrace. How good to see him again and to let the closely drawn fibers of her nature expand and rest in his warm presence!

All was fine at Saint Elzear, though of course *maman* could be stronger, Zoë and Elodie were not so skilled in the carriage shop as Esther had been, but then, he himself was in the shop very little now that Joseph and Stanislaus were running the business. Most of the work was being done at Saint Martin de Laval where Pariseau Brothers were coming to be highly respected. Now and then he and George took a turn, because it would be regrettable that there should grow up a Pariseau who did not know the feel of wood in his hands. One understood more about God's goodness when one knew the wheel, and the ash and oak and tempered iron which made it. They all had their hands full with the baby Moyse, assuredly; without doubt they were too indulgent with him; as well, he was the last—except for the grandchildren who were beginning to arrive, as she knew.

They would miss Julie as they had missed Esther, but he and their mother had been particularly blessed in that God had wanted their two fine daughters. They were proud, too, that they were here at this house, working with the great lady who was its superior. One knew at a glance that she had quality—fine grain, strength as well as flexibility, and intelligence. Had she not had the good sense to take his word about his daughter?

Sister Joseph relaxed under the genial flow of his thought. She had no need to reassure him about her own happiness. He knew without being told that all was well with her, and this knowledge gave him strength to part with Julie. After all, ther came a point beyond which no parent, not even a Pariseau, could go with a child. For the rest, that was God's department.

When he left in the late afternoon, Sister Joseph felt a wholesome renewal of spirit. He had brought with him an invigorating freshness which blew through her like a bracing wind blowing away the small conceits and fripperies with which good people so often try to delude themselves and others. How wonderful to be a Pariseau! How much more wonderful to be beloved of God in this holy house! She must help Julie to this realization, though there was little that she or anybody could do to mitigate the desperate loneliness of these next few days. Dear Julie, now another Sister Pariseau, lost in the anonymity of the postulant's habit.

· · · · · · · · ·

By the beginning of the year 1847 there were at the Providence some twenty-six professed sisters and sixteen novices and postulants. Their works now included the care of orphans, aged and invalid priests, and mental patients, in addition to their original service to aged and infirm women and teaching. The demands of charity were far in excess of their personnel. The greatest strain was yet to come when the little community was barely five years old.

There had been a disquieting rumor during the late winter and early spring of 1846–1847 of frequent and sudden death among those arriving on ships from Ireland. Ship fever, it was said. The Irish had suffered for two hundred years the ills of tyranny and famine and plague, all of which threatened their extinction as a people. A supine and selfish government which was not much interested in their survival did little or nothing to mitigate these ills because the once glorious isle of saints and scholars had clung with unearthly tenacity to the ancient faith. In one last heroic effort to save themselves, millions of them turned toward the new world in the early decades of the nineteenth century. Wave after mounting wave of immigrants reached the seaboard cities of the United States and Canada only to find that they had brought death with them for themselves and for those who would have befriended them.

Irish ague, typhus, ship fever–these are three names among many for the deadly disease which recurred on this side of the Atlantic in the late forties. It could always be expected in the wake of extreme poverty and famine. Squalor, crowded quarters, and filthy clothing are the breeding ground of the disease, the typhus virus being transmitted by the body louse. Foul air offensive odors, destitution, and dirt are not in themselves the cause of typhus, and neither are war and famine. But starving human beings and starving rats in search of food migrate in large numbers and being thrown closely together spread the lice which carry the disease. The unfortunate Irish fleeing from their homeland were crowded into dirty ship quarters on their desperate journey across the Atlantic. Wherever they went, death stalked them. Many died en route, and many more reached America only to find there a quick-limed grave.

Monseigneur Bourget had left for Rome on September 29, 1846. By the time he reached the Eternal City on December 15, the ills of the Irish people had increased alarmingly. The Holy Father, Pius IX, had asked that public prayers be said in Rome for the deliverance of that race which had endured poverty and oppresion but which had never faltered in its loyalty to the head of the universal Church. Piux IX had also authorized the collection of funds for Ireland, and Monseigneur had preached on that subject at the Roman Church of Saint Louis of France. By the time he returned to his own diocese in May, 1847, the typhus had reached alarming proportions in Montreal. Heroic measures were necessary to halt its spread. To supplement the steps taken by Monseigneur Prince in his absence, Monseigneur Bourget first moved to see that additional spiritual assistance be brought to the stricken. He called upon the priests of his diocese, diocesan and religious, to come to the aid of the Priests of Saint Sulpice, who had gallantly borne the brunt of the burden until then. The Canadian government hastily erected temporary hospitals called "sheds" at Point Saint Charles. To these sheds, the Grey Nuns went on June 8, 1857, to be followed on June 27 by twelve Sisters of Providence.

All had volunteered the evening before, Sister Joseph among them; but the choice of who would go had been left by Mother

Gamelin to the physician. Young Doctor Louis F. Tavernier was Mother's nephew and possessed the confidence of them all. The superior herself was detained from going by Monseigneur who felt that she should remain at the Asile for the over-all direction of affairs during the emergency. Besides the Asile with its many works, there were three branch houses, Hospice Saint Joseph's for priests, the school and house for mental patients at Longue Pointe, and the hospice at Laprairie; this meant that extreme care must be exercised in the management of the works of the young community.

In the tense hours while she was awaiting word of the assignments to Point Saint Charles, Sister Joseph was torn between her desire to help the afflicted and her revulsion for the disease. Only love of our Lord and faith in the supreme goodness of His will helped her to exterior and interior control. At twenty-four, death is unlovely in all its aspects, and death from the typhus was horrible. Yet why should she be spared when others who had had so much less in life were stricken? There was no reason, except that God in His goodness had seen fit to deal gently with her. As she waited, she prayed for courage to want suffering if the Son of God who had endured the ultimate in agony should ask her to share His passion . . .

As it turned out it was not she but Julie who went to the sheds, Julie the beloved–it seemed as much as she could bear. The postulants went almost gaily, dressed for the occasion in the novice's garb, leaving Sister Joseph to reflect ruefully that it would have been easier to go herself. In humility and confusion she prayed with Saint Peter: "Lord, Thou knowest all things; Thou knowest that I love Thee." Did she imagine an answer like an echoing overtone to her perplexed thoughts?

Amen, amen, I say to thee, when thou wast younger, thou didst gird thyself, didst walk where thou wouldst. But when thou shalt be old, thou shalt stretch forth thy hands, and another shall gird thee, and lead thee where thou wouldst not . . .

There could be no living at all were one not to trust God. He was the Lord of the universe, the arbiter of life and death. She could and would rely on His wisdom and goodness for this present moment, and for the years ahead, if there were to be any such. By the time she was forty, she would, she prayed, have the grace no longer to fear death-certainly, by the time she was fifty. And by that time, assuredly, she would gladly lay down the burden of her years. It was unthinkable that she would live beyond so advanced an age.

In the meantime, there was the present, and in it many times her capacity of things to do. With Sister Caron gone to the sheds, she had to assume her duties. Somehow they would manage.

Manage they did, in spite of the increasing demands on their personnel. The number of typhus victims in the sheds or ambulances mounted to 1,291 on the single day of August 18 alone, with twenty-five deaths there on that day. Long before that, the plague had spread throughout the city, sparing neither the great nor the lowly, the rich nor the poor. On July 16, the novice Sister Wilson fell ill of the typhus, and on August 18, Sister Assumption died of it in the community infirmary. In an interval of three months, twenty-five others contracted the disease, among them Sister Julie Pariseau.

On July 19, Monseigneur Bourget came to them at the Asile and in their name pronounced the following vow to our Lady of Seven Dolors:

We, the undersigned, Sisters of Charity and Servants of the Poor, fearing the effects of the typhus fever now afflicting our young Community, turn to thee, O Mary, our good and tender Mother. We vow for ourselves and all those who shall come after us in this community to burn seven candles every Friday of the year before the holy statue which reminds us of thy Seven Sorrows. These seven candles shall be for us the symbols of the seven principal virtues which we must practice after thy example and in thy honor; namely, simplicity, humility, obedience, confidence in Providence, abnegation, generosity, and charity . . . .

Before the fever had run its course, two other Sisters of Providence, Sister Belouin and Sister Antoine, were dead from it, and many others were weakened by it for months to come. Monseigneur Bourget and Monseigneur Prince both contracted it, and recovered; but the Vicar-General, Canon Hyacinthe Hudon, died as did Monseigneur Michael Power, Bishop of Toronto, and thirteen priests of Canada. In Montreal alone some 3,862 immigrants were buried near the spot which one day would be the northern terminal of the Victoria Bridge. One of the last victims in 1847 was the Mayor of Montreal, the Honorable John Easton Mills, who had worked unsparingly among the immigrants. The disease lingered on, but its greatest force was spent before the year was over.

Monseigneur Magloire Blanchet who with his vicar-general, Abbé Brouillet, and two clerics had left for his new diocese on March 23, 1847, reached Fort Walla Walla on September 51 they learned afterwards at the Asile. Oregon had grown remote and unsubstantial under the pressure of the weeks and months from which they had just emerged; but gradually things came into proper focus, and Sister Joseph again felt her heart turn within her at the mention of Oregon. She wondered if the decorous ecclesiastic whose stocky figure had looked so well-groomed as canon of the Cathedral might not now welcome a few homely ministrations. In quick pity for every maladroit man of God, she speculated about the rule of religious women like herself in that distant land. Surely one justification for their being there was that they might help poor priests to the external dignity to which they were entitled by their sacred office. She herself would spare no pains with needle and thread, nor with soap and water, for that matter.

But there were more immediate considerations than Oregon, and she was not sure whether her preoccupation with it was a temptation or not. It would certainly give her much natural satisfaction to see that far-away land, and to lend her native abilities and vigor to build there a small compact community wherein the' Heart of Christ would be made known, where He would be honored and loved. In that little world there would be order, goodness, prayer, and beauty.

She pulled herself up short. Thought of Oregon was like a two-edged sword. With one edge the blade hewed out a new kingdom for Christ in the wilderness; with the other, it cut through every natural tie to home and country that she had as a

Pariseau and as Sister Joseph. To leave this Asile and its beloved superior, to leave her father and mother and Stanislaus, to leave Julie with her new white wings-she trembled and sickened at the thought. How foolish to be dreaming thus of Oregon, when neither Monseigneur nor Mother Gamelin had said anything to her about it. Certainly, not of late, with all their other bewildering problems. She would have done with this "Oregon" as a vain thought. In the meantime, there was the new year of 1848.

It was a year made memorable in the Ville Marie by public devotion to the Blessed Virgin, most frequently under her title of Notre Dame de Bon Secours. Gratitude to God and to their lovely patroness for deliverance from the typhus impelled clergy ,and laity to public demonstrations in the form of processions and fetes on land and sea. One great spectacle after another bespoke the homage the city lavished on its heavenly queen.

Sister Joseph was at Mother Gamelin's right hand planning the share that the Asile took in each solemn event. For days she helped embroider the crimson velour which was the Providence offering to Notre Dame de Bon Secours. With sure and delicate stitch, her needle plied in and out of the rich fabric until it was highlighted with the tawny glint of golden lilies and roses in designs brought long ago from old France. She was grateful to her mother who had taught her needlecraft-grateful, too, to the Sisters of the Congregation for passing on the art of making vestments to the sisters at the Providence. It was all very well to be capable and healthy so that one could scrub and cook and launder and grow a garden, and she enjoyed all those things, just as she enjoyed the work in the roberie which had been her first charge. But to create something beautiful out of a yard or two of silk and an assortment of thread was even more to her liking, for it resolved the occasionally tangled skein of her vehement thoughts and emotions. She liked to meet the challenge of fragility as well as that of strength; hence, her enjoyment of the work in wax. The small, delicate figurines, when she had finished them, were sheer delight. It pleased her that Julie too had light, sure fingers for the wax work.

Before the year ended, Julie took her vows. On November

26, 1848, the second Sister Pariseau became Sister Martin. Sister Joseph's duties had become weighty. She was infirmarian, pharmacist, community seamstress, and, after Sister Caron was appointed to the new Saint Elizabeth's in Joliet, general bursar. In all these functions, Sister Martin was now named her assistant. It was pleasant that they could work side by side as in the old days, and not be constrained by the barriers which set the novitiate apart from the rest of the religious household. They had not suffered too greatly, of course, but it was easy to be betrayed by natural affection into violations of the rule, and both wanted to give God perfect service. Now the good God seemed to accommodate Himself to the ties of blood between them.

CHAPTER 7

T HE FOLLOWING SPRING, Montreal was revisited by sickness, this time by a recurrence of cholera. As they went from family to family, the sisters learned to recognize the dread symptoms: the sunken countenance, the hollow eyes, the pinched, livid features like a death's mask; the thready pulse, the cold, moist, corrugated skin; the nausea and spasms; the insatiable thirst; the clear integrity of the intellectual faculties coupled with extreme anxiety and restless, ineffectual movements of the body. They learned to fear the hot, humid days of summer as "cholera weather," and to dread the hasty summons during the night and early morning.

Again it was the poor who suffered first, and again Mother Gamelin offered the slender resources of her community to assist them. In the house of her cousin, Madame Agatha Nowlan, which was some distance southwest of the Asile in the old Saint Laurent district, a temporary hospital was set up under the title of Saint Camille de Lellis.

Monseigneur laid down the rules governing the conduct of the sisters—rules which mitigated as much as possible the ordinary austerity of their lives at the same time that they provided the nuns with protection and guidance.

Separate apartments shall be given the sisters named . . . . while braving every danger, they shall not expose themselves unnecessarily. Hence they must never inhale the patient's breath, nor lay out the dead as ordinarily, simply seeing to have the corpses put in the coffins as they were at the moment of death, and taking care to have them cov-

ered with the quicklime furnished with the coffins by the Corporation.
. . . The sisters, especially those detailed for the care of the sick, shall
be given good, nourishing food. All the dispensations, even from fast
and abstinence, are granted them in this regard. . . . They all follow the
doctors' orders. . . . In very urgent cases, and whenever necessary, the
sisters may go alone to visit their patients, relying on their good angels
to accompany and assist them everywhere.

Between July 3 and September 20, there were 138 patients
cared for at the little hospital of Saint Camille. By the fall, the
cholera subsided and again life moved along at a more normal
tenor.

News from the Pariseau home was disquieting; their mother's
illness had grown steadily worse, and there was now no hope
that she would ever recover. Sister Joseph and Sister Martin were
allowed to visit Saint Elzear, and they found Françoise Pariseau
with the marks of death already on her. She had always been gentle and quiet; now there was a detachment, a withdrawal of spirit,
which made one feel that she gave attention to those around her
and to life itself only after a return from great distances. Though
she loved them, she was already slipping ahead to the heavenly
country, to God, and to small Eulalie, Salomie, and Seraphine.

In April, 1850, Mother Gamelin sent the two of them back to
Saint Elzear, and they were with the family when the end came
on April 30. The priest had been with her, and as they prayed
around. her bedside, she suddenly left them. A door had been
closed silently and conclusively, with her for the first time in all
their lives, beyond their need for her. She had seen God, and it
was they who were lonely.

In the meantime at the Asile, Sister Joseph had lived through
a painful experience of a different nature. The last two years had
been a period of stress for the sisters. Fears and tensions arose
from sickness and overwork. The demands of external activities
had made inroads on the life of prayer. There could be but one
result—dissension among themselves.

It was a whisper of criticism, then a sudden outspoken dis-
agreement, then a chorus of vehement censure. It became clear

that the focal point of the whole unhappy dissonance was the very person who more than any other was the living embodiment of the idea of the Providence–the superior of the house. It was said that the Institute of the Daughters of Charity, Servants of the Poor, was a weak excuse for a community when so many relaxations were allowed in it. The old orders of Montreal would certainly not tolerate such constant fraternization with the world and its votaries. Why were so many dispensations from the rule allowed? Fine furniture, fine clothing, fine food were not for the servants of the poor. Moreover, the superior did not seem to know her own mind. She reprimanded today for conduct which she had commended yesterday, and she did it with severity and coldness.

At first Sister Joseph was appalled at the rising tide of opposition against Mother Gamelin, and then she was angry. In her youthful devotion, she could not distinguish between cause and effect; since all the fault-finding was so patently unjust, she wanted to lash out at the critics. She did, only to find herself the more unhappy. God seemed to leave her to herself, and her prayer became difficult and disturbed. In her inexperience she did not realize that much of the umbrage was due to taut nerves rather than to reflective judgment.

Had the critics done more thinking and less blind feeling, they would have remembered that the Providence had been founded to fill needs in society not sufficiently met by the older communities; hence, though its spirit was to be as deeply religious, its form had to be more flexible. The Mother Superior was forced by circumstances to have frequent recourse to friends and notables for the very subsistence of the Providence. Because her health was delicate, she was under obedience to take the special food which she required, no matter how embarrassing this consideration proved. As a woman of taste and affluence, she had seen to it that the furniture of her own home had been good; it seemed only sensible to her that it should now be used at the Asile. The rule was not too clearly defined, and it had been given to them piecemeal, with the result that it was sometimes subject to various interpretations and quotations. Beyond all this, was the anomalous position in which the superior was bound to find herself. She was

Placed between two authorities, both of them strong-minded ecclesiastics, very zealous for the success of this new community. Monseigneur Bourget himself undertook its direction, and he also gave it an ecclesiastical superior in the person of Monseigneur Prince. Without knowing it, the policy-makers sometimes disagreed, and sometimes their jurisdiction overlapped. Mother Gamelin was a reserved and dignified person, not given to easy explanation, and thus it was that her management seemed at times autocratic, and at other times erratic and inconsistent.

Sister Joseph needed no explanations from her superior. Her own direct and forthright nature made her endorse whatever helped towards expediting the work at hand. She understood the reserve of her superior, too, having understood her own mother. Besides, she loved her sincerely and deeply.

After finding Mother Gamelin in tears on several occasions, she was ready to call down fire on the heads of the critics. When Monseigneur Bourget announced late in 1849 that he would make an official visitation of the community, she rejoiced because she was sure that her superior would now be exonerated and the malcontents silenced.

What was her consternation to hear him, at the conclusion of the visitation, place the blame for the whole unhappy business squarely on the shoulders of Mother Gamelin and hold her responsible for the necessary amendment. Bewildered and humiliated, Sister Joseph was impelled to protest hotly the manifest unfairness of his verdict. But some prevenient grace restrained her. She had the clear memory of herself and Julie and Stanislaus on a warm summer's day along the country road on the way home from church. Again she heard her father speaking gravely and authoritatively, "This is the voice of God speaking." She did not understand, but she would bow her judgment in acquiescence. When the quick anger had died within her, she realized that her superior was leagues ahead of her on the path of sanctity. She had not remained merely silent under the reprimand. She had publicly accepted the censure and had pledged herself to correct the abuses which had come into the community as if through her fault.

Sister Joseph found that she held no resentment against Monseigneur. Perhaps he knew that the only one among them with virtue enough to suffer his reproof was the superior. He had wanted the Providence to survive, and that it could never do if there was internal dissension.

Surprisingly enough, the air was cleared and life at the Asile settled down to a conventual calm. Sister Joseph hugged to her heart a new bit of wisdom; namely, that the way of peace is the way of sacrifice, particularly the sacrifice of one's pride. She knew whom to thank for this restored peace–God first, of course, and then His faithful servant who had allowed God's grace to work among them through her. From that time on, Sister Joseph knew that she was privileged to be working side by side with a saint. Time was running out, had she known it.

. . . .

The cholera struck again in August, 1851. Mother Gamelin went to Saint Elizabeth's in Joliet County in September, and commented that they were having "cholera weather" even there. On her return she was, as usual, busy with her duties as superior. General elections were coming up, and there were other weighty matters to consider. On September 22, she presided for hours at a meeting of the council. Sister Joseph was, for the most part, intent on her duties as bursar, but was relieved, for her superior's sake, to note that the council meeting seemed to have gone to Mother's satisfaction.

For some time now she had shared Mother's bedroom, and this gave her opportunities for small, personal services which eased the burden of office. After the long day, the heat still seemed oppressive and it did not surprise her to find Mother Gamelin restless during the night. But suddenly at four in the morning, she was startled from her own rest to hear a moan and then a sharp, agonized cry of pain.

"I have the cholera, and I am going to die," Mother gasped. At a glance, Sister Joseph saw that she was acutely and violently ill. Moreover, she had indeed the symptoms of the disease which they had come to recognize so easily. Sister Joseph hastened to rouse Sister Vincent, the assistant superior, and others who might help. Dr. Tavernier was summoned, as also Dr. Deschambault, physician of the Asile.

By the time she returned to Mother's room, she found her up and trying to walk.

"I desire to go to the sisters' infirmary and share the same treatment others have when they are dying," she said.

In terrible weakness and distress she was assisted to the community infirmary and was scarcely there when Dr. Tavernier arrived.

"Dear Aunt, don't be frightened; I shall save you," he reassured her.

But she knew she was dying and begged that he would give her no sedatives which might obscure her mind. After an hour or so, her natural fear of death and the agitation which is the concomitant of cholera were succeeded by a period of prayerful calm. At eight o'clock she asked for the priest.

It was Monseigneur Prince who responded, he who had proved the steadfast friend as well as the severe mentor. It was he who administered the Last Sacraments, he who gave her the Holy Viaticum, which by some mercy she was able to receive. Monseigneur Bourget arrived at her bedside before her communion and anointing; in his presence she reaffirmed her faith and asked pardon for the human frailties by which she had grieved her community. Then, when those about her would have had a last word, she murmured, in one final compliance to their will, "Humility, simplicity . . . char-". She lapsed immediately into unconsciousness, and died at four in the afternoon.

There followed for Sister Joseph a period of confusion and bereavement so painful that all the world seemed grotesque and horrible. The very air at the Asile was fetid and contaminated. To her shocked sensibilities it seemed as if life were lived crazily on the edge of a nightmarish abyss yawning under the feet of the unwary. How could one be prepared against such a death? How forestall it? That Mother Gamelin should have had to suffer the final macabre spoliation of the quicklime, be disintegrated before their very eyes, and hustled into the tomb in dreadful and unseemly haste was a thought which did violence to reason itself. She would twitch her mind away and try to find God's will through prayer, only to find herself back again turning over the tormenting memories of those bitter hours. Nothing could touch her searing grief–not the Masses said by bishops and priests, not the tributes that were made to Mother Gamelin, not the sound of sorrow which she heard on Saint Catherine Street–nothing save God's grace in His own good time. When the passing years had done their healing work, imperceptibly and slowly, she was able to realize that the mystery of pain is impenetrable, and to know by faith that the passion of Christ, the Son of God, is never in the past but always in the everlasting now, being perpetuated in the members of His Mystical Body.

That September, she afterwards realized, she left youth behind. Sorrow would touch her again, but never so corrosively. There would be deprivation and disappointment and events of catastrophic proportions, but though she might feel grief or anxiety or pain, still no adversity would wound her so intimately and sharply.

When the great fire devastated Montreal in 1852, halting as it did on the very doorstep of the Asile, she knew fear again, and her heart bled for the victims and for those made homeless; yet had the Asile itself been swept away, it would have been nothing compared to the desolation of September 23, 1851.

In April of 1852, His Grace, Monseigneur Francis Norbert Blanchet, Archbishop of Oregon City, and his brother, Monseigneur Magloire Blanchet, now Bishop of Nisqually, came back to Montreal on their way to the Second Council of Baltimore. With their coming, Sister Joseph found herself roused from the routine of her duties and a little diverted from her sadness. Her position as bursar of the community was an important one. Moreover, the new superior, Mother Caron, leaned heavily on her practiced wisdom in the guidance of affairs and people. The two of them were in accord regarding Oregon, and both were interested in the work of the bishops, though still vague as to the geographical background of their work. Saint Paul, Oregon City, Walla Walla, Vancouver, Nisqually–these were names only, but names both would be glad to know first hand.

It was obvious from his first visit to the Asile that the Bishop of Nisqually had plans in mind which involved the Sisters of Providence. They had not long to wait for the disclosure of his desires. Monseigneur Bourget asked him to preside at the profession ceremonies on April 2. His Lordship used the occasion to speak of his diocese and of the crying need for sisters. Never an eloquent speaker, he nevertheless spoke so simply and sincerely of the work to be done there that no sooner were the ceremonies concluded than the two newly professed, Sister Mary of the Sacred Heart and Sister Mary of the Angels, hastened to His Lordship and volunteered to go to Oregon, if their superiors would allow them to do so. That same day he made an official request to Mother Caron for a Providence foundation in his diocese.

This, then, was where God was leading, Sister Joseph reflected. His Lordship of Nisqually's need was part of God's divine plan. She had had a premonition years before that some day she would work in that raw new country for the glory of the Heart of Christ. She had become steadier and older in the seven years since she had first tried to put Oregon aside as an idle fancy.. God had severed some of the ties that bound her heart to her own land, and she did not doubt that He would give her strength to break those which remained. So it was that she offered herself for Oregon, and knew again in her mind that deep surge of happiness which had made her life complete and whole with her first clear knowledge of her vocation.

To her dismay and confusion, on May 1, she heard the council decide against her, because, of all things, she was too much needed as general bursar in Montreal. Five others were chosen, and forthwith plans were made for their setting out in the fall.

Again Sister Joseph found that peace was possible only by submission to what the Divine Will had made manifest through obedience. It had seemed so sure a thing that she was the one who had been beckoned by grace, and yet she had been passed over for the trifling excuse of her spurious indispensability! Had she been entirely wrong in believing that she had the qualifications of a missionary? Certain it was that, whatever her particular abilities, they were not now to be used in Oregon. She resigned herself as best she could, and then plunged into the preparations which had to be made for the departure of Sister Larocque and her companions.

As bursar, she had plenty to do for the five of them. They had

to have secular clothing for the journey, and though they certainly should not be too fashionably attired, she would see that
they were presentable. By a wise purchase here and a discreet hint
there to a friend who had money, the wardrobe was accumulated:
dresses of black, dark green, gray; hats and veils; shawls, gloves,
and scarves. She smiled to herself afterwards, thinking that the
general result was not bad. They looked like gentlewomen of indeterminate means. On October 18, she was glad that their strange
apparel did not make them ridiculous because there was enough
to bear without that.

The leave-taking was a painful experience for those who remained as well as for the new missionaries. Sister Joseph found
herself weeping freely. Monseigneur Bourget had put the voyage in charge of Father Gedeon Huberdault who was to go to
Oregon with them. Moreover, Mother Caron and Sister Theresa
of Jesus, two priests from the cathedral, and several friends accompanied them to New York. Every possible provision for their
safe arrival in the diocese of Nisqually seemed to have been made,
and they were off.

The ranks at the Asile seemed pitifully thin to those left behind.
They missed their sisters, and they missed, too, the buoyant activity of the days preceding the departure. That was little enough to
suffer for Oregon, Sister Joseph reminded herself as she settled
down to await some news of the venture.

After several weeks, letters began to reach Montreal from San
Juan del Norte, from Acapulco, and finally from San Francisco.
From the accounts of the missionaries, it had been a painful and
dangerous voyage. Moreover, the prospects about the rest of the
trip were none too encouraging, and there was a general note of
uncertainty. Evidently His Lordship, the Bishop of Nisqually,
was still away from his diocese on a begging tour in Mexico, and
would not be home to receive them. Oregon seemed to have
become more remote than ever, and there was no clear-cut idea
of just what their destination was in that general area. Sister Joseph began to be worried about the vagueness of their objectives,
and Father Huberdault's letters did little to reassure her. They
were full of interesting detail, which she read avidly; but *where* in

Oregon were the sisters expected to go? They had been destined for the diocese of Monseigneur Magloire Blanchet and his. episcopal see in Vancouver. The next letters were not from Vancouver but from Oregon City which they had reached, by some mischance, on the boat up the Columbia. Once there they could not get back to Vancouver because of floods in the Willamette and Columbia areas.

Then in the spring of 1853 what was the dismay of everyone at the Asile to receive word that the Sisters of Providence had left Oregon City in company with the Sisters of Notre Dame de Namur, and that they were all in San Francisco awaiting further orders. Sister Joseph knew that someone had bungled, but it was only much later that the whole story came out. At best, it was a confused situation, with everyone in Oregon seemingly taking flight to the gold fields of California. When even those who had been in the country were differing violently among themselves as to what could be expected in the immediate future, it is not surprising that the little caravan of Canadian missionaries had taken fright and departed in lamentable haste.

. . . .

In God's plan even human misadventure plays its part. Another three years elapsed. The Bishop of Nisqually came back to Montreal, knocking once more on the doors of the Asile and asking for a Providence Foundation in Vancouver. From the painful episode of the previous failure had come the establishment of the community in Chile, but His Lordship's disappointment in 1853 community in had left him a little touchy on the subject of the South American venture. The events of 1853 had taught him to leave no detail to chance, and this time, in November, 1856, he himself headed the caravan.

This time, too, Sister Joseph went along. She had been named the superior of the new foundation, and Monseigneur Bourget, to console and strengthen her, had given her a new name along with her new dignity. She was now *Sister Joseph of the Sacred Heart*— she who had been Esther Pariseau.

Twenty-five years later, writing of November 3, 1856, she said:

Very soon the bell tower of Providence, our happy home, was lost to view. We went to the ferry, and on to Saint Lambert, where we took the train to Rouse's Point. From thence we went by boat over the calm and placid waters of Lake Champlain and the Hudson River. The moon was bright and gave evidence of a fair day to come. The peaceful trip offered no inducement to sleep. How happy we were to have our beloved Mother Caron still with us whenwe arrived in the great city of New York.

CHAPTER 8

THE SIGHTs, sounds, and smells of New York assailed the eyes, ears, and nostrils of the travelers, as they were jostled by the crowds along the pier. To the south of them was the harbor where the Hudson moved swiftly and silently to meet the grey expanse of the Atlantic. At their backs beyond the river lay the Jersey shore, obscure and indefinite in the mists of the morning; before them was the unkempt and restless city reaching as far as eye could see. A good stiff breeze to landward carried the tang of the salt sea and mingled its freshness with the malodorous smells of the wharves and warehouses. Beyond the waterfront, a welter of roofs and chimneys was poised above the cobbled streets, now made turbulent by the hackney cabs and their importunate drivers.

The shrill cries of the cabbies were enough to intimidate even the seasoned traveler, and they thoroughly confused the little group from Montreal. His Lordship of Nisqually and his clerics hastily accepted the service of the nearest cab. The sisters followed in the vehicle of the next most raucous driver to whom they gave the name of a hotel which had been recommended. They went careening at top speed through strange streets while the cabbie called insolent remarks to any and all who impeded their progress. Finally they arrived in a down-at-the-heel neighborhood and were landed before a rooming house whose interior soon proved no more reassuring than the exterior. The room to which they were conducted had no pretensions to either cleanliness or order, and the bedding was neither fresh nor inviting. Mother Caron tried to make the situation more bearable by reminding them that the servants of the poor should be housed no better than the poor themselves.

Although she was willing to share the poverty of her masters, Sister Joseph was relieved to have the situation improved by the arrival of Mr. Dennis Sadlier, a Catholic gentleman known to the Bishop of Nisqually. Mr. Sadlier and his brother, Mr. James Sadlier, were publishers with business houses in both New York and Montreal. He had been notified of this expedition and had hoped to meet the travelers on their arrival; by the grace of God he had finally overtaken them before they had settled in these miserable surroundings. They must leave this district and this boarding house immediately, he told them. The place was disreputable and dangerous. They would certainly be robbed of their baggage, if nothing else of a worse nature befell them. He had made arrangements for them to stay at another place, and had cabs at the door to take them there. Indeed, they needed little persuasion.

So once more the party found themselves being jolted along the streets of New York, though this time with more assurance, if not more dignity. Sister Joseph found that she could smile when the passersby first stared at them and then broke into laughter.

"Look at the Quaker ladies," some called after them.

They did look queer in their somber, out-moded clothing, even to themselves. Madame Proto's green veil and engulfing boa might have been the last word in elegance thirty years before, but worn now by Sister Wilson, it did little to relieve the absurdity of her costume. As well, the Sister Servant reflected, she had done a better job for the nuns in 1852, but no matter. This time she was on her way to Oregon, and that being so, she did not mind the derision. Only a few days ago she had made a compact with her Lord on that very subject, and there still remained to her the precious task of getting it duly recorded for Monseigneur. If there was time, she would complete that bit of business here in this city.

Mr. Sadlier brought them to the comfortable and affluent Delmonico Hotel, where they were received with kindness by its generous-hearted Irish Catholic proprietor. The latter bade them remember that this day, November 4, was Election Day, and that they should not be alarmed by the noise in the street below. There had been plenty of anti-Catholic feeling in the city in the last few years, with the Know-Nothings stirring up prejudice and violence; but the party was being checked, thanks be to God and good Archbishop Hughes, and most people wanted nothing but peace. With the North and the South glaring at each other over slavery there was enough trouble in the country already without stirring up the Irish.

The Bishop of Nisqually had left the arrangements for their voyage in the hands of Father Quinn, pastor of Saint Peter's on Barclay Street. He obtained passage for them on the SS. *Illinois* which had been due to sail November 5. But because of the presidential elections, its sailing was delayed until November 6 so that their ship could carry word of the outcome of the elections to the West Coast. The travelers thus had the opportunity of seeing some of the religious houses and churches of New York. They were well received by the religious of the city. The annalist notes that on this occasion the superior of Manhattanville gave Mother Caron a sewing machine which was the first to be used in the community.

Their visits and their hours together in the hotel rooms were made more pleasant by the fact that they were again wearing their religious habits. The proprietor had assigned a special dining room to the Bishop's entourage. When the sisters showed up the first evening in their embarrassing and antiquated attire, the waiters had been convulsed with ill-disguised amusement. After dinner the genial mâlitre d'hotel spoke to the sisters and assured them that they would have nothing to fear were they to wear their religious habit in the hotel, on the boat, or for that matter, in the city itself. To the great relief of all, the precious black habits were unpacked and donned at once.

Sister Joseph found that her spirits rose immediately. She had again the sense of belonging to a community; though she was to exile herself from so much that was dear, yet she knew she was taking with her a vital portion of their religious family. She and

her companions were living branches which were being transplanted to grow anew in Oregon-for the glory of God! The habit was
the outward symbol, and the sight of it comforted her.

She was full of hope for her own spiritual life. Monseigneur
Bourget himself had spurred her on in her aspirations after holiness, and with his approval she was making this time of sacrifice
the occasion for the complete oblation of herself. She would step
out boldly from this world of petty things and trust all to the
redeeming love of her Savior. To honor His Precious Blood she
would reach for highest sanctity. At the same time that she gave
her mind and her body to labor for the Lord in Oregon she would
give her heart to the perfection of every interior and exterior act.

So now, in the hotel room on the eve of their departure, with
the babel of American voices in the street below, she painstakingly
wrote out for Monseigneur Bourget the promise she had made
under his guidance. She wrote it with his pen, remembering the
compassion in his face as he had given it to her. She had been on
her knees before him, begging that she be spared the superiorship.
He knew she had not the qualifications; he knew she was rash
and impetuous and difficult in spite of her efforts to be humble
and dignified. Besides, her education was meager. She wrote so
poorly, in spite of Mademoiselle Broyèes's careful training. She
remembered the gentleness of his smile as he reached for his pen,
given him by His Holiness Pius IX himself. He blessed it again and
handed it to her.

"My child, this will help you with the writing."

Strangely enough, the writing did seem to be easier, even in these
distracting surroundings. Slowly and precisely she formed the words,
hoping for that miracle of grace she would need for their fulfillment.

I, Sister Joseph of the Sacred Heart, wishing to increase love for the
Precious Blood of Our Lord, promise in the presence of the adorable
Trinity, the Blessed Virgin, Saint Joseph, my Guardian Angel, and the
whole heavenly court, to do always according to the light of my conscience, that which seems to me the most perfect, by binding myself to
the practice of the third degree of humility, recalling always my role of
victim to the Sacred Heart of Jesus.

Made at the foot of the altar of our Mother House with the authority of my ecclesiastical superiors. All Saints Day, in the year 1856.

. . . .

Down the harbor, past Bedloe and Governor's Island, through the Narrows, and out into the open sea, moved the *SS. Illinois* with gathering speed. The painful partings, with their last lingering look at dear ones receding so quickly on shore, the storm of tears, and the dreadful blind desolation were all behind. There remained this emptiness of sky and water to match the interior exhaustion of all feeling and emotion. It was a calm sea, rolling gently and lifting them always toward the ever receding halfcircle of horizon. The motion of the ship was pleasant enough to begin with, and if the expanse before them soon grew monotonous to the view, there were other things to claim the immediate attention of the travelers. The steam packet was the bearer of the great good news that the world's most promising democracy had compromised on the burning issue of slavery by electing James Buchanan as its fifteenth president. There was no fanfare aboard. Neither was there the drama and romance of the clipper ships. No great white sails were spread out overhead to catch the wind and send the ship forward swiftly and gracefully. Instead, plumes of dark smoke moved up from the stacks and sent cinders and smudges down on the upper deck, as engine and paddle wheel worked mightily to keep the ship plowing ahead.

"*La rue du cheval noir*" . . . Black Horse Street, the sisters called their location. A wild stallion it was, too, with untamed, iron hooves beating mercilessly against their tired senses. The kitchen racket was on one side of them, and the wheel of the ship on the other, with the engine directly below.

With the Bishop of Nisqually was his secretary, Father Louis Rossi, a young Belgian, who had accompanied His Excellency on his European begging tour and had, even before his ordination, prepared for missionary work in the Far West. In New York, these had been joined by Mr. Hardy, a clerical student, bound for the San Francisco diocese. The final member of the Bishop's party was Moïse Loisel, a banker's apprentice, who had served at

Monseigneur's house in Montreal and also with the sisters at Longue Pointe.

In the Sisters' cabin, along with the five nuns, were a Mrs. Kelly and a little girl eight years old. Kind Father Quinn of Saint Peter's had arranged for the child who was an Irish Orphan also bound for San Francisco.

"We welcomed this addition to our group," their journal records piously, "because we considered ourselves happy to exercise our work of charity, despite the inconvenience and burden this created." A nice sentiment, Sister Joseph later reflected and much like Sister Blandine, poor child. At eighteen one needs to have one's little sacrifices prettily labeled. She was glad that the Council had chosen two very young sisters to come along. She liked young nuns. Both Sister Blandine by her quick sensibilities and Sister Mary Ellen Norton with her delicate beauty and quiet young dignity, would serve our Lord well in Oregon. As for the others, they, too, were invaluable—Sister Theriault, so truly humble, and Sister Praxedes, already proved capable and reliable in the community's work.

On the first evening out, the sisters left their crowded, noisy cabin to go on deck for a breath of air. It was their last respite for many days. The following day the sea in spite of its calm laid its ascendancy on them. One after another, they succumbed to sickness. Sister Joseph had thought herself the hardiest of the five but she noted with surprise that it was the ex-superior of Longue Pointe, Sister Praxedes, who alone remained well enough to give the others care.

In spite of the misery of the experience Sister Joseph emerged from it with the worst of her heartache drained away. For a week she had been so dreadfully ill that only the exigencies of the moment could claim her attention. Now that she had survived physically, she found her mind, too, cleared of its wretchedness, God had not spared her; she had felt the full weight of sacrifice; yet she had lived, and now again she was finding the world about her beautiful and interesting.

As they moved farther and farther south she noted the increasing mildness of the air, into which quick storms swirled up out of nowhere, pelted them with rain, and were gone again. Dusk came more suddenly, too, lingered briefly, and merged into nights made luminous only by the stars overhead. The color of the sea seemed to change. Thinking of the Saint Lawrence, she remembered it as always carrying with it the tint and texture of the melted snows of springtime. This water absorbed all color and gave back to the eye hues which only the imagination had known before. Then there were islands floating mirage-like against the horizon, or near at hand, with flashes of unbelievably white beaches washed by seas ablaze with light and color.

Where had she seen trees like these before? Here were none of the pines and firs of the Laurentians, nor the brooding greens and blues against Mont Tremblant or Mont Royale. Ah yes, she remembered . . . those incredible pictures of Paradise with Adam and Eve shuddering conscience-stricken and afraid in the foreground. When she was young, that was as good a setting for Paradise as any other. Now she knew Heaven would not be like that at all. Rather she would walk with God and the saints and her dear ones over the ordered and gently rolling fields of home, or perhaps some of the time along a brown country road like that to Saint Martin de Laval. But Heaven was not yet, and in the meantime there were these new vistas to be enjoyed. It was so like God to entice them away from their sadness. Surely she could do no better than follow His lead.

As they sat quietly together one afternoon, Moïse Loisel suddenly. appeared among them. Poor Moïse! He, too, had been ill and they had not seen him for days.

"How are the sisters at Longue Pointe?" Sister Praxedes asked him with wry humor.

With good grace, he made up a little story of each of the nuns there, for all the world as if he had just stopped in at the Asile for a brief visit. Sister Françoise made wonderful fricassee as Sister Norton knew. . . . Sister Mary of Bonsecours had a new pupil. . . . Sister Zotique had had him bake some barley bread. Punctuating his narrative with an occasional Gallic shrug or an uplifted eyebrow he regaled them with familiar names and places until they were shaken by quiet laughter.

"This gave us a moment of recreation," commented Sister Blandine in her journal.

Their first and only port of call aboard the *SS. Illinois* was Kingston, Jamaica, which they reached on November 13. Had they known it, they were entering a harbor made historic by a long line of adventurers and swashbuckling buccaneers -from the days of Christopher Columbus and the whole astounding breed of Spainards on down. It was into Kingston that Henry Morgan, the most brutal of all the Caribbean pirates, sailed to hold the island for the English, and for his pains was given a title instead of a halter. Here, too, a brace of English admirals, Penn, Rodney, Nelson, fought the battle of empire again and again. But in the late fall of 1856, there was no drama in the harbor, though the stupendous backdrop of natural beauty remained and was not to be entirely obscured even by a heavy rain. The ship made its way into port past a long finger of land which curves inland to form the breakwater for one of the most beautiful harbors of the Western Hemisphere. When the tropical downpour abated, the sky above the island was a clear, pale yellow. Against it towered the Blue Mountains which rise abruptly from the coast in heavily wooded foothills.

Everywhere in nature there was exotic profusion. Giant fans of the palm and the banana merged with flowering trees cascaded with blossoms in the most delicate tints and the most brilliant colors.

XaYmaca, "Isle of Many Waters," its original inhabitants, the Arawaks, called it. To the mixed population of modem times, it is still the isle of many waters; and while it looks like an earthly paradise, its great harbors have contributed to its prosperity at the same time that they have been the source of much of its misery. Black, mulatto, buckra depend on trade for their living, and the degree of color determines how good the living is to be. Usually white means rich, and black means poor. The black Jamaican, however, suffers from no inferiority complex, and his bearing shows it. He speaks the King's English, he maintains order, and he is clean, even though he is poor. The abundance of the earth is near for food. He has but to reach out his hand to pick the bread fruit, the mangoes, the papayas, the oranges, and the bananas with which his island is so lavishly blest. Of clothing, he needs but little because of the mild climate. But the spirit of man looks for more than provision against hunger and cold.

An innate Christian sense gave the Montreal travelers a perceptive insight which made them view the city and its poor with pity as well as interest. From their steamer's location along the dock, they looked out on this new world.

Sister Blandine, who did most of the writing for them, recorded it thus:

On the 13th we were at the Isle of Jamaica, at a little town called Kingston. Negroes form the population there. About fifty Negro women, carrying on their heads large wooden baskets of coal, walked in close single file up to the wharf. They were led there by Negro men. Although these women were performing a similar task, each was different. Some were laughing, some were singing, some were gay, and some were sad. As we watched we had ample matter for reflection.

During the whole day, other Negroes brought fruits of every kind, which were beautiful and cheap. Fruit constitutes the principal item in the diet of these poor people. We cannot but admire the infinite goodness of God Who has caused this -abundance of fruit to grow here without cultivation for the sustenance of the poor natives.

With hearts still torn by homesickness, they found that the past and the present were often in juxtaposition in their observations:

We saw trees which resembled palms; they made us think of Biblical scenes. There were also the most beautiful flowers, like those we have in Canada in the month of July. We would have liked to send some to Sister Mary of the Nativity, for her garden; then she could give a bouquet to Sister Rose of Lima for the shrine of Our Lady of Seven Dolors. This is one more thing for our list of self-denials.

His Lordship, Father Rossi, and a young Irish deacon, Mr. Hardy, who is traveling with us as far as San Francisco, went ashore to visit the five Jesuit missionaries who are evangelizing these poor people. It was one of the major Jesuit feasts, that of Saint Stanislaus Kostka. We celebrated it next day, as that is the date fixed for it in the Diocese of

Nisqually; the fact that these Jesuits are laboring in this far-away land gave us new courage and zeal in the work for the salvation of the souls of our separated brethren.

We almost forgot an interesting thing. From the Jesuits' garden, Mr. Hardy brought us a branch bearing fruit.. It is said to be the "forbidden fruit," like that in the Garden of Eden. The branch had six beautiful fruits like our largest oranges in Canada.

Like the woman Eve they were not content merely to look, because the journal continues:

They were similar in size and color, but the taste is not so savory. The presentation of this branch made us remember the fall of Mother Eve . . . .

. . . . Our voyage was resumed at 7:30 A.M. on November 14 . . . . On this great day, we attended Mass in spirit at the Providence, arriving at the last bell for the Community Mass.

Four days more, and they were carried across the Caribbean bound for Colon, then called Aspinwall. Each morning the sky above them was drenched with color—violet, amber, scarlet, then a somber grey and saffron, dispelled by a tropical sun. Light and heat beat down on them until they longed for the melancholy twilight, the sudden night, and the end of their journey.

Along with the others Sister Joseph of the Sacred Heart recalled the lurid accounts of the Isthmian experiences of the missionaries in 1852, and shuddered at the prospects which lay ahead in the dirty little port city known to her generation as Aspinwall. This was still the day of the gold-seekers, argonauts bound for quick wealth in California, coming in hordes by this route. The group docked at Aspinwall on November 18, at 3:00 P.m. and were conducted along with the others of the Bishop of Nisqually's party to Hotel Aspinwall. There, they found the hotel was so crowded that the only available space was turned over to the sisters, and His Lordship and his companions were forced to find less favorable lodgings elsewhere. Their accommodations were far from attractive—a crowded room on the top floor, with inch-thick mattresses on the beds and no pretense at cleanliness. Fortunately they had only one night there, and were off next day for Panama.

In 1855, a narrow-gauge railroad had been built between Aspin-wall and Panama, and the missionaries were thus spared the peril-ous journey on mule-back which had caused the 1852 group so much fright and misery. In comparative comfort except for the humidity and heat, the travelers now made the forty-seven mile trip in five hours. It was indeed an alien land through which they passed. Rank growths of strange tropical leaves and shrubs grew out of the swampy soil. Orchids clung to the great trees, and bril-liantly-plumaged birds and chattering monkeys were disturbed by their passage. They reached Panama City at 11:30 A.M., and caught their first glimpse of the Pacific lying deceptively blue and placid.

The Bishop of Nisqually made immediate inquiries about the next lap of their journey and, discovering that their ship would not be ready for them until late afternoon, rescued them from the great, hot depot in which they waited. Gathering his party about him, he ushered them along the quay, drove a brisk bargain with one of the native boatmen, and in short order had them rowed across a strip of water to one of the best hotels along the shore.

As their boat and others approached the beach, they were surrounded by the glistening brown bodies of boys diving for coins. Never having been encumbered with clothes, these Negro urchins were not now going to endanger their powers as swimmers in so competitive a business. For a horrified moment, Sister Jo-seph did not know what to do with her eyes. Then she was highly amused to see the Bishop of Nisqually belaboring the little beggars with forceful pokes of his umbrella and to hear him saying, in the mode of Abbé Blanchet, *"Allez-vous-en, petits salops!"*

The hotel proved a haven of comfort. They enjoyed an ex-cellent meal, well cooked and well served, in pleasant, cool sur-roundings. They roamed the garden, delighting in the beauty of the flowers and shrubs, in the variety and novelty of birds and fishes. Rested and refreshed, they returned to their waiting room near the dock. The uncertainty of their sailing kept them from visiting the city; but they could see above the palms the great Spanish tower of the Cathedral; and they could look out over the busy harbor and see the ceaseless movement there, with many clippers, steamers, and small fishing vessels cluttering up the bay.

At 5:00 P.M. they embarked once more, on a lighter into which they were crowded with hundreds of others on their way out to the *Golden Age,* which would carry them to San Francisco.

This was an unpleasant hour, as they stood shoulder to shoulder in the intense heat and dying light with tired children crying and men cursing noisily and violently. In the dark they clambered up rope ladders to the deck of their steamer, to find to their great delight that it was luxurious and spacious, after the discomforts of the *SS. Illinois.* To the music of a band and a round of cannon, they were off at 10.00 P.M.

Sister Blandine had pleasant details for her account of the sea voyage:

Our cabin, Number 25, was as commodious as possible. We had three little beds and a comfortable double bed. The lady (Mrs. Kelly) had another cabin, but we kept the little girl with us.

The crews on both the Atlantic and the Pacific showed us all respect and courtesy, especially those on the Pacific. There was a young Irish Catholic woman, the Captain's maid, who sent us delicacies–canned sardines, nuts, figs, bananas, hot pies–by Moïse. We had breakfast at 5:30, lunch at noon, dinner at 5:00, and tea at will.

It was, as they wrote home, "a delightful, calm, uneventful trip of seven days to Acapulco."

Into the shimmering blue bay, the *Golden Age* sailed on Sunday morning, November 23. Acapulco was a little town in those days with the church easily visible from the wharves. Thither the travelers hastened; there the Bishop of Nisqually and Father Rossi said their Masses, and the sisters received Holy Communion for the first time since they left New York.

Sister Joseph found her heart wordlessly at home in this church among these strange people. Heavily veiled women made up the bulk of the congregation. Though their faces were scarcely visible she felt the warm friendliness and courtesy which they gave her along with the faith they shared. There was comfort and peace in the thought. She realized that some day, when her own heart and mind were rightly disciplined, home would be wherever God is. Now He was corporeally present as the Divine Guest of the Eucharist, come to be her strength and safety, as He would come one day, she prayed, to see her through the dark gateway. How often at the Asile, she had heard the voice of Mother Gamelin singing clearly and truly the beautiful hymn of the liturgy:

"Behold the bread of angels, made the food of travelers."

Ecce panis angelorum
Factus cibus viatorum

And that other simple hymn she had loved so well, sung in their own tongue:

O douce Providence, dont les divines mains
Sur nous en abondance, repandent tous les biens!
Qui pourrait me connaitre l'auteur de ses présents
Et ne pas remettre entre ses bras puissants?
O gentle Providence

She was conscious of neither her tears nor the passage of time until Sister Praxedes touched her, and she realized that the church had emptied. Looking about her she thought what an ugly church it was, really, with no communion rail at all, and with the altars and their linens in Latin disarray! In the niche above the high altar was a statue of Our Lady clothed in a rich, stiff fabric embroidered in tarnished gold thread. On her head was an ornate, bejeweled crown, tipped slightly forward and giving her the appearance of leaning toward all below. How friendly was this little Virgin of Acapulco, with the doll-like features. Suddenly she saw the church as its spirit made it—the dwellingplace of beautye—Eternal Beauty. There was no ugliness here.

At the entrance of the church she was greeted in Spanish by an elderly lady who bowed deeply and presented her with a book of devotions to the Sacred Heart. The kind old pastor, too, was there to meet them. He had them all go to the parish house next door. It was an adobe house without windows and without floor or carpet, but cool and clean. Two Negro servants spread a beautiful white cloth before them, with delicious pastry-like cakes and cups of strong black coffee.

By then it was eleven o'clock, so we each enjoyed a good breakfast, Sister Blandine continues. "We could not help being moved when we visited the house because it corresponded so exactly to the description given of it by our sisters in Chile. We felt so at home . . . . The houses are very low because of frequent earthquakes. The good curé tells us that the country resembles Chile in climate as well as in many other respects."

The travelers went aboard the *Golden Age* shortly after noon. Looking back to Acapulco, across the dreamy blue of the harbor, Sister Joseph prayed in quiet thanksgiving.

· · · · · · · · ·

They reached San Francisco on December 3. This part of the voyage had not been without incident. On the evening before they were due in port, they were disturbed by strange noises aboard ship, but having again been sick, they had not investigated and had tried to sleep. Then about 11:00, the ship halted with a tremendous lurch, and they thought the end had come. The partition of their cabin collapsed and fell on Sister Norton's bed, frightened her badly but doing her no further harm. The governor of California, Mr. James Bennett, came to their rescue, wrapped the little sister in a shawl, and carried her to the salon. It was discovered that one of the wheels of their ship had been badly damaged but that there was no immediate danger; so when the captain had assayed the situation, he ordered the ship ahead with the help of sails. The all-clear was sounded and the nuns fled back to their cabin, very conscious of the irregularity of their attire. Two days later, at daybreak, their ship limped through the Golden Gate and they saw before them the city and behind it the barren, brown hills of California.

Bishop Joseph Alemany's secretary, Father Michael King, had carriages waiting for them. Very shortly they were with the Sisters of Mercy at Saint Mary's Hospital. It was the feast of Saint Francis Xavier, the patron and model of missionaries, and they arrived on time for Mass and Communion.

CHAPTER 9

TO THE END of her life, Sister Joseph never forgot the Sisters Of Mercy and the wonderful days spent with them in San Francisco. There her heart found an oasis in the desert of renunciation which separated her from the things of home. Like her four companions, she busied herself with parallels and comparisons between the day of life of these Irish nuns and the dear community she had left in Montreal. There were many points of similarity–the basic pattern of religious life, the work with the poor, the sick, and the orphans, the little community customs. The warm mantle of hospitality which protected them in this brash, raw city was reminiscent of the same mercy the Sisters of Providence on Saint Catherine Street extended to others in need. They were made to feel at home and by that very fact their sacrifice became poignant and new again as they remembered the Asile.

Father Michael King constituted himself their guide in the city. Even before the gold-seekers had swarmed through the Golden Gate, the Church had lived long, mellow years in California. This was the land of the brown Franciscans who had built a mission-studded rosary from San Diego to Sonoma. To the old Mission Dolores built in 1776 Father King conducted the travelers on December 3. It was a three-mile walk from Saint Mary's Hospital and as they went they recalled similar excursions in other days to Montreal's Mont Royale. The Mission had fallen on evil days when they viewed it in 1856. Gone now were the rich vineyards and grasslands; gone the great herds of cattle and sheep, which had once been the part of the material abundance won by the toil of the friars and their Indian charges. The missions had been secularized in 1834, and their abundance dispersed and depreciated. But the Mission church had survived; its four-feet-thick adobe walls, its ceiling of heavy timbers with Indian designs in deep reds and tawny yellows, its high altar with rich panels and quaint, hand-carved statues still spoke of other times and other ways.

On the main altar there was a statue of Saint Francis of Assisi. There were many others representing the saints of that order. In the sacristy, we saw a crucifix, with an expression of such sorrow it is capable of softening the most hardened heart. The corpus had a bluish tint, like bruised flesh. There are wounds in the knees from which blood runs to the floor. It is a perfect piece of workmanship. . . . We went to the cemetery which is like that on the Mountain (Mont Royale). The tombs are decorated with flowers arranged with taste and symmetry. Each family has a plot as large as they wish enclosed by wood, iron, chain, or even by marble. We thought that if Sister Thomas were here she would have many models for her parterre and for the ornamentation of the grounds.

Father King conducted them to the Sisters of Charity of Saint Vincent de Paul where they enjoyed a concert given them by the orphans. There, too, they saw the little room which had been occupied by Mother Larocque and her companions in the fateful year of 1852.

At the Presentation Convent they heard the story of these nuns lately arrived from Ireland. San Francisco had not received them with its customary hospitality and had rebuffed their good offices because there were already "enough religious in town." But the sisters had stayed on, giving education to those who would accept, and teaching music, drawing, painting, needlework, and classical subjects.

At Saint Mary's Church, on Grant and California, they saw Bishop Joseph Sadoc Alemany's new cathedral which had been solemnly dedicated only two years before. Its wood and granite had come from China, its brick and iron around the Horn from the Atlantic states, its stained glass from Europe, and its fine organ by clipper ship from New York. The sound of its great bell carried the time of day across the city below, and its square tower looked down with peace and dignity on the turbulent life of the crowded port town where peoples of every race and tongue jostled one another in their mad quest of quick riches. "Son, observe the time and fly from evil," the church admonished all. Sister Joseph wrote:

On the day of our departure, we had many little things to buy; so we spent the forenoon in the city streets. There we saw people of all nations, among them Chinese in native costume. They are distinguished by a braid of hair which begins at the back of the head and extends to the heels.

The precious five days of respite were drawing to a close. The missionaries had been allowed to participate to the full in the life of the Sisters of Mercy. There had been grand recreation given both communities in their honor. There had been music and dancing every evening; and like the Providence novices at home they had asked and obtained a quarter, postponing the night prayer in favor of an added interval of shared merriment. As always, at such times, Oregon was remote and Montreal was near in spite of geography. Montreal they knew, and they could turn to it with well-etched remembrances, whereas Oregon was part of the great unknown. Father King, who had been in the Northwest for a year before his health had given out, tried to tell them what it was like. He told them how best they might succeed in working with the Indians whom he had found coarse and degraded; but in the last analysis, they would have to find out for themselves how to handle the work which would be sent them by God. If only they could put down roots in the new land as the Sisters of Mercy had done, Sister Joseph prayed—or better still, as the Franciscans had. Perhaps they could cultivate a farm for themselves and their charges; along with the work on the land, they could develop other crafts which would make the art of living a civilizing process. Her hopes rushed ahead to a carpenter shop, a print shop, a flower garden, as well as to the school which they most certainly must undertake-perhaps in good time' a hospital, too.

Then she pulled her thoughts up short. After all, they were going to Oregon to help His Lordship, the Bishop of Nisqually. It was he who would direct their undertakings and indicate what should be done. She could only hope that in due time he would leave them freedom for the garden and the carpenter shop. Both would be good for the soul as well as the body. That was the very reason she was so highly pleased with the gift of an accordion presented them by the Sisters of Mercy. Sister Blandine with her quick sensibilities and delicacy of feeling had need of a legitimate channel for pouring out the ardor of her nature. Music would do that for her, just as the touch of finely grained wood satisfied the Pariseau at the core of her own being.

San Francisco, the city of "little hills and earthquakes," was left behind on December 5. Their ship for the last phase of the journey was the *Brother Jonathan*, named after Washington Irving, the American historian of the Astor expedition. Looking back with affection and gratitude toward the enchanting city that was even now partially veiled by the fog drifting in from the bay, they singled out the landmarks they would never forget. Beyond the forest of masted ships along the wharves were Telegraph Hill and Russian Hill; there, too, were the great streets cutting awayfrom the waterfront, and somewhere along them their friends, the Mercies and good Father King.

Aboard ship, the Oregon group should now have included His Lordship and young Father Rossi, the five nuns, and Moïse. Yet when the final check was made, Moïse was nowhere to be found. In dismay, they remembered that he had been with them on the wharf; yet now he was unaccountably missing. Both the Bishop of Nisqually and the Sister Servant made inquiries, and the ship was searched for the missing member of their party. But no Moïse!! Sister Joseph thought she detected an odd silence on the part of the two younger nuns, but the matter was not pressed, and they resigned themselves to the fact that somehow Moïse had not taken the boat with the rest of them.

The nuns had two comfortable cabins among them, and the

trip should have been pleasant enough. But no sooner had they left the shelter of Golden Gate harbor than the sea turned rough and frightening. Seasickness descended upon them immediately and once more Sister Joseph thought she was going to die.

In early December the Pacific is not an ocean to be traversed without challenge, and it now reared alarmingly against the *Brother Jonathan* and tossed it about with heavy fury. On December 6, the weather took on storm proportions, and for two days they endured its full blast. Between the roar of the sea and the high winds which buffeted it, the whole world seemed engulfed in violence and confusion. Trunks and baggage were thrown about, as was every other object not lashed securely in place. The steamer creaked and groaned at every joint as it strained to buck the mountains of water hurled against it. In the middle of the night the mainmast was blown down with clatter, injecting an added note of alarm to the general tension. Even had they wished, the sisters could not have left their bunks because it was impossible to stand. Writing of their voyage some time later, Sister Blandine says:

All through that night, Sister Praxedes kept asking me if I were afraid. I pretended to be brave and said that I had slept very peacefully. Besides, were we to perish, we would have a bath and be very presentable before going before the heavenly court and Our Lady of the Immaculate Conception. In the meantime, I was praying with all my might, saying to our Lord: "Do for us what you did for St. Peter and calm this storm." But He did not seem to hear me; so I importuned the Blessed Virgin, the Angels, and all the Saints of Heaven and earth. I had not been that fervent for a long time.

About 5:00 A.M., Sister Praxedes said, "I have exhausted all my prayers." "Dear Sister," I replied, "it is an excellent time to begin them over." I did all in my power to reassure her, but the poor nun seemed to be dying of fear. She was chilled through and through, and several times she was so overcome by weakness that she was faint.

Sister Praxedes was not the only one succumbing to fright. When the ship's mast fell, young Father Rossi, thinking that the end was near, rapped on the door of His Lordship's cabin, crying out:

"My Lord, don't you know that we are perishing?"

The Bishop of Nisqually emerged from his cabin to go to reassure the sisters, even though so short a trip across deck was hazardous.

With much difficulty Monseigneur Blanchet came to our cabins, encouraged us in a fatherly manner, promised a Mass in honor of the Immaculate Conception, and returned to his own cabin, strong in his confidence in the protection of our Blessed Mother.

Christ had not come to them walking on the water, the Sister Servant reflected, but He had sent His good servant. Gathering the sisters about her, she proposed to them a novena to the Sacred Heart to supplement the promise made by the Bishop, and somehow the terror that had gripped them subsided.

At last came the dawn, and with it calm to the waters. The captain announced that we were about to cross the bar of the Columbia, that grave of so many valiant ships.

This was one of the most difficult passages in the world, dreaded by every mariner who approached it. Hidden shoals and shifting sands had long ago earned it the ominous name of "The Grave Yard." In the thick, grey morning light there was little to see except occasional glimpses of distant headlands to the north and south of them and directly ahead, the heaving sea and a long line of breakers which formed and hurtled and broke and formed again in interminable, frothing fury. The *Jonathan* crept into the gap between the spurs of land on either side, turned east, and began fighting the current of the river. The swells increased and the ship rolled and pitched; yet it inched forward length by length feeling for the channel. This was the ultimate test in seamanship, and only skilled bar pilots could be trusted with it. Gradually the skies lightened, and the tension lessened among the ship's crew. The chant of the leadsman up ahead became less a moan and more a cocky triumph. Suddenly the ship was idling in clear green water and a river bank seemed near enough to touch. Passengers came on deck smiling relief. Back to the north of them was the jutting crag of Cape Disappointment, to the south lay the desolate sandy wastes of Point Adams and across the great width of the river ahead was Astoria, the old American Fur Company fort.

With the lifting of fear, the world looked fresh and new again to Sister Joseph. This was Oregon, this green expanse of fir and cedar pressing down to the river's edge. Here were trees so tall that the fog still lingered in their heights. Here were forests leaning out over their ship so dense that surely they were impenetrable to the ways of man. This was the Oregon which had troubled her thoughts these many years. She could only repeat to herself, "This is Oregon . . . This is Oregon." Looking across to the wooded banks on her left, to the land north of the great river, "There," she thought, "lies His Lordship's diocese . . . There lies the new vineyard of Providence . . . and somewhere, ahead of us, we will some day build another Asile."

Her heart kindled at the thought. Looking about her, she found Sister Blandine. Could they not dedicate even these first hours to their holy patroness with a hymn in her honor? Remembering the Asile, remembering the gentle mother who lay buried there, remembering above all the devotion which had formulated and crystallized everything which she had hoped for herself and her daughters, could they not sing to the accompaniment of the new accordion which Sister Blandine had already begun to master?

So while the *Brother Jonathan* plowed steadily upriver sending white spray back from its bow, the five of them gathered in a sheltered spot on deck facing the northern bank and sang the ancient hymn to Our Lady of Sorrows, the *"Stabat Mater."*

. . . .

Imbued with the importance of these hours and convinced as they were that they were making history, they lingered on deck so as not to miss either the beauty of this new world of theirs or the inner significance of everything they saw and heard. One day when there was time they must write it all in great detail to Mother Caron and the sisters at the Mother House, the Sister Servant reminded them. Nothing was unimportant, because all had been planned by the Lord Himself. Those who came after them would want a clear and detailed picture. They must make them see through their words and impressions the Columbia Valley as they were seeing it this very day. This country could be made intelligible to others in terms of things they themselves knew.

"This river reminds us of the Chambly (Richelieu)," they would write to Montreal. And again in the annals, they would record:

We admired the river banks, but we could not admit that they rivalled the banks of the majestic Saint Lawrence. In vain we searched the banks for the pointed church spires. . . . This happiness we could hardly expect in this vast new land of our Father's vineyard.

With pious effusion they were to remark on—

. . . so many little waterfalls coming down high cliffs on the mountain sides. These crystal clear streams lost in the peaceful Columbia seem symbolic. The prayer which arises from our hearts is that the waters of grace fertilize the vine confided to our planting.

Finally, at 3:00 in the afternoon on the Feast of the Immaculate Conception, the travelers reached Vancouver. The river channel had not yet been penetrated by a permanent pier; so they stepped from their larger ship to a small vessel which served as a wharf. Back from the river lay the little town, larger really than they had expected. Once the bustling fort of the Honorable Hudson's Bay Company, it was now an American military post occupied by two companies of soldiers and a small group of civilian families of mixed origins.

Near the landing a few people had congregated to greet their arrival. A distinguished gentleman with long white hair down to his high collar stepped forward and knelt to kiss the hand of the Bishop of Nisqually and then turned to young Father Rossi and the sisters. It was the vicar general, the Abbé Jean Baptiste Abraham Brouillet, they were startled to learn, in this unaccountable attire. A strange country, indeed, in which priests did not wear soutanes.

Up the incline from the river lay the December landscape; a light white frost covered the lawns, which were even now green as in springtime. On the slopes beyond the clearing made by the town towered virgin forests of blue-black fir and pine, and not far removed from one such stand of timber was unmistakably the mission, with its cross-surmounted church and humble episcopal residence. As they moved away from the shore there was heard the clear, high peal of the church bell welcoming them from the long journey.

Not so fine as Great Bourdon, Sister Joseph thought, nor as jubilant as the voice of "Marie-Elizabeth-Genevieve"; but an authentic voice, nevertheless, speaking the language of the universal church whether on the Ile Jésus or Saint Catherine Street or here in the Diocese of Nisqually. How good to be home where gentle Providence had led them!

CHAPTER 10

Exactly five weeks and some six thousand miles of travel lay between the sisters and Montreal. They had become more knowledgeable as a result of their contacts with strange places and strange peoples; yet essentially they remained the same—French Canadian women with the love of their race for orderly living and for cleanliness. Almost over night the mission felt the impact of their arrival, and by Christmas 1856, the episcopal palace of His Lordship, Augustine Magloire Alexander Blanchet, had great gusts of energy breathed into it.

His Lordship and his priests had found the bishopric comfortable and adequate and had enjoyed there a modest degree of rumpled, male well-being. But, alas, the place had not been built to house sisters. In fact, no provision whatsoever had been made for them in spite of the Bishop's express commands to the contrary. The situation on their arrival was therefore painfully awkward.

This embarrassment had come about because of the Vicar General, Abbé Brouillet. In the year's absence of Bishop Blanchet, Abbé Brouillet had been instructed to make the necessary preparations for the coming of the sisters. But he had been busy at his own missionary pursuits, and besides, he had not been convinced of the wisdom of the Bishop's orders and had hoped to make him see that the place for the nuns was not Vancouver, but Olympia, the capital city of the newly organized Washington Territory. Abbé Brouillet was right in foreseeing the growth in population and importance of the Puget Sound area, but another fifty years was to elapse before the Diocese of Nisqually would become the Diocese of Seattle, and, as the chronicles 1856 record, "The Bishop did not agree with his Vicar, and wanted the sisters near him in Vancouver which was already the center of Catholicism, that the kernel planted there might be cultivated and let grow."

It did not take the nuns long to realize that His Lordship was faced with a real problem on that late afternoon of December 8. While they were consecrating themselves anew to the Blessed Virgin before her picture in the Vicar-General's room they overheard sharp words between the two ecclesiastics next door. There was not a place in town for the sisters, except a shed not far from the bishop's residence, Abbé Brouillet said. That was none too good, because it was open to the wind and rain, and at that season, the weather could be unpleasant. Why on earth hadn't the sisters gone to Olympia? In the midst of the discussion, the baggage arrived and was piled high awaiting further disposal.

Sister Joseph could stand no more dispute. She entered His Lordship's room and told him that her party would most willingly retire to the shed; they would be satisfied with that.

"You may be satisfied," young Father Rossi chivalrously interposed, "but we are not."

"Bring in the baggage," the Bishop of Nisqually said in a tone of finality. "The sisters will remain here tonight."

Remain they did. There was an unfinished attic in the episcopal palace, which His Lordship proposed as their sleeping quarters. It was cluttered up with acquisitions made by His Lordship on his various begging expeditions—broken furniture, carpets, and old blankets and quilts which both Indians and whites had used as bedding the previous winter, when there had been much going and coming in the old fort during the troublous times of the Indian wars. The Bishop was embarrassed as he showed the nuns into the crowded, airless upper room, but they attacked the situation in good- natured merriment. Soon the whole house reverberated to the sound of cleaning and rearrangement going on overhead.

That was the first of many house-cleanings in Vancouver, and as such it became not only the herald but the symbol of how the sisters would put their impress on the mission. There was more for the Lord in a house which was clean and orderly; so it was no unusual feat to make the attic habitable. Sister Joseph of the Sacred Heart found other arrangements more difficult to accept.

There was the matter of eating at the Bishop's table, with Abbé Brouillet and young Father Rossi. The first evening meal was a generous one, with what should have been a holiday air about it. The Vicar-General had butchered a pig for the occasion, and there was an abundance of good food. After the sea voyage, all appetites were sharpened. But somehow the meal lagged, and tension at the table seemed to grow palpably. For a few minutes, the Sister Servant wondered what could be wrong. Then after flashIng a glance at her nuns, she knew. Sister Norton and Sister Theriault were paralyzed with embarrassment at the unwanted honor of sitting at the same table with His Lordship and his clergy. They were so tormented by shyness and at the same time so hungry that the meal became more frustrating by the minute. There was nothing to do but see it through as best they could, but other arrangements would most certainly have to be made on that score.

Supper once over, the table was cleared, and at His Lordship's request this same table was prepared for the following morning's Mass. The change was lovingly and simply made. Consciousness of being so intimately in our Lord's own household eased the constrictions of heart and mind. In confusion they had eaten at the Bishop's table; now they laid the linen and the furnishings which made it our Lord's own altar where He Himself would become not only their gracious Host but their sustaining food. the world of faith once more superseded the world of sense. On the following morning tears were shed when the Bishop of Nisqually gave them Holy Communion. It was not that they lacked faith or courage. It was only that human nature was torn by the knowledge that finally they were here where they had come seeking God and He too was here waiting for them. The eternal reality of God was being made accessible to them for the first time eucharistically in this new land between the ageless forests and the great river.

Speaking of this even twenty-five years later, Sister Joseph of the Sacred Heart would say:

Our hearts uttered endearing words to our Mother Immaculate and to the dear Sacred Heart to whom we had pledged our souls and the work of our apostolate in this adopted land. What more could we desire? He who created the universe is satisfied with the little we have to give. The Bishop's Mass was followed by Father Rossi's. After these acts of worship we broke our fast in this same room which the sisters again converted into a refectory. This state of things continued until the little house which the Bishop had built for us was completed sufficiently to be used as a chapel. The church was undergoing repairs.

After a trial period of a housekeeper hired by the Vicar-General, the matter was talked over with the Bishop, and at the Sister Servant's suggestion the care of his house was handed over to the sisters. Off the kitchen was the housekeeper's room which measured some ten by sixteen feet. This became the sisters' abode. Calling on her Pariseau ingenuity, Sister Joseph now set about seeing that it was made habitable.

With money given her by His Lordship she purchased some boards, some simple tools, and a few basic supplies. Soon measure and square were much in evidence, and one could hear the rasp of the saw and a hammer industriously banging away. Sister Theriault's nimble fingers were busy sewing up oblongs of ticking and filling them with clean straw which young Father Rossi had gotten from somewhere—probably the fort. The other three embarked on an orgy of washing and scrubbing. From all their labors there emerged a combined dormitory-refectory-community room. In it were five narrow bunks complete with fresh straw mattresses and clean blankets. There was a rough table hinged to the wall and a well-scrubbed box to serve each nun as her chair. A box nailed on the wall held their dishes and tableware; and another, the few books of piety given them by the good fathers of the seminary and their other friends in Montreal. Simple calico curtains at the doorway and windows gave them a minimum of privacy. In a protected spot stood Sister Blandine's treasured accordion.

The finishing touch was a surprise sent them by our Lord Himself. It could be from no other, Sister Joseph reflected. While she sorted the contents of the attic for whatever they would need downstairs, she had come upon a piece of yellowed linen. Holding it to the light she saw that on it was a richly embroidered representation of the Sacred Heart, done with delicacy and skill. The Bishop of Nisqually had collected all sorts of things in his travels, and this piece had been stored away and forgotten. Here was one more sign of our Lord's loving and timely solicitude as well as of His divine condescension to her. She had vowed to bring others to His Sacred Heart; He would help her even in the crude cenacle they had prepared for their own simple needs.

She brought her discovery to the other four, and noted with gladness in her heart that they too were moved. How often in the old days had the nuns at the Asile clustered admiringly about a fine bit of needlecraft! How often, too, had they made a little ceremony of offering some piece of lace or brocaded silk to beautify the altar of Saint James Cathedral or the shrine of Notre Dame de Bonsecours! There had not been time for any such luxuries in Vancouver, but there would come a day for that later. In the meantime, they would formally enthrone the image of the Sacred Heart of Christ in their community room, as He seemed to wish.

Sister Joseph freshened the embroidered linen and tacked it on the wall, while Sister Praxedes improvised a vigil light which she placed before it. Sister Blandine found an act of consecration in one of their prayer books and got out the accordion, while the two postulants flew outside to find a few sprigs of evergreen for a bouquet. Then they knelt on the newly scrubbed floor, and in the mild light of the December day they thanked the Son of God for having protected them so lovingly. Once more they consecrated themselves and all their future labors to His Divine Heart. The world outside their walls was full of elemental dirt and primitive vulgarity; but here they would guard His Kingdom clean and undefiled and here in their meditations on His love they would find solace and renewal.

Providence Academy, Vancouver, Washington

Sister Blandine was doing very well with the accordion, Sister Joseph noted, as they concluded with the old community hymn.

O gentle Providence,
From thy caressing hands
In limitless abundance
On us all good descends.

Who would not but proclaim
The author of all gladness!
Who would not rise from sadness
To bless His holy name!

. . . .

Shortly before Christmas the mystery of Moïse Loisel was cleared up. Sister Praxedes was about to begin supper when a vigorous knock sounded at the back door. She had no more than partially opened it, when she was greeted by a torrent of French and Moïse himself. Where had he been? In San Francisco, of course, as they must surely know. The sound of his voice was a signal for an excited gathering–Sister Theriault from the laundry, the Sister Servant from her sewing, and the two young nuns somewhat hesitantly from their studies. As they gathered about the pleased and eager center of their interest, the story came out. He could not find the popcorn that day at the dock.

"Popcorn?" the Sister Servant queried.

"Yes, the popcorn for Sister Blandine and Sister Norton," Moïse reiterated.

At that there was nothing for the two youngest to do but to acknowledge in confusion that they had seen this novelty displayed as they had gone aboard the *Brother Jonathan*, and thinking there was plenty of time they had asked the faithful Moïse to get some for them. But alas, he had strayed too far afield, and to their chagrin the ship was under way before he returned.

What had he done when he found that his ship had sailed? He had had an hour of real panic, he told them, until he thought of good Father King. That kindly and practical priest had taken him in tow, and had gotten him work with a baker. Surely the

Lord had allowed the eyes of her two youngest to wander, Sister Joseph reflected. She could not reprimand them because, after all, Moïse had profited by his apprenticeship. Years later she observed, "He had learned to bake good bread."

That was a happy ending to the popcorn incident, and Moïse was welcomed back among them. He was immediately given ample opportunity to prove his new prowess and thus became the first of a long line of bakers at the House of Providence in Vancouver.

There the baker was to be held in affectionate respect by all the growing and hungry small fry who through the years would smell the heavenly savor of baking bread and pastries. He would emerge from the bakery, flushed and hot, with flour still clinging to his bare arms and with white cap askew. Before him he pushed his cart, piled high with the long, brown, crusted loaves and the spiced and sugared rolls. He was a figure to follow with avid, hopeful eyes for sometimes he was known to dispense a favor here or there, in spite of his air of studied incorruptibility. In December, 1856, the Sister Servant could not foresee the timeless patience and tact she and Sister Praxedes would spend with the men who baked the bread; but she knew even then that they would be important enough in the scheme of things to merit not only careful training but forbearance for their human weaknesses and eccentricities. Any good workman, no matter how crotchety and captious, could serve the Lord's cause, if he were managed correctly.

The return of Moïse was timely. Before another day had elapsed Sister Joseph had his duties mapped out for him. The approaching feast of Christmas meant more work for them all, and he must do his share along with the others of her religious household. No matter how hard they toiled, their ordinary tasks for the mission were never done; yet the great religious festival must be made as solemn as possible.

There was His Lordship's wardrobe as well as their own to be put in order. This along with the endless laundering fell mostly to Sister Theriault, though Sister Joseph and the two youngest gave her a hand from time to time.

There was this abundance of food at hand to be prepared for the clerics and themselves. To the frugality of the daily fare, Sister Praxedes and Moïse now added whatever special pastries and dishes they could contrive or improvise.

To Sister Blandine and Sister Norton were confided the up-keep of the Bishop's quarters, as well as the thorough cleaning of the rooms of the two priests.

Sister Joseph reserved the renovation and care of the vestments as her own particular task. As her needle flew in and out of the raveled lace of the linen A or the poor elegance of the chasuble, she remembered Monseigneur Prince who had sent her and Sister Choquet to the Congregation nuns to learn the art of making vestments. Her nuns here in the West must establish and preserve that art, she promised herself. When there was time they would learn to apply the gold embroidery and the liturgical designs to the stiff brocaded fabrics; they would make strong, patterned laces for altar linens. When there was time? They must make time for so beautiful a service to our Lord's own altar. Nothing could be more important than that. She herself would some day make the altar. In the meantime there was the cathedral church which somehow must be made splendid for Christmas.

Everybody helped with that, to the great pleasure of the Vicar-General. Never well cast in the role of a mere onlooker, Abbé Brouillet found himself working side by side with the sisters, and set himself to keep up with the brusque energy of the Sister Servant. Together they assayed the situation.

The old Hudson's Bay Building had been converted into a church and was now in the process of being renovated. Formerly it had been a barn which the officials had used for the storage of furs. A new roof had been put on it, and other rudimentary repairs made it habitable; but rough, discolored walls left the interior squalid and unattractive. There was neither lumber nor labor nor time in which to finish the building; so the two of them decided to cover over what they could not remedy. Bolts of house lining were tacked to the blackened walls and the whole interior was made to look fresh and clean.

As Sister Joseph went up and down the uncertain ladder, she was glad that God had brought the fir and pine forest so near. That would supply their decorations. Abbé Brouillet brought in armloads of evergreens which they used in profusion throughout the main body of the church and in the sanctuary. There were graceful festoons for the walls, great sprays on either side of the altar, and, above the large, darkly hued painting of the Immaculate Conception which His Lordship had brought from Mexico, a wreath of interwoven pine and spruce.

The result, when the freshly-dipped candles were added, was very commendable, the Vicar-General and the Sister Servant agreed. Each now knew a healthy respect for the capacity for work in the other, and whatever strangeness had existed between them was banished by their common effort to make the church a place of wonder and beauty.

It was a lowly Bethlehem indeed, but the glory of the Lord descended on it in the mystery of the Mass on the feast of Christ's nativity. Sister Blandine's young voice and that of an American soldier from the Army post made a satisfactory choir, with the accordion supplying a simple accompaniment.

Mingled with the few townsfolk who came to the Midnight Mass, Sister Joseph and her sisters were indeed pilgrims far from their beloved mother house-pilgrims, but not strangers. One never got beyond the warm hearth of the faith where there were always to be found good Saint Joseph and the Blessed Virgin with the Infant Christ in her arms. Where, indeed, was there room for loneliness?

· · · · · · · · ·

The old year was officially ushered out and the New Year in by His Lordship. It was an occasion of impressive gravity when on December 31 he paid the sisters a visit in his role of spiritual lord of Holy Mother Church and made the five of them the object of a solemn mandate on their purpose and status in his diocese. With the loftiness of the episcopal rhetoric, the poor, shabby little community room assumed regal splendor and dignity. It was a glorious and privileged vocation to share and lighten their bishop's burdens. It was also a calling which elicited the versatility of each one of them in that it demanded skills in so many fields.

To Our Very Dear Daughters, the Sisters of Charity of our diocese, Greetings and Benedictions in Jesus Christ, our Lord:

From the moment when, by the admirable judgment of God, We saw Ourselves charged with the heavy burden of the episcopal dignity. We cast about for means and co-operators to aid Us in the accomplishment of Our terrifying duties. A religious establishment was not the last to come to mind.

We considered that the civil and Christian education of the young, as well as the care of the poor and the sick would contribute greatly to the formation of families where our holy religion would become known and practiced, and bring back to the paths of truth and virtue those who had had the misfortune of falling away.

Nor did we forget the poor Indians whom Divine Providence had especially entrusted to our care; for the establishment we wished to make in our place of residence seemed to us like a cradle whence would come forth "daughters" filled with the spirit of their vocation to carry to those poor creatures, along with the knowledge and love of their Creator and Redeemer, the way to live honestly among themselves and with their neighbors.

To these motives was joined another contributing not a little to make the necessity felt of having a religious community in our diocese; namely, that of having the care of our Mission and of the sacristy of our Cathedral.

Sister Joseph of the Sacred Heart felt her heart bum within her at his words. The Abbé Magloire Blanchet had come a long way, indeed, since those days on Saint Catherine Street. He was now this resolute prelate speaking with deep vision and exalted language of the tasks to be done. If God had done so much for him, surely He would do as much for her, plagued as she was by her human weaknesses.

She felt her pitiful inexperience, her imperious disposition, her abysmal ignorance crowding in on her. Surely, poor Sister Blandine had reason to harbor rancor and resentment against one so clumsy in the art of command. She could only pray that Sister Norton, that lovely, flowerlike soul, and Sister Theriault, who was the essence of devotedness, would not be corrupted by her own blundering and tactless heedlessness, would not be drawn to share in Sister Blandine's inner rebellion against a superior so inept. She thanked

God that Sister Praxedes was mature enough not to be shocked by the too human brusqueness of her superior.

Every one of them was so different from the other, and each had been shaken these months by her own particular loneliness; somehow she must learn to share and lighten the personal heartsickness of each. With God's help she must show Sister Praxedes that she relied on her prudence and wisdom. She must elicit the natural gaiety and courage of Sister Blandine. She must warm the piety of Sister Norton, and she must show appreciation of Sister Theriault's quiet and humble constancy. This was her duty as superior. This was what Monseigneur had asked of her. This was what Emmelie Gamelin had done for her in those difficult days of her postulancy. This was what her father would expect of his daughter, Esther Pariseau. With such a program there would be no time to think of herself.

She hoped that the Sacred Heart of her Lord would understand that there might not even be much time for quiet prayer in the new year of 1857, if they were to begin all the works which His Lordship was even now enumerating for them . . . a school, a hospital, a mission for the poor Indians, the sacristy and the bishopric! The five of them had better get busy . . .

CHAPTER 11

WINTER in the Oregon country could be disagreeably wet and cold, Sister Joseph of the Sacred Heart soon discovered. Though there was never the heavy weather which they had known in Canada, there was some snow in December. But worse than the snow was the steady downpour of rain which, while keeping the grass green, also kept the sisters confined to the house. There was the advantage that this afforded them of time to consolidate their position indoors. It also gave the two youngest some leisure in which to prepare for the school which His Lordship encouraged them to open in the spring. Education of the young held first place in his program for the evangelization of the area, and he lost no time in setting events in motion to that end.

There was to be a new convent first, and for the immediate future that would provide space for a small classroom, too. The building began as soon after the new year as the weather would permit. The annals of 1857 record the outcome.

On Ash Wednesday, February 22, we took possession of our new convent—a small wooden building 16' x 24', with four windows and a glass-paneled door. A stairway led to the attic which served as our dormitory. A partition walled off a small room which we fitted up temporarily as a chapel. With a few boards, Sister Joseph built a suitable altar; from a candle box she made a gem-like little tabernacle, painted and decorated with delicate gold ornament with the best material she could afford for a tabernacle veil.

The sisters beheld their small habitation with great interior joy. Here was our home!

Our kind bishop said the first Mass and for our comfort reserved the Most Blessed Sacrament there. The God who descended to our altar also came into our hearts. How happy the morning which enabled us to possess our Lord within our dwelling.

Here we were privileged to observe privately our community devotions—the forty hours of Our Lady of Sorrows, the month of St. Joseph, and that of the Sacred Heart. Here we pledged ourselves anew to advance the kingdom of Christ. We envied the lamp that burned night and day before the Blessed Sacrament. We chanted the Te Deum, and with renewed energy took up our burdens.

Now the order and regularity which prevail at the Mother House was possible among us.

It was in the new house that Sister Theriault and Sister Norton were clothed with the holy habit on March 21. Young Father Rossi directed their retreat. It was an oasis of quiet in the midst of the flurried activity of the mission. Looking on from the periphery of the intense stillness the Sister Servant was awed at the peace and interior beauty reflected in the faces of her two spiritual daughters. How extraordinarily visible even to the human eye were the effects of prayer! She saw the foreshadowing vows touch the humble maturity of Sister Theriault and transform her into her own faithful companion; as Sister Vincent de Paul she would be her helper and co-worker in a thousand Martha-like tasks for long years to come. She saw the vows also reach out to clothe the youth of Sister Norton, now Sister Mary of the Precious Blood, with an unearthly loveliness which must surely soon bum away the vessel of clay which housed so intense a spirit. Was this the girl who so lately had sent Moïse on his fool's errand looking for popcorn? Seeing the light of grace in her face the Sister Servant was glad that Sister Mary of the Precious Blood was to be entrusted with the guidance of the minds and hearts of children. She would be a good teacher. If only our Lord would spare her to them for long enough to get the school well under way! She was young, but she had had good training with Mother Seton's daughters in New York, and she had had some experience as a teacher at Longue Pointe.

While she watched and listened from her post as Sister Servant, Sister Joseph was busy with preparations for the school. She knew their resources for such an undertaking to be slender indeed. She and Sister Praxedes and Sister Vincent were handicapped in not knowing the English language. Try as she might, she could not master that barbarous tongue with its difficult consonants and its deceptive diphthongs. She could make herself understood and that was about all. But if there was to be a school, there was need for more sisters who could speak English fluently and teach the fundamentals of speech and written composition. Sister Blandine had a natural aptitude for it, and of course it was the native language of Sister Mary of the Precious Blood. They, at least, were equipped for beginning the school, but she could not be satisfied with mere introductory measures. If they were to accomplish anything of value their work must be not only thorough but also suited to the needs of the children who would come to them. This was not French Canada, and much as she might secretly lament that it was not, she knew that she would have to measure the effectiveness of their school against the standards set up in this remote little town. That town was largely American and Protestant. Any Catholic children entrusted to the sisters must receive at least as good a training as that given other children in the town. Otherwise they would be hampered by the very fact that they were Catholic. The faith was meant to be part of a bright heritage which would guide not only the soul which chiefly reflects the image of God but the hands and intellect of man through which God also works to effect His purposes in the world.

Certainly if any people needed to be regenerated in the heritage of the faith it was those of her own race who lived in Fort Vancouver and its environs. Sister Joseph thought of them with shame and faint hope. In her visits about the town she had been saddened to find so many French Canadians living lives incompatible with the Christian principles in which they had been reared. Perhaps through their children they could be won back to the sacraments and to decent living. His Lordship had done much to regularize their marriage alliances and to baptize their children in the seven years he had been Bishop of Nisqually, but

the force of bad habit reclaimed too many of them to careless-
ness and evil. True, there were a few faithful ones, and it was
wise to capitalize on the power of good example. With zeal and
the grace of God supplementing their poor human deficiencies,
the sisters would begin the school after Easter to do what they
could.

Both His Lordship and the Vicar-General had spoken from
the pulpit about the sisters' school. There had also been a quiet
advertising campaign by word of mouth throughout the town.
Catholic parents were urged to send their children to the sisters,
(and non-Catholics were also encouraged to consider placing
their little girls with them. The instructions would consist in the
rudiments of learning, but basically, it would comprise much
more than that. It was a matter of training small hands and hearts
and minds to good habits, and above all, of instilling knowledge
of God and of His Holy Mother, Mary. Imagine a child who had
never heard of the Blessed Virgin! Alas, there were many in Vancouver. There would be the three R's taught slowly and painstakingly and, for those who wished, some French—that language
which set apart those who mastered it as persons of refinement
and good breeding. There would be needlework of a practical
nature, and when one did fairly well with that, there would be
embroidery. Always there would be prayers and the catechism.

If only all this could have been supplemented by music! Sister
Joseph resolved to write both Monseigneur Bourget and Mother
Caron of their real need for a music teacher at the very earliest
date. It was clear to her that their school would have its critics
and she knew that as teachers her sisters were without much experience; hence she would make them as competent as possible
in as many fields as they could manage. Lessons in music caught
the public attention, and it was necessary to gather pupils by
whatever attraction they could offer, not for the sake of the sisters and their reputation, but for Holy Mother Church.

While constantly advising the sisters what the conduct of their
school should be, the Vicar-General was maintaining his own
small school for boys. There was an interchange of services between the sisters and Abbé Brouillet. He helped them with their

plans and instructed the young sisters; they in their turn provided his students with their meals and did their laundry and mending. Each grew to respect the zeal of the other, and the bond grew stronger with the passing weeks.

On March 16, Sister Joseph, who kept a vigilant eye on the approaches of the convent, saw a woman with a small child open the gate and move toward the porch. Before the knock was completed the Sister Servant had the door open for them. So was ushered in three-year-old Emily Lake, the first pupil of the first Catholic school in the Northwest.

The scene that followed was awkward and painful. It was obvious that the woman had only one aim—to get rid of the little girl as quickly and as completely as she could with as little encumbrance as possible from her in the future. The child was a fatherless waif, of mixed blood, whose appearance indicated that she had been neglected during most of her short life. Sister Joseph's heart sang within her because she knew that the school would be a success no matter what their shortcoming at Providence. Had not a child significantly called Emily come to find refuge among the daughters of Emmelie Gamelin? Moreover, our Lord had said that whosoever received a child in His name would be receiving Him. She reached for the small, grimy hand and drew the child protectively close.

Somehow they would manage to care for Emily, she reassured the unfortunate mother, who showed nothing but relief that the matter could be arranged so quickly. The door was scarcely shut on her, when the Sister Servant looked down on her first orphan and made a resolution which called for immediate action. She couldn't tolerate dirt.

April 15, 1857, was the day set for the opening of school. Sister Blandine and Sister Mary of the Precious Blood waited tensely at their posts, as teachers had done from time immemorial, fussing over last-minute arrangements and wondering what the day would bring. The convent room was bare to the point of austerity, but it fairly shone with well-scrubbed cleanliness and good order.

Before the day was out, seven little girls were admitted as students for Sister Blandine and Sister Mary of the Precious Blood.

From that Easter Tuesday on, there was heard at Providence the sound of the alphabet being given in timid lisps or in mighty chorus, of numbers recited haltingly and then in proud triumph, of words recognized and spelled, of primers laboriously read, and of the "Our Father" and "Hail Mary" ascending in slow and precise syllables to Heaven above.

In fair weather there were wonderful times outdoors, with "London Bridge" or "Farmer in the Dell," "Skip to the Loo," and sometimes that other game that Sister Blandine taught them called "Sur le Pont d'Avignon." Often as not, the little girls clustered about the nuns as closely as possible and enjoyed with their teachers the sharp edge of spring in the air. By some wordless process they now knew that if they had come to worship the sisters, the sisters had grown to love their pupils and to find joy their response and progress.

But it was Emily Lake who remained the jewel of the house old and the delight of the Sister Servant. Out of the small resources left by the child's mother and her own slender purse, she clothed the child in garments which were warm and clean, and she lavished affectionate and protective care upon her. For the first time in her life, Emily knew that she was wanted. Her small body became plump with proper food and rest, and very shortly she learned to use her baby wiles to extract an extra sugared cookie from Sister Praxedes in the kitchen or a bright ribbon from the Sister Servant. When both Sister Vincent and Sister Joseph conspired to make her a Sunday dress with a bit of embroidery on it, Emily with true feminine instinct admired both the dress and herself for hours together. The dress was blue, of course, for the Blessed Virgin. No opportunity was lost to instill in the child's mind the simple truths of faith. If she was to be seen at the heels of Sister Joseph, who was busy at the church sacristy or in the garden, she was also to be found near her in chapel, very much at home in the Eucharistic Presence.

Since Emily was to be the ward of the sisters in every sense but the legal one, Sister Joseph saw no reason why she should not have the child baptized as soon as possible. The month of May would be an opportune setting in time for the administration of the sacrament to one whom Our Lady must shield particularly. The blue mantle of the Queen of Heaven was needed by small Emily more than by most children, the Sister Servant believed. She prayed that its warm goodness would securely enfold their own little one. She would not only pray, she would do her part in a solemn pact with Our Lord and His Mother. The sisters would join her in making the occasion unforgettable.

The four responded to Sister Joseph's plan with spontaneous interest and generosity. Sister Blandine built the May altar. She selected a corner of the sanctuary for her shrine. The base of it she covered with mosses and delicate maidenhair ferns which the children had brought in from their trips with Sister Mary to the garrison woods. Garlands of tea-vine were hung in a background, and bouquets of trilliums, dogwood, and sword fern formed a beautiful bower for a statue of our Lady of the Immaculate Conception which His Lordship had brought from Mexico.

During school hours there was heard the thin, uncertain treble of childish voices learning to sing "Immaculate Mother . . . Ave! Ave! Ave Maria!" And there was also heard the frequent admonition to be very clean and to wear one's good dress for that day. In June, after the event, the Sister Servant paused long enough to write Mother Emily Caron, the Superior General, of those things nearest her heart:

Please accept my apology for not having written in advance to offer feast day wishes. . . . I must say that neither the Sisters nor I had the time. But with all of the family of Providence we joined you that day. For those far away there is always a note of sadness, but do not think we spent the day less gaily for that. Strengthened by the grace of God, we renewed our sacrifice and celebrated the day most happily. At the same hour that Sister Charles was presenting her kindergarten to you, we offered dear little Emily Lake for baptism. Out of our poverty, dear Mother, we had this precious thing to give- the first of our little orphans. May St. Emily be her protector and give us too a share in her tender love-especially a love for poor children.

Once more the Lord appeared on their doorstep. Sister Joseph was again called to the door, and before she quite realized what was happening, a boy who was scarcely more than an infant was thrust into her arms. The poor mother begged in a few broken words that the sisters take care of her child, and fled before Sister Joseph could obtain much information from her. Well, here was another to follow Emily to the sacred font of baptism. With His Lordship's permission, they repeated the ceremony for James Wilks, this little scrap of humanity, and made him the equal of kings and pontiffs as the child of the Heavenly Father.

The chronicles of the year speak often of Sister Blandine's shrine before which they found oneness of heart and a shared consecration.

Here the community and the children gathered daily for our May devotions. Here our first orphan girl was baptized Emily, and here also was baptized an orphan boy whose mother had abandoned him to the care of the sisters.

And as it so often happens, several significant beginnings emerged in the intertwined events of the same period–this time, the month of May 1857. Not only youth but crabbed age came knocking on the door of the Vancouver Providence, and both subsequently lived together amicably under its roof in spite of the proverb. A man whose eighty-five years had left him both feeble and penniless asked the sisters to take him in. It was not a plea that any daughter of Mother Gamelin could dismiss with a quiet conscience. Though there seemed no room for him in the crowded quarters of their convent school, Sister Joseph and her assistant, Sister Praxedes, considered carefully. There was so little required by old age–a little warmth, a little food, a bed to sleep in, and in fair weather the out-of-doors in which to putter about.

Sister Praxedes measured the kitchen with her eye, and thought that perhaps the space by the stove was large enough for a bed. Could they let him sleep there? The good Saint Joseph, who was after all their bursar, must have perceived just that spot as fitted to his purposes.

The Sister Servant loved her dependable assistant more than ever before at the suggestion, and let the complexities of the situation disappear in a sigh of relief. Of course, the old man could be accommodated with them, and no doubt he could help a bit with the vegetables and with the garden just outside the door. Perhaps poor Moïse who had lately received news of the death of his father would welcome his company.

They were never to regret their decision; out of it would grow one of the works with which the Sisters of Providence were to be integrally associated in the Northwest. Because of it many an aged person would spend the last flickering years of life in the steady light of morning Mass. With the sisters they would find the security and protection needed to face death confidently and serenely.

At the close of June, 1857, the following cold statistics were sent to the Mother House. Behind each item lay the secret history of souls in their search for God—their sacrifices' their tears, their faltering and uncertain quest, their growth in holiness, and their faith in their vocation.

STATISTICS FOR THE YEAR 1856-1857 FOR THE HOUSE OF PROVIDENCE, VANCOUVER, WASHINGTON TERRITORY

Personnel and works

Sisters	5
Boarding pupils	2
Orphans	2
Day pupils	10
College students (boys) boarded	2
Sick persons cared for in their homes	10
Sick persons visited in their homes	25
Night watchings in homes	34
Baptisms	2
Conversions	2
Servant	1
Ecclesiastical boarders	3

The Sister Servant had a sense of triumph as she painstakingly put her signature to the report. They had at least made a good beginning, and put down a few roots. The Mother House would most certainly realize that the West must have more Sisters.

CHAPTER 12

IN SPITE OF the unceasing labor and the thousand distracting problems which filled her days, Sister Joseph of the Sacred Heart wrote her Superiors in Montreal with a surprising degree of regularity. She owed it to the Mother House to keep them informed on the progress of their works and on the state of the sisters. After all, this was a community undertaking and all were interested in its outcome. The sisters in the West were bound by race and blood to those on Saint Catherine Street. They were all Emmelie Gamelin's daughters. As such they had an innate sense of family, even though at times they disagreed heartily among themselves and manifested disparate character, as members of a family often do. Loneliness harassed the hearts of the missionaries at being so far* from home, and lay like a burden on their good intentions to serve God wholeheartedly.

In April 1857, Sister Joseph had written Father Truteau, their ecclesiastical superior:

We have not yet received any reply to the letters we have written since our arrival; they must have been delayed on the way; if not, our people must have forgotten to answer us. I dare not complain, despite our extreme desire to hear of our relatives and friends, our sisters and venerable superiors.

The gloom was dispelled with the arrival of mail in May. Not all the news from Montreal was good. Mother Larocque, one of the foundresses, had died in Chile, and many of the sisters were ill, but Monseigneur was better; but bishop of Saint Hyacinth was convalescing, and the work with the aged and the poor was being visibly blessed by God. Just to know that they themselves were fondly remembered by their sisters was inspiring.

Sure that she would be comforted by her dear ones, Sister Joseph could now put on paper a thought she had scarcely dared allow in her own mind. Her next letter to Mother Caron gave an intimation of how acutely they had suffered in Vancouver. "Beginnings are always trying," she said, - and here the devil is so enraged he frightens me."

Now it was a great relief to dispel her misgivings by dwelling on those small, homely services which Mother Caron had done them, or would perhaps do when she could. There were the music books Mother had taken the pains to send them. There was good Marie Beauchamp who was to be sent to their mission as a servant, and there were inquiries about the faithful Moïse Sister Joseph let warmth and gratitude surge through her reply to her Superior. By thus manifesting the dependence of the missionaries on the Mother House for little things as well as for the greater ones she was binding each group to the other as closely as possible. So her letter continued:

I beg you, dear Mother, to send us a spindle, a flange, and some wire. I shall try to make a spinning wheel. It is hard to get woolen stockings here, but we can get all the wool we need at low cost. With a spinning wheel, we can reduce expenses. Forgive me if I also ask you to send the lives of Saint Francis de Sales, Saint Aloysius Gonzaga, Saint Stanislaus Kostka, and other young saints whose biographies will form profitable reading for the novitiate. We have a number of books already, but not those I mention.

In her next letter to Mother Caron she was delighted to pass on one item of news which would show those back home that their sisters in Vancouver had not grown lax.

A regulation bell like the first in the community has been blessed. May its sound recall the voice of our Mother, and may it unceasingly remind us of the observance of our Holy Rule.

Some day in the new House of Providence in Vancouver, they would, she hoped, have a beautiful clear-toned bell more like "Marie-Elizabeth-Genevieve." It would have a bell-tower from which the Angelus bell would speak to their little world of Mary, the Immaculate Virgin. The village would learn to set its clocks by the convent and put its children to bed by the quiet tones of the retiring bell. And when the slow doubles of the passing bell were heard they would bow their heads for the departing soul. That was not yet, the Sister Servant reflected. Now the town went by the garrison's bugler with his importunate reveille or his drowsy taps, as if one should be hauled out of bed or lulled to sleep without any thought of God! The present bell, at least, made for precision and punctuality in her community, and both Sister Blandine and Sister Mary were able to ring it correctly.

She only wished there were more of them like Sister Blandine and Sister Mary. The school was a source of worry. For that reason, the constant refrain of her letters to Montreal was the need of more sisters, particularly of those with specific training or aptitudes for their works. How amused Joseph Pariseau would be to know that his daughter spent so much time with pen and paper! She was sure that he would applaud her efforts, since that was the only means by which she could influence the thinking of those at the helm. Her father had taught her to adapt the method to the means available, though he would perhaps smile at the trick that God had played on her in forcing her to write, write, write. Letters to Monseigneur Bourget, to Father Truteau, to Mother Caron written with all the precision and patience she could muster went with every steamer putting off for the long voyage home. Wryly she wondered how much she had suppressed her own over-urgency in asking for help. Surely that man of God, the Bishop of Montreal, divined that she had no patience at all, because she had never been able to conceal her intolerance of work half planned or poorly done. Strain as she might she could not feel that things were well ordered and efficient in Vancouver.

The results were that she was waspish toward Sister Blandine and apt to construe many of her legitimate observations on the state of affairs as discontent or moodiness, so that the poor nun "had lost all confidence in her superior. For comfort or under-standing she turned wholly to Sister Praxedes. Thank the good Lord her assistant was a well-balanced religious. Her counsel to both Sister Blandine and Sister Mary was admirable, and often saved the day for the little community. The Sister Servant shud-dered to think what it would be like had our Lord allowed the whole pattern of their religious life to be left to her own clumsy efforts. All generations coming after would have been marked by the stigma of her failures. Things she could manage, but so often people were beyond her. She affronted them and trod on their small susceptibilities; and when she begged pardon on her knees, she was conscious of the fact that they were not always appeased. Even the evidence of her tears did not convince them of her real sorrow at having been offensive. Would she ruin all for the Sacred Heart in the land she wanted as His own province? Part of the trouble lay, she felt, in their insufficient personnel; so she must write those interminable letters for which she had neither genius nor inclination.

In midsummer, she wrote at great length to their ecclesiastical superior, Monseigneur Joseph Larocque. Theirs was a great oppor-tunity in the Oregon country, if this raw new land did not com-pletely swallow up the five of them before they had maded their own position.

Our Lord Himself was our first poor one. Had you seen His altar, my Lord Bishop, His sacred linens, and even His tabernacle you would have been moved to pity.

. . . it looks as if we can count on a good number of children. Our first pupils are very docile. Generally speaking, these poor children have been left to themselves. Their ideas are neither religious nor moral, their ignorance is pitiful. Even the Catholics know nothing of devotion to the Holy Virgin. Our little Protestants are not at all prejudiced. Their parents willingly allow them to go to church and learn the catechism.

We have the consolation of visiting the sick from time to time. We are happy to profit by such occasions whenever we can. The Protestants receive us cordially, and they are the predominating element in Van-couver.

I hope that Providence will find a place for us to live among the

Indians. These unfortunates have been driven to the mountains by the whites. just a few days ago Father Brouillet said that there will be important missions to be founded among the Indians. We expatriated ourselves to do God's holy will; that God knows well. But we are weak instruments, unworthy to make Him known and loved by these poor people. . . .

More and more I feel that I shall be happy only in contacting and relieving the destitute. Divine Providence seems to favor my wish. The greater number of our boarders are orphans, and we can expect many more. This class of children is most to be pitied. They are placed out under guardians who have every right of tutorship over them and who often maltreat them and bring them up without principles of any kind. They do not mind coming hundreds of miles to get rid of the poor little ones. Any institution with sure means of subsistence which could receive such children would do a great deal of good . . .

Everywhere they looked, there was work to be done. Circumstances were so ordered that the time did indeed seem propitious. Yet here they were, handicapped by the fewness of their numbers and frustrated by their own miserable shortcomings. She was the most wretched of the five, because it was to her that Monseigneur had committed the whole venture. Along with her own faults she had to bear the burdens of the others. She worried over Sister Praxedes' ill health and her own inability as Sister Servant to see that the good nun had the assistance in the kitchen and the rest which she so sorely needed. She was disturbed at Sister Blandine's continued depondency, and disquieted at the loneliness she saw in the young eyes of Sister Mary of the Precious Blood. Were it not for that dear soul, Sister Vincent de Paul, she would have been panicky for them all. While she was at it, she might just as well let His Lordship know how abysmal was her own dejection.

I am the one who deserves pity, my Lord. With sorrow I see myself relaxing and losing hold. I am incapable of doing any good. The least temptation to immortification or dissipation causes me to fall. I no longer keep my devotional prayers to the Blessed Virgin or St. Joseph. . . . What will become of Me? From time to time I seek to hide myself in the Heart of our Lord, to cleanse my soul by His Precious Blood. Will He have mercy on me? I no longer hear the voice of my Beloved, nor taste His sweetness, no doubt through my own fault. I often cast myself before the altar of the Sacred Heart which our Bishop allowed me to set up in the cathedral. There remembering the good intention which brought me to these shores, my confidence revives a little. If I can but bring glory to God, even at the expense of my own spiritual interest, I will rejoice. Yet my courage fails. Our confessor, Father Rossi, no longer permits me daily Communion. . . . Neither will he allow me to renew my particular promise, about which my Lord, you already know. . . . My heart is broken. Yet at the same time, I am happy to be here, and to make these sacrifices for our Lord, and to allow my life to be consumed in His holy service. The only practice which really binds me is that of the third degree of humility which you counseled at my departure; but even this is, I fear, more in my mind than in my practice.

Thus it was that she who had been Joseph Pariseau's beloved daughter, she upon whose strong, young arm Emmelie Gamelin had leaned for friendship and assistance, she whose imperious will and generous heart had been curbed and trained so carefully by Bishop Bourget and by Canon Prince' now entered on her own dark night of the soul. Though she felt herself to be very much alone, she was joining the noble company of the saints.

There was evidently a certain catharsis in getting it all down on paper to her religious superior, because in the fall of the year she was able to write Mother Caron words with faint overtones of a hard- earned peace.

I greatly encourage the Sisters who are generous to come and share our sacrifices. If the missionary has her difficulties, her trials, and her vexations, she also has her consolations. Our Lord never lets Himself be outdone in generosity. The missionary knows this well.

Moreover, the same letter shows unwonted restraint in the matter of the desired additions to their personnel.

Knowing your own needs at the Mother House, I hesitate to ask for anyone since you have been obliged to send recruits to other houses.

While I am writing to you, the Bishop of Nisqually is in receipt of a letter from the Bishop of Montreal, announcing that he will do all he can to send us a sister with Bishop Demers. I leave it to you, dear Mother, to guess how eager we are to know if this is true.

You see how silent I am about a sister for whom we asked to take charge of the music; she would be most useful for the offices in the church. But as she is not of absolute necessity for the support of the establishment I should be very indiscreet to mention her, knowing as I do how short the Community is of subjects. As for the Bishop of Nisqually, he asks with confidence and hopes in spite of all. . . .

By that time, too, Father Rossi seems to have become less a cause for interior pain and could now be spoken of with equanimity.

I have nothing new to tell you unless it be of the departure of our good Father Rossi. This esteemed priest has directed our community with great prudence. He gave us solid instruction and took real interest in us. We are very grateful to him. The Vicar-General, Father Brouillet, will be our confessor.

The Sister Servant was thus assiduous in correspondence which kept her religious superiors informed about Vancouver. She also put herself to great pains to write the missionaries in Chile, saying, "I write so poorly and with so little enlightenment that I am hesitant. I need time to write well and I have so little," adding with a hint of complaint, "Sister Blandine does so much better than I, but she delays."

But though she was faithful in the use of the dear Monseigneur's pen in all these matters, she refrained except on rare occasions from writing to those of her own family. Perhaps it was that she could not trust herself to give over her thoughts to the remembrance of those who were so dear to her. Perhaps, too, it was part of the pact she made with her Lord when she had solemnly promised to choose the way of renunciation because He had chosen the way of suffering for her. Whatever her reasons, letters to the Ile Jésus were so rare as to be almost nonexistent. Somehow her father would understand. It would be unworthy of his daughter as a Pariseau and a servant of God to put her hand to a task and look backward over the long furrows to the sweet dependence of childhood. He had known how to abide by his bargains in the old days at Saint Elzear. Now that his hair had grown white in seventy years of faithful allegiance to

God, he would not approve of a partial adherence to duty nor of anything which looked like regret. Joseph Pariseau would know that there would be time enough in eternity for every solace to the human heart. It was scarcely befitting either of them to cling to all the small comforts to be had now. So Sister Joseph of the Sacred Heart wrote at long intervals to those at home and was answered many times over by Elodie, who was now a sedate and matronly figure in her own household.

Somewhere in the fall of 1857 one letter in particular must have been written by Elodie to her sister in Oregon. There is no record of it, nor is there any evidence of any reply; but the stark statistics at the Hotel de Ville in Montreal bear mute testimony that some correspondence must have taken place.

"Pariseau, Joseph, died August 23, 1857."

At what secret place of the heart Sister Joseph met her kindred to share a common grief, no word of hers remains to tell. Of the nine living children of Joseph and Françoise Pariseau, she was the farthest from the Ile Jésus, and to a strong, ardent nature such as hers the distance could only add sorrow to sorrow. In not being with her loved ones to partake in the last rites of him who had given her not only his blood but his temperament was true bereavement. God Himself had wrought this spoliation, as He does each time He removes a beloved parent from the filial ties which bind together an earthly home. Sister Joseph could only have acquiesced lovingly though sorrowfully in what the hand of her dear Lord had laid upon her. Since there were no words, there could at least be her silence. Evidently the silence mounted until she must have wondered within herself if she had ever been a Pariseau. Could she ever again endure to be reminded of those simple, uncomplicated family relationships? Would it not be better to curtail once and for all those attachments which when cut off bled so profusely? This was evidently the decision she reached.

It was Sister Martin, her beloved Julie, who rebelled at this spirit of retrenchment. She counted the months and years which slipped by and later reminded Sister Joseph of how long time could be.

It is to my own dear Sister, from whom I am separated by many leagues that I am writing. Distance brings our hearts closer, for in sacrifice love grows stronger. However, I only half believe that truth, because your detachment seems to me as vast as the ocean. I see in you nothing which would hold the chain which should link our hearts, one end of which should start in Vancouver and the other reach Montreal. I do not wish to be reproachful today, but your love seems too well voiced by two years of silence, which was interrupted only to ask a service. For the moment let us forget. All is forgiven. Your short note touched the very fibers of my heart. I must avow that I am not indifferent in all things. You are too dear to me to allow that in two short years I would forget you to such a degree.

There is in her letter an intimation that the holy indifference of her older sister had made her recoil from the idea of following in her footsteps.

The missionary spirit has not yet come to me. I do not know if this indicates a lack of fidelity to grace, but it is true that the attraction has not come.

She still remembered the anguish of their parting and the desolation which followed.

I recommend myself to your prayers that I may obtain the gift of tears. Perhaps at your departure I shed them too abundantly. Since then I have had none for any cause whatsoever. I assure you that there are times when I feel the need of them. Pray for me. I never forget you before God. Your name is graven on my heart . . . So at the foot of the cross, you will find your affectionate sister, Sister Martin (Pariseau), Sister of Charity.

The gift of tears, indeed. Sister Joseph longed for the time when she could build the shrine she had promised for the Sacred Heart of Jesus. His was a pierced Heart, and she would not mind shedding tears before the emblem of His compassionate love.

CHAPTER 13

BELOW THE MISSION the great river moved toward the sea. Looking across it on clear days, the sisters could see Mount Hood with the eternal snows of its slopes now ivory or ice blue, now flushed rose. Behind it at sunrise and sunset, unbelievable color washed the skies, making the earth beneath a place of mystery and hazard. This country was too new and too distant for one ever to be lulled into a sense of security about it.

There were dangers from the forests behind them where the solid evergreen wall towered malevolently about their cluster of houses. The gigantic stands of fir, cedar, and spruce were beautiful with the sun highlighting their deep hues of green and blue; but so often they were nothing but impenetrable masses of shadow and fog which glowered and threatened a thousand unspoken evils. True, each year the forest was pushed back a little as the land was cleared for cultivation or settlement. But roads through the great timber were for the most part only wilderness paths soon made impassable by the heavy rains of fall and winter—just enough road, as Father Joseph M. Cataldo reported of Captain John Mullan's famous Mullan Road, to find one's way back.

Beyond the clearing, one sometimes stopped in quick horror at the sight of a tawny-coated cougar slipping noiselessly through the underbrush, interested, thank the saints, in more strongly scented prey. On quiet nights, and which of them were not, the nuns sometimes wondered if the lonely howl of the coyote had not merged into the hysterical and unholy racket set up by the vicious

135

bobcat. The imagination could not be allowed to follow down that disturbing pathway.

"Ab Omni malo, libera nos Domine!"

The time had not been far distant when the forest held other terrors. Now one saw few Indians, as Sister Blandine reported in her journey, and most of them were squalid, inert figures about the town. Occasionally a small group in full- feathered regalia and gaudy blankets rode into the garrison, but they were not a common spectacle. Usually it was the military folk or the governor who went to the Indians for council or powwow of one kind or another.

When the sisters first arrived in Vancouver there was much going and coming among the people of the fort because of the Yakima wars, but Sister Joseph and her four sisters had been too absorbed then in their own immediate problems to be aware of the significance of this activity. Passing their door on his way back from the Cascades, there could have come a young lieutenant –brisk, black-haired Phil Sheridan whose exploits were said by many to have saved Vancouver itself from Indian attack. There could also have come Lieutenant-Colonel Edward Steptoe. His precarious deliverance from massacre was to change the whole thinking of the military on the deadly serious nature of the contest being waged with the Indian tribes of the Big Bend and Yakima country. The Steptoe Disaster of May 1858 was followed by the influx into Vancouver of many a weary United States officer wearing a dusty blue uniform. General Newman S. Clark arrived from San Francisco in the early summer and called a council of his officers at the fort. Here Colonel George Wright was briefed for his famous campaign against the Spokanes, the Coeur d'Alenes, and the Palouses. In time the sisters came to know Colonel Wright well when he was commandant at Vancouver, and they were to receive many kindnesses at his hands. But in 1858, they knew only that he and his dragoons rode out of the garrison, traveling eastward, leaving a great cloud of dust to tell the mission and the town that an important expedition was under way.

All the Big Bends was aflame with a revolt stirred up by

Kamiakin, the astute and tragic Yakima chief. Against the Indians was sent no mere frontier, volunteer force, but regulars of the United States Army whose leaders had finally come to agree with the Indian policies of territorial governor Isaac Ingalls Stevens. Now it was either subdue the hostile tribes once and for all, or close the interior area between the Cascades and the Rockies to white settlement.

Right or wrong, the whites had come into the Oregon country to stay. The government had pushed the Hudson's Bay people north of 49°, and it had encouraged its own settlers by the Donation Land Act which paid scant attention either to Indian susceptibilities or to Indian rights. It was not surprising that the Indians bitterly resented the influx of white settlers who assumed that the earth was theirs for the taking; it is also understandable that the whites were easily stirred to retaliation against a series of horrible acts of primitive ferocity. Between the white man's vengeance and the red man's barbaric cruelty, the governor had tried to build a span of justice by his treaties with the various tribes, but the government was slow, and passions were high. Now there was no other way but conquest possible against the hostile tribes.

A ripple of fear tore through the whole northwest frontier and reached even the portals of the young Providence and Vancouver. Other missionaries in other times had been engulfed by similar uprisings. The vicar-general, Abbé J. B. Brouillet, had often spoken sadly of those difficult days a decade ago when the Cayuses had shocked all Oregon by the atrocity of the Whitman Massacre at Wailatpu. His Lordship had arrived in his new Walla Walla diocese just in time to be drawn into that dreadful event. For a time it had seemed that the work of the Church would be completely paralyzed by the savagery of the deluded Indians on the one hand and the bigotry of Christians on the other. With dogged, French Canadian purpose, poor Bishop Blanchet and his scattered priests had patiently explained their position to those who would listen, and had kept silence in the face of the campaign of vilification raised against even their most humane activities. In God's time they would be exonerated. In the meantime, they had used their influence to temper justice with mercy toward the unfortunate Indians whenever they could.

In the earlier warfare that had surged across the Yakima Valley in 1855 the Oblate Mission of the Holy Cross at Ahtanum was wantonly destroyed by American soldiers. But though the Indians had carried off their friend and protector, Father Charles Pandosy, O.M.I., they had done him no harm. In the war of 1858 it was the Jesuit Fathers who, having remained among the Indians, counseled them whenever possible and acted as intermediaries between them and the whites. Colonel Wright's military exploits at the battles of Four Lakes and Spokane Plains finally convinced the Indians that their cause was hopeless. One by one the tribes made their peace with the white man. Gradually the main body of the army returned to Vancouver, and the fort came under General William S. Harney in September 1858.

But if the Indian wars disturbed the whole Northwest and interfered with the progress of the missions, it was mainly the Indians who suffered. Captain John Mullan, to whom was committed the task of supervising the survey and building of a road between Walla Walla and Fort Benton, had accurately appraised the effects of the impact of white civilization upon the Indians. His view has been justified by history.

The only good . . . that I have ever seen effected among these people has been due to the exertion of these Catholic missionaries. Many of these missions might have benefited by the government allowing them the charge of the schools and hospitals, for they actually take care of the Indians when sick and educate them when well, and all this with the mere pittance at their disposal, not a moiety of what they need; while hundreds and thousands are squandered on paper for the benefit of the Indians which they never receive. The Coeur d'Alene mission has the Fathers Joset and Gazzoli, and Brothers Francis, Maguire, and Campapiano. They have chosen a beautiful site, on a hill in the midst of the mission valley, and it has proved to the weary traveler a Saint Bernard in the Coeur d'Alene mountains. I fear the location of our road, and the swarms of miners and emi. grants that must pass here year after year, will so militate against the best interests of the mission that its present site will have to be changed or abandoned. This, for themselves and the Indians, is to be regretted; but I can only regard it as the inevitable result of opening and settling the country. I have seen enough of Indians to convince me of this fact, that they can never exist in contact with the whites; and their only salvation is to be removed far, far from their presence. But they have been removed so often that there seems now no place left for their further immigration; the waves of civilization have invaded their homes from both oceans, driving them year after year toward the Rocky Mountains; and now that we propose to invade these mountain solitudes, to wrest from them their hidden wealth, where under the heavens can the Indian go?

To this question the little group of nuns at the new Vancouver Providence could give no solution, even had they understood the scope of the problem. They had come to the Northwest to do whatever work His Lordship would confide to them, and his directions from Bishop Joseph Provencher of Red River had specified that the missionaries were sent first to minister to the Catholic whites of the Northwest. But their hearts yearned over those small fragments of humanity, the metis, who came to them as orphans or boarders or sometimes as patients desiring the white man's medicine.

In August of 1858, Bishop Blanchet wrote from Cowlitz to his "dear daughter in Christ," the Sister Servant:

Toward the middle of next week I shall travel to Vancouver, but not alone. Two orphans, a boy and a girl have claimed my sympathy, if I can take them from the disorderly Indian house, a public nuisance, where they are. I ask your Sisters to be mothers to them . . . . I have told the good people here that I desire to have the Sisters here, etc. . . . . Who can say?

The old records of the Vancouver orphanage and school are evidence that the Sister Servant received many such children, some of them staying with the nuns a few months and some remaining for years. Sister Joseph found no answers to the over-all problem Of the clash of one race with another less civilized; yet she did what she could to care for those individuals whom the Lord confided to her. That she was stepping down to minister to the Indians was a thought completely foreign to her way of thinking. In this, as in so many other inherited traits, she was like her own people, who found it easy to live among Indians without any delusions of racial superiority. Rather she longed for the time when His Lordship would allow the Sisters of Providence to go directly to the Indians in mission schools; but in 1858 she knew that that time had not yet come . . .

Both His Lordship and the Abbé Brouillet held opinions on the Indian question which were neither popular nor orthodox in the late 50's. Most Americans of the era were convinced that it was their nation's "manifest destiny" to extend from ocean to ocean, and let those who stood in the way of that impulsion beware. Anything else was nonsense. So if the Bishop and his vicargeneral were to accomplish anything for the faith they had to get along with the Americans, among whom they had chosen to live, and work patiently and unobtrusively for a more Christian treatment of the Indians. Justice to the tribes was slow in arriving; but in the meantime, there was charity.

To Sister Joseph charity must be practical. It meant first of all helping the wretched and needy to help themselves whenever they could. While the tumultuous world fought its passionate warfare beyond the picket fence enclosing her little world, she cultivated a new orchard and an ample mission garden. She saw to it that the half-breed children who came to the sisters were trained to work at her side. Perhaps she could make a few good farmers out of these incipient followers of the camas, the huckleberry, and the salmon.

That there were so few Indian children grieved her heart which longed keenly for the extension of the Kingdom of Christ. But it was worse than useless to attempt what she had neither authority to undertake nor resources to accomplish. God was patient, and she would bide His time. In her heart she felt that some day both the Abbé Brouillet and the Sisters of Providence would be given their opportunity to help these pitiful, slow-spoken children of the Heavenly Father. Ile Abbé was all for a head-on attack to take the case of the Indian to the citadels of the mighty and make the government come to some recognition of these people as human beings. She herself would be content to serve them and to teach them, and so to bring them finally to the summer of God's eternal country.

As a child she had been very sure how that country looked–not much different from Ile Jésus, in the long warm July days. Now in middle age she knew that Heaven is wherever one has the clear vision of the Triune God when one's being has been re-created to endure that vision. Because she remembered how she had felt about heaven as a child, she thought she could make the poor savages understand what Christianity could do for them. They already believed in the Great Father and the fertile land to which He would bring all good Indians.

There were so many who did not yet understand that the Heavenly Father had done much more, so many souls for whom Christ died who had never heard the sacred name of their Divine Benefactor.

Monseigneur Modeste Demers had spoken of the tribes of his spacious diocese which swept northward from a land so like their own to the ominous snows of Russian America, and Father Pierre de Smet, the Jesuit who had been in Vancouver for no better than a day in September 1858, was full of plans for more missions in the Rocky Mountain area. Only by the slow and gradual process of missions and mission schools, he told them, could the Indian be taught to accept the white man's civilization. For that matter, only thus could they be taught the art of survival as a race. What a giant of God that blonde Belgian was! How her heart had followed him as he hastened eastward to the Coeur d'Alenes to allay the fears of the defeated tribes! In this sentiment, at least, she reflected wryly, she and Sister Blandine were in complete agreement. She knew for a fact that her secretary longed as much as she to work among the Indians. But both of them had just now become more effectually bound to Vancouver. In a limited sense, they would have the Indians brought to them, for had not the good God already sent to their new Saint Joseph Hospital one small, dying Indian child?

As with all works of God, the hospital had come into being without much fanfare. The idea of founding a hospital had had a natural growth. From the very first the sisters had made it their duty and their happiness to visit the sick in Vancouver and to do whatever they could to care for them in their homes. Here, at least, there was no language barrier, for suffering needs no interpreter. The Sister Servant found her small, poor store of English words growing as she visited one family and then another. Those who were afflicted received her services gratefully, and she frequently visited Protestant families as well as Catholic. Often she and a companion looked in on young John Lloyd, a consumptive, who was clearly in the last stages of disease. People came to rely on the sisters in time of sickness, and to find security as well as healing in their ministrations and simple remedies.

On the feast of Saint Joseph, 1858, the Abbé Brouillet found a small coin as he came from town.

"Here," he said to Sister Joseph of the Sacred Heart, "is the first donation to the hospital."

With that, the two of them began seriously to examine the possibilities of such an undertaking. Tuberculous John Lloyd became to them and to other well-meaning folk in the town the living testimony to the need of a hospital. A number of people begged the sisters to take him under their care, not only because he was ill but because he had no home of his own and was left to the charity of first one person and then another. It was not that the Sister Servant nor her companions were unwilling to take over John Lloyd. But where to lodge him? To the Vicar-General if an action was commendable, it was forthwith to be put into motion. He immediately obtained legal approval. If the nuns by themselves could not initiate a hospital, then they must have help. He therefore set about prodding the women of the town to form an organization similar to that which had aided Madame Gamelin in Montreal. The result was that on April 6, 1858, the Vancouver Ladies of Charity assembled for the first time. Mingled with a majority of Catholics were Methodists, Episcopalians, and Jews. Sixteen were actually present, and thirteen others who could not attend asked that their names be registered for membership. The Sister Servant was present as was also the Vicar-General.

At this first meeting the Ladies of Charity discussed and disposed of three pieces of main business, with Abbé Brouillet presiding and handling the initial questions with dispatch. The very fact that the Ladies had assembled was sufficient for them to presume without any further discussion that there was to be a hospital. The first issue was, therefore, what to call it? A good Methodist lady proposed, in the spirit of the time, that the new institution be named *Washington Hospital*. Sister Joseph of the Sacred Heart had nothing against the Virginia gentleman who had led Americans to rebellion against a fatuous English king, but there were others to whom she would turn with greater familiarity and confidence. She caught Abbé Brouillet's eye and was quickly relieved to know that he had rightly interpreted her glance. With perfect composure and courtesy he told the group that he saw no objection to calling the hospital by the proposed name among themselves. However, in the act of institution it was designated as *Saint Joseph Hospital*. At this, the meeting quickly agreed that so it should be, and as the annalist concludes, "There was no further question of Monsieur Washington."

The hospital had now legal being and a name but no location in the world of real things. It would have been easy enough to find land on which to build, but to build at that particular time seemed out of the question. Prices of both construction materials and labor were prohibitive. "Lumber at forty dollars a thousand, and a working man at eight dollars a day," moans the annalist.

The eyes of the Ladies of Charity began straying toward Sister Joseph of the Sacred Heart. What of those little houses, those cabins, she had been putting up in the Providence enclosure? Could not one be spared? Sister Joseph had just completed a small building she had intended for both laundry and bakery. The partitions were not in yet, nor the interior finished. The whole building extended only sixteen by twenty feet, and was eight feet high; but if such a humble structure would serve the purposes of a hospital, she would gladly turn it over to that end. Her offer was accepted with alacrity and visible relief. They left her part of the little house for a bakery, and pledged themselves to begin immediately to complete and furnish the rest for occupancy.

The third bit of business that day was the election of a president.

Here the group showed tact and tolerance. They elected Mrs. William Rodgers, one of Vancouver's highly respected Protestant ladies, knowing that she would interest a wider circle of friends in the functioning of the hospital.

On April 9, began the work of bringing the Northwest's first hospital into being. Sister Joseph and one of her workmen put in a ceiling of rough lumber. Walls and ceilings were covered with a light weight muslin fabric and then with a simple wallpaper. The ladies had four beds put in the room, with four accompanying bedside tables. and chairs.

Twice a month the Ladies of Charity met at the convent to sew for the hospital. At the same time each pledged herself to contribute twelve and a half cents a week for the cause, and to undertake general collections for the support of the poor who would not be able to pay for hospitalization. For each sick person sent to the hospital by Mrs. Rodgers, the president, the association agreed to pay the sisters a dollar a day.

News of the hospital spread and interest in it grew. Among others, John Lloyd waited as patiently as he could for its opening. But even before it was ready to function, those in distress began to knock at the door. On May 19, two men from some distance came to the sisters for help. One had a badly mutilated hand , the other was a consumptive. Though the hospital was not ready to receive them, Sister Joseph had not the heart to send them away. She turned, as always, to the Bishop, knowing that his quick sympathies would find a way to give aid to the sick men.

"The Vicar-General is absent," the Bishop said. "Put them in in his room for the present."

Not without reason, the annalist pauses to comment on the aging bishop as their "vigilant shepherd, devoted father, and sincere friend."

The Bishop looked both elegant and paternal when on Saturday, June 7, he came to bless the new Saint Joseph's Hospital. John Lloyd, who was waiting on the doorstep for the simple ceremony to be over, followed the bishop without observing the formality of removing his hat. However, after looking on with astonishment as the bishop sprinkled holy water about the room and reverentially invoked the blessing of God and the protection of the Blessed Virgin and the saints, the Protestant soul of the first patient gradually succumbed to the solemnity of the occasion. Slowly he removed his hat and lowered his head.

The sun seemed to shine more brightly than usual, the air was purer, the scent of the flowers more delicate. It was one of those days on which the heart was carried on waves of memory and of hope. . . . Our humble room seemed a holy place—a place consecrated by suffering and repentant tears. It would be a *port of salvation* opened for all poor sinners; a *tower of David* where every sufferer would find sanctuary and protection. This small corner of the earth unknown to the great ones of the world would become the *haven of the weak and the infirm.*

The Sister Servant wrote the sequel somewhat later to Bishop Bourget in Montreal, who followed from afar the progress of their works. John Lloyd, who had never bothered much about his relations with God, began to develop an interest in the Catholic faith. He was baptized on the feast of Saint Vincent de Paul, and died shortly afterward. The second person to die was a small Indian child who had known the sisters and returned to them "for their medicine." He was speeded on his way to the Heavenly Father by that best of all medicine, Extreme Unction. The third person to die was none other than that estimable lady, Mrs. Rodgers, president of the Ladies of Charity. They had not known the proprieties, in that instance. How were they as Catholics to conduct themselves in the event of the death of one not of the faith? Sister Joseph begged her father and friend to lay down the rules of proper behavior. Should they stand? Should they kneel? Should they pray aloud, or should they remain silent? There is no evidence that the Bishop answered her questions, but he must have done so, because the Sisters of Providence subsequently assisted many a poor, non-Catholic sufferer through the dark gateway without any disquietude as to decorum.

The hospital had been filled to capacity from the very beginning, Sister Joseph told the bishop. She hoped to extend its effectiveness by finding another room, perhaps by additional building, in which to house convalescents. The ladies had by early fall provided a small pharmacy. All took turns with the sick, but the greater part of the burden fell upon Sister Blandine and Sister Joseph. The physicians must also have been interested in the work of Saint Joseph's Hospital. At one time in an earlier letter she had written of an unnamed, former Hudson's-Bay-Company physician who had spoken encouragingly of the good to be accomplished by the sisters, and she subsequently had warm praise for her good friend and adviser, Doctor David Wall. But in 1858, the care of the sick was looked upon rather simply as one of the corporal works of mercy. One did whatever was possible, without much help from either the medical science or the wonder drugs of that day. When one did one's best, the rest could safely be left to God, the Sister Servant often reflected, and since the hospital was named after Saint Joseph, had they not made assurance doubly sure?

The forest behind them continued to glower, and occasionally heavy storms beat down upon them. But a sense of security came to the Sister Servant when she heard the cheerful bugler in the fort next door, and the sound of their Angelus bell sending the praises of Mary out over their garden, over the poor sick ones at Saint Joseph's, over the children safely cared for at the school, and over themselves as the daughters of Our Lady of Sorrows.

CHAPTER 14

AUTUMN, 1858, was ushered in by the Feast of Our Lady of Sorrows, September 21. It was a golden day to all five sisters, but more particularly to the two of them who made profession of vows. There was no community chapel for this intimate conventual ceremony; but there was the Bishop's cathedral church, poor as it was, and there was the Bishop himself offering a pontifical Mass as solemn in intent and sacred in character as any in Christendom.

Whatever richness of ornament Saint James Cathedral possessed in 1858 was donned and the altar was made splendid by flowers and lights. Sister Joseph of the Sacred Heart had trained six choir boys and vested them in new lace surplices and red soutanes. But all agreed afterwards that the most beautiful adornment of the church that day was the two novices themselves.

The people of Vancouver had seen nothing like it. They were visibly moved by the youthful beauty of Sister Mary of the Precious Blood. There seems to have been ample reason for their being impressed since even the community chronicler permitted herself enthusiasm on the subject.

Allow me to remark on the rare beauty of Sister Mary of the Precious Blood. Since our dear sister has left this worldfor heaven one runs no risk in speaking of her attractiveness. Our young novice possessed extraordinary beauty of feature and expression, joined with intelligence and liveliness of spirit. She was so remarkably beautiful that on her departure from Montreal several priests remonstrated at Monseigneur Bourget's imprudence in sending so lovely a girl to a land both protestant and savage. Later, a Jesuit said to the superior in Vancouver, 'Send that young novice back to Montreal. She is too beautiful for this country!' Hence it is not surprising that dear Sister Mary on the day of her profession, in all the lustre of youth and beauty, drew the attention of all as she made her oblation at the foot of the altar.

That such observations were allowed to remain in the chronicles above the approving signature of Sister Joseph of the Sacred Heart, that they were not deleted as bits of fulsome nonsense, shows something of the mind of the Sister Servant. Sister Mary was beautiful and good. Why not put it down so that all might read about what God had wrought? She loved the little sister, and had she been faced with the charge she would have admitted honestly that she loved Sister Mary largely because she was intelligent and lovely to look at. As she grew older those around her knew very well, often at the cost of their personal feelings, that Sister Joseph liked good-looking, keen-witted nuns.

In the fall of 1858, the Sister Servant could not afford to be over- particular in her choice of co-workers at the Vancouver Providence. The taking of vows had not multiplied the accomplishments of either Sister Mary or of dear Sister Vincent de Paul. Both were working to capacity, as were Sister Blandine, Sister Praxedes, and Sister Joseph herself. The new hospital taxed their energies to the full. As in previous years, too,, they were plagued by the absence of a music teacher.

They were conscious of their shortcomings in the field of education, and suffered from the knowledge of their lack of preparedness and from the criticism to which they were subjected. The Abbé Rossi had, as her director, admonished Sister Joseph about her vanity. The realization that the English school was not as efficient as she could have wished was a condition which she accepted as a corrective to her own self-complacency in well- doing. She could not remedy the circumstance, but she could bow to the arrangements of Divine Providence which forced both her and her little community into a situation which left no room for vanity. But since God so patently desired them to undertake that which was beyond their present endowment, she would trust Him. God would be their adequacy.

Gradually, He was teaching Sister Joseph to curb her burning urgency for activity–for activity of any kind-rather than for stillness and inner quiet which so often feel like emptiness and aridity until God manifests Himself therein. She had long known by precept that God is not in the whirlwind, and somewhere in those first busy years in the Oregon country, she learned how she must incorporate that knowledge into the practice of daily living. She could not longer allow herself to be blown along on every gust of energy which stirred her. She must instead learn how to wait on God's will. Certainly it was He Himself who had put in her heart the desire to build here in Vancouver a realm in which Christ could freely reign. The thought of it persistently recurred and filled her with a joy and peace which could come from God only.

Yet there appeared so little scope for her dream in those early days. It seemed rather that they would all die surrounded by mountains of unfinished housework. Endlessly, the cleaning and laundering, the sewing and cooking, had gone on day after day, encroaching on the time for sleep and even on the time for prayer. But by the grace of God the Sister Servant discovered that it became not only bearable but refreshing to approach each fearful stack of dirty dishes, each tub of steaming clothes, each heap of ragged garments as God's request for her services now. After all, He could use a dishpan, a washtub, a sewing basket to further the designs of His infinite love. In times past He had used the simple, lowly things of daily living on which to rest the whole structure of the Redemption. Had He not dealt with water pots, fishing nets, and even with thirty filthy pieces of silver in a worn purse? Even His speech was rich in allusion to such things as patched garments, burnished lamps, and salt without savor.

"For some of us," she wrote Bishop Bourget in late 1858, "the idea of being engaged only in housekeeping was painful. There should have been less eagerness for our works and more abandonment to Providence."

By that date the housework had multiplied many times over,

though they were gradually bringing it under a more definite schedule. One wonders how a handful of sisters could manage the care of the bishopric, the church, the hospital, the orphanage, and the boarding school, provide meals for the clergy, the children, and the boys from Abbé Brouillet's college, and care for the linen and the laundry of all these. Added to this were the garden, the constant building projects of one kind or another, the visits to the sick and the poor, and last but certainly not least, the school.

Their vocation as Sisters of Providence made them servants of the poor. Sister Joseph worried frequently about the whole business of education. Of however imperfect and humble a nature now, was it not committing them to a program of studies beyond the scope of their rule? Her practical good sense made her see that circumstances altered their position and what was possible in Montreal could be thoroughly impossible in Washington Territory. But in any event, she would have the blessing of obedience on all their undertakings. Hence she wrote again and again to Bishop Bourget and Mother Caron explaining her temporary adaptations and begging their counsel and approval:

The Bishop having taken the rule into consideration finds nothing contrary to that which forbids advanced teaching, music not being so regarded in this country where it is taught in the lowest schools. His Lordship found it painful, and we too, Monseigneur, to see their education in lax institutions because of not having found with us the music which their parents demand so urgently. In spite of these considerations, he has told me that he will have us discontinue it (the music) at the next vacation if it has not your approval.

We have had some prejudice to overcome; our incompetence was openly discussed in our first years, particularly by the public who proclaimed that our school was of no value except for beginners. That pleased me because I feel confident that this little humiliation is good for us. . . . I believe, Monseigneur, that we must exert ourselves to become better equipped for teaching.

According to appearances, works of charity must be established slowly and in a small way until the population increases. While waiting we try to help our neighbor on all the occasions which present themselves.

The difference in age, sex, and condition multiplies the work many times, but without this condition we could do little for our neighbor. It seems that this is the means Providence is using to attract the attention of the public to works of charity. But the two older sisters are not always ready to accept this view, and I sometimes must oppose their thinking. I do not believe that we can wait for those works to be organized as they are in the East in communities of long standing. It seems to me that we must be happy to suffer inconvenience in doing good and that the sisters must come to understand this. These little miseries are not acute. I should be happy Monseigneur, if you would advise and encourage us in this regard.

To the great joy of all, aid from Montreal arrived on October 6, 1858, in the persons of Sister John of God, Sister Mary Peter, and a postulant, Sister Mathilde Fissiault. Without delay each assumed her duties at the Vancouver Providence, the first at the hospital, the second in the classroom and the pharmacy, and Sister Fissiault wherever her mistress of novices directed. Both professed sisters had just made their vows; having lived these last two years on Saint Catherine Street, they brought with them not only intimate and personal news of the dear ones, but also that aura of distinctive religious spirit which pervades the birthplace of the community.

Sister Joseph believed that she could discern in the choice of recruits which the General Council had made for the Western mission a tacit approval of her policies. Her superiors had shown their affirmation of Saint Joseph's Hospital in sending little Sister John for immediate service with the patients. And thanks to God and all the saints, they had sanctioned the teaching of music by listening to her repeated requests for a music teacher. All disquietude regarding her own adherence to the spirit of the constitutions was dispelled. Her painstaking explanations of the situation in Vancouver and her arguments for the need of adaptation had convinced those in authority, and now she could proceed with clear conscience. The last thing she wished was any change in the basic character of her beloved community, or any weakening of its safeguarding virtues of humility, simplicity, and charity. She rejoiced that her superiors had concurred in her judgment that the essential character of the institute could sometimes be best safeguarded and its distinctive works made more effective by modifications in non-essentials.

But this was not a matter on which to offer herself congratulations. Neither would she belabor the point with either Monseigneur or the Council. It was sufficient that God smiled on their works through the approval of her superiors. Had they withheld their assent, that too would have been His Will.

The immediate improvement in their teaching removed all cause for apology and embarrassment. She looked ahead to a time when she and her companions would have an expanded sphere of influence. There were always so many poor, so many sick, so many children, so many afflicted who had not been brought to our Lord and His Blessed Mother. It was a relief that the shortcomings of the sisters themselves no longer hindered their approach.

In the following spring, Sister Joseph of the Sacred Heart wrote the ecclesiastical superior, Bishop Larocque, letting the facts speak for themselves.

The mission is making headway more rapidly than we had hoped. But we do not manage it by ourselves. I have given it over to Saint Joseph. Since Father Brouillet will be going to Canada soon, I shall not enter into details. He understands the spiritual and the temporal concerns of our little community. . . .
The care we give our patients, especially those who die, favorably impresses them (non-Catholics). There is a great deal of good to be done here. . . . We do all we can. . . . Our dear little orphan girls have only a small corner for their dormitory; we have nine, and they give us much consolation. So do our orphan boys. Our young postulant, Sister Fissiault, is as zealous in training them to piety as Sister John of God is in the conversion of her patients. . . .
Sister Mary Peter is in charge of the boarding school. She, too, is very devoted. I am surprised that she accomplishes so much in her state of enfeebled health. There are always between twenty-four and thirty boarders. She also has thirteen music pupils, and has to study much that her pupils may progress. . . .
I sincerely thank you, my Lord, for having sent us these three sisters. They give good service and are exemplary. I hope the com-

THE BELL AND THE RIVER

munity will grant us two more at the request of Father Brouillet. If he succeeds in collecting enough money for us to maintain a larger hospital, we shall transfer the patients to a house we bought for that purpose last year. The present hospital will then be given over to our orphans.

We are praying much to Saint Joseph during his month to obtain funds for the payment of certain debts contracted for the care of the poor at the hospital. Devotion to this good father, Saint Joseph, is growing here; it will have fine results.

Very shortly the good saint was going to find himself further embroiled in temporalities. The day would come when he would be maneuvered into matters of high finance, and who is to say that he has not done a better job than the Rothschilds, the Vanderbilts, and the Morgans of the world?

The Vicar-General, Father Brouillet, having watched the expansion of the Vancouver Providence with enthusiastic approval, decided that the enterprise needed the protection of the law of the land to give it permanence and freedom of action. Time was when Young Abbé Brouillet had viewed the sisters and all their works and pomps with a measure of skepticism; the nuns had reciprocated by distrusting this clergyman who looked so unclerical in waistcoat and cravat. All that was two years ago. Now there was seasoned friendship between the Vicar-General and the nuns. So in December 1858, Father Brouillet had had a bill presented to the territorial legislature in Olympia for the incorporation of the Sisters of Charity of Providence. To his dismay, the bill was quickly defeated. But the good father was not easily daunted, and on the advice of a Catholic legislator the bill was rewritten with some minor alterations. Father Louis Rossi, who at the time was in the Puget Sound area, was asked to use his influence at the state capitol. The bill was introduced again in modified form and, through the good offices of Father Rossi and the political support he was able to rally, this time it was passed without difficulty.

Sister Joseph of the Sacred Heart was named in the Act of Incorporation as forming the corporation with the authority to take into partnership those sisters whom she so disred. the legal title was "The Sisters of Charity of the House of Providence in the Territory of Washington." The act specified that this body could acquire property which would yield up to twenty thousand dollars in annual revenue. The third section was worded thus:

"The ends of said corporation shall be the relief of needy and suffering humanity in the care of orphans, invalids, sick and poor, and in the education of youth."

Quick to see special significance in this singling out of the one among them named "Joseph," the community felt it only fitting that they should pay particular honor to the great saint to whom they had entrusted the matter. With Sister Praxedes, her assistant, and Sister Blandine, the secretary, the Sister Servant made the following act of council:

This nineteenth day of March, 1859, we, the Corporation of the Sisters of Charity of the House of Providence in the Territory of Washington, wishing to testify our confidence in the protection of Saint Joseph, most humbly request him to be the protector and guardian of all our works, our property, and all the business transactions in which we may engage. By these presents, we declare him to be the Father and President of the Corporation.

Moreover, with the consent of the Superior General, we promise to support, lodge, and maintain a poor person in the name of Saint Joseph for all time to come.

Made and passed at the House of Providence, Vancouver, W.T.

SISTER BLANDINE, *Secretary*
SISTER JOSEPH OF THE SACRED HEART,
Superior.

Never was a president of a board of directors held in greater esteem, consulted more frequently, or entrusted with a wider variety of business ventures. Certainly only a saint would have allowed himself to be so often importuned. With her boundless energy and her constant drive to expand and improve the material scene for the spiritual and corporal works of mercy, the Sister Servant set the pace; she certainly expected Saint Joseph to do his share. As a child under her mother's tutelage she had learned to trust those great ones of God who now stand before His throne, and it had become a habit to turn instinctively toward the saints in the exigencies of daily living. Now that she was a mature woman, she never doubted that they bent lovingly and solicitously about her when she needed them. The Church Militant in Vancouver was sometimes straitened. What was more natural than that they look for assistance from the Church Triumphant, particularly from that just man, Saint Joseph? The comfortable thing about him was that though they had made him a financier he would always retain the working man's point of view. With him she need not disguise the satisfaction she felt in wielding a hammer or a saw.

CHAPTER 15

Pariseau affairs obtruded themselves on the attention of Sister Joseph of the Sacred Heart in the early summer of 1859. Sister Martin had written in haste of George's troubles. As a young man of family he was finding it hard to make a living and conceived the idea of leaving Ile Jésus for the West and Vancouver. His was the old dream which had obsessed so many French Canadians—the dream of greater opportunity and quick wealth to be had in the easy-going, less ordered areas on the far rim of the continent. But his level-headed older sister knew from what she had seen in Vancouver that it was the rare French-Canadian who found fortune and well-being in the rootless society of pioneer settlements and wilderness trails. She also knew that she could not allow George to lean on her for the strength he must find within himself.

The letter she wrote Sister Martin is almost harsh in its determination to halt all deliberation on such a course. Without doubt some of the vigor of her expression is due to the distress she felt in refusing to come to the aid of her own kin. It is an anguish every religious experiences when she must abstain because of her vocation from trying to help those dear ones of her family who normally would have first claim on her charity and attention. For their good, she must not let them depend on her; for her own good, she must remember that she has left father and mother, brother and sisters for Christ, and that she cannot be more concerned for her own flesh and blood than she is for God's other poor or sick or unfortunate ones. She can only trust them all to

God's care and providence; and invariably, when she does, she finds in this as in all else the hundredfold of her vocation. Despite her heartache, Sister Joseph wrote Sister Martin:

The message about our brother George which you sent in the letter to Sister Mary of Providence has been carefully considered. I hope you were not hurt by the reply I sent through Mother Caron. But the more I reflect on the subject the less encouragement I can offer. Though I would not try to prevent George from coming here to be with me, I cannot approve of his desire to do so.

You know, dear sister, that since I entered the community of Providence, I have taken no part in family affairs. How could George depend on a poor missionary such as I who today is here, and tomorrow is where? From the look of things we shall be establishing an Indian mission in two years. Perhaps I shall be one of those happy ones chosen for that work. Then our brother would be left alone.

George speaks no English, and there are few Canadians here with whom he could associate honorably. To my confusion I must admit that our poor countrymen here are without faith, without principles, and without honor. . . . There are no exceptions. Protestants are more sober, but without faith, without religion. Only a miracle could save George and his family from association with Protestants, who will be in the majority for a long, long time to come. What a sorrow for parents of a Catholic family to lose the faith!

You tell me the children are young. I surmise that it is for their future that he is willing to sacrifice family ties and country. The climate is good. It is easier to make money, though more difficult to keep it. A good workman can draw down good wages, but often he is without steady employment. An excellent Canadian mechanic who has been here two years now has had only a few days' work during the last two months. Let George reflect on all this and choose what seems best to him. . . . God will take care of him if he is faithful to his religion. . . .

I pray that having accepted the sacrifice of our separation on earth, the family may one day be united in heaven. Be sure to tell George that I sympathize with him in his present unhappiness and assure him of my continued prayers. My remembrances to all the family. I love each one most tenderly. . . .

There is no record that George ever came West, nor that his family suffered unduly for his having heeded the advice of his older sister. But much later other Pariseaux came, among them George's daughter, Sister Adrian, as a sister of Providence.

And today, a cherished heirloom in the Pariseau family is a small statue of Saint Joseph. Mother Joseph on her last visit to Montreal gave each of her nephews one, saying, "Ask Saint Joseph to help you make a good marriage."

The House of Providence at Vancouver was set on the edge of a wilderness, and every steamboat arriving from up or down river was an event for the sisters as well as for the little town. Hence, departures and arrivals play a prominent part in the chronicles, and one has the sense of much coming and going at the Mission, no doubt because such events loomed large to those there. It could not have been easy to house visitors when living space was so constricted and furnishings were so meager. Yet all visitors were freely welcomed, and if His Excellency or one of the fathers was away, the absence created a real void.

Accordingly when Father Brouillet went East on business for His Lordship in 1859, his departure was keenly felt. A man of intellectual energy and many activities, he was bound to be missed by the sisters. However, they rejoiced with him that this journey provided him opportunities to visit his own people. His letters, arrived with great frequency from various points along the way, and showed warm interest and affection for the sisters and their charges.

The good father had been given many commissions. His Lordship had asked him to secure the service of the Viatorian Brothers as teachers for the boys' school, as well as to intercede at the Mother House for more sisters for foundations in the Northwest. And Sister Blandine had evidently put in a special request, because from San Francisco, he wrote:

> Mr. Robbins will bring you the farina for which you asked, that is, if I have translated correctly. I had no dictionary, and my Washingtonian pride refused to have recourse to a California translater; so I took oatmeal to mean the *farine d' avoine* of Sister Blandine. If that is correct, fine; if not, too bad; but correct or not, it is enormously expensive.

The Viatorians could not accept a Vancouver foundation, and the boys' school accordingly endured a fitful existence, dependent on whatever migrant men of learning Father Brouillet could lure to his wilderness academy.

The pleadings of His Grace, Archbishop Francis Norbert Blanchet, along with those of Bishop Magloire Blanchet and of Bishop Modeste Demers, of British Columbia, formed a mighty chorus to which those in Montreal neither could nor would turn a deaf ear. The Vicar-General arrived in Montreal in time to second the requests of the bishops. This barrage of petition had immediate and generous response.

Sister Joseph received the word in far-off Vancouver on August 5, while she was writing Father Brouillet.

His Lordship just came to announce that two of our sisters are coming with six Holy Names. Our sisters are overjoyed. Our contacts with the Sisters of Jesus and Mary have always been friendly. They are well prepared for their work. They, too, are the daughters of the Bishop of Montreal. Should you see them before their departure, tell them we expect their company for a few days' rest in Providence after their long journey.

Not only the promptings of her own heart inclined the Sister Servant to do all in her power to smooth the way for the new comers. Both Monseigneur Bourget and Mother Philomene, the superior general, wrote her letters of wise counsel with regard to the Sisters of the Holy Names and the Sisters of Saint Ann. The arrival of new communities in the Northwest was an occa sion for establishing precedent along well-defined lines so that God would be better served by all.

The three communities had much in common. Each of them had been founded by the venerable Bishop of Montreal in those difficult years of the 1840's when economic hard times had followed political upheaval for so many French Canadians. The work of each religious group had a particular emphasis; the Sisters of Charity of Providence, for the poor, the sick, and the abandoned; the Sisters of the Holy Names of Jesus and Mary, for the

Christian education of children; and the Sisters of Saint Ann, for schools in rural areas. Yet there were no hard and fast limitations for each community. At the request of the bishops, the Sisters of Providence sometimes conducted schools, the Sisters of the Holy Names maintained orphanages and creches, and the Sisters of Saint Ann were engaged in hospital work and a far-flung missionary enterprise.

In the Northwest, the activities of the three groups were at first somewhat loosely determined by geography. The Sisters of Providence were sent to the Diocese of Nisqually, the Holy Names Sisters to the Archdiocese of Oregon City, and the Sisters of Saint Ann to the Diocese of Victoria. Very shortly all such boundaries disappeared because there proved work enough for each community many times over, particularly when, after the Civil War, the tide of population moved westward in a great upsurge from the eastern United States.

However, in 1859 it was important that the policies be clearly laid down. Hence Mother Philomene wrote to Sister Joseph:

> Soon you will have as neighbors our dear Sisters of Longueuil. It is my hope that the greatest cordiality will be maintained between the two communities. Let us remember that our good father Saint Vincent, regarding his own congregation as the least of all, held to the principle that it was his duty to do what he had to do to the best of his ability without being -envious of those who could do more. Take particular care, dear Sister, that the greatest intimacy reign between your sisters and the Sisters of Jesus and Mary, knowing that should you do otherwise you would fail to maintain the spirit of Saint Vincent de Paul and you would be acting against the intentions of your superiors, particularly the Bishop of Montreal. All will go well if each works only to procure the greater glory of God. Our good Bishop desires that you go to the assistance of the Sisters on their arrival in Portland.

Monseigneur himself had taken a hand in establishing an ordered pattern for the group of missionaries. On the journey, the eighteen religious were to regard themselves as belonging to one community, with Sister Mary Alphonse, of the Holy Names as superior, Sister Agnes, the Providence sister as her assistant, and Sister Marie de Bonsecours, of Saint Ann as councilor.

"Obey with joy and love in all things those named to conduct and guide you, having but one heart and one soul."

The three sisters so constituted temporary superiors of the missionary group soon discovered that theirs was a fairly restricted field of authority. The party which left Montreal in mid-September included Archbishop Francis Norbert Blanchet of Oregon City, and an entourage of priests, Father J. B. A. Brouillet, Father Jean Flavien Malo, and Father Zepherin Poulin. There were twelve Holy Names sisters, two Saint Ann's with a prospective postulant, and two Providence sisters and a postulant. After a journey which paralleled that of the original five in route they reached Vancouver on the morning of October 21, 1859.

Sister Joseph of the Sacred Heart who kept a sharp eye on the river was alerted by a deep, prolonged whistle. There on the lower river was the *Uncle Sam*, moving grandly upstream, its great side wheel churning the green waters of the Columbia to white foam. As the boat put in slowly to anchorage directly below the Mission, Sister Joseph and Sister Blandine hastened to the embankment. They were at the landing long before the ship was in position to unload its passengers. To their amazement, the sisters saw that the company of missionaries along the deck rail was twice as large as they had expected. There was their good friend and monitor, the Vicar-General, next to His Grace of Oregon City! And there was the beloved Providence habit worn by two sisters they had never seen before. In the midst of busy calculations, a sudden exclamation from her companion interrupted the Sister Servant. Sister Blandine had recognized among the Holy Names nuns her own sister, Sister Mary Florentine. From then on, all was joyous confusion. For the travelers, the fatigues of the long journey were abated; for those on shore, the old loneliness at the heart melted away as they reached forward to welcome the newcomers.

His Grace of Oregon City offered Mass at Saint James Cathedral and gave Holy Communion to all in his party. The small pioneer church with this unwonted number of clergy and religious was reminiscent of the churches and chapels back home, where so often the great functions of the liturgy were attended by rank after rank of priests and nuns.

The sight of this noble company kneeling at the altar railing to receive Holy Communion, and prostrate before the shrine of the august Mother of God, rekindled our courage to continue the warfare against evil. Never was the *Te Deum* chanted with more gratitude.

So Sister Joseph of the Sacred Heart wrote later to Bishop Bourget, the beloved father and friend in Montreal, whose benevolent approval had speeded the new missionaries on their way to Oregon. The chronicles of Providence make us believe that the Sister Servant's hymn of praise was perhaps broken in upon by other considerations. There was the matter of food for those who had had only ship's fare for several days. While Mass was in progress, she no doubt slipped over to the convent to marshal her forces there and to take a hand with the cooking. At any rate, the breakfast which followed was sufficiently memorable to be mentioned in the annals.

The three communities mingled companionably, exchanging messages and greetings, questions and answers. . . . The Vancouver sisters were eager for news of Canada, the beloved homeland; those lately arrived were more full of inquiry about the West and intent on what might be ahead for themselves. All too soon the hour of departure arrived. At eleven o'clock the Uncle Sam's whistle was heard again, and the Archbishop and the twelve sisters of the Holy Names bade a reluctant goodbye. They resumed their voyage to Portland, where they arrived at three o'clock in the afternoon.

The Sisters of Saint Ann lingered for two reasons. First, there was, for the time, no ship to Victoria; secondly, their postulant Mademoiselle Adelaide Archambault, had contracted Panama fever or malaria and was unable to travel. Sister Joseph of the Sacred Heart insisted that she be placed immediately at Saint Joseph's Hospital. There her condition grew alarmingly worse, so that when the sisters received word that there was a ship to be had out of Portland for Vancouver Island on October the twentythird, there could be no question of taking her with them.

Sister Mary of Bonsecours and her companion were transported across the Columbia by row boat. The poor sisters were frightened at the prospect of another encounter with the treachery of the

Columbia bar and of the perilous equinoxial seas awaiting them off the northwest coast. Even more painful was their grief at the necessity of leaving their dear Adelaide already so clearly marked for death. Sister Joseph tried to reassure them, knowing all the while that every heart must bear its own burden and vanquish its own fears. She and her sisters could not stay death or deter their friends from the difficult voyage, but they could and did give service to the dying and abundant sympathy to the living. This shared sorrow forged strong bonds between the two communities which neither time nor vicissitude has been able to shatter.

Adelaide Archambault died October 25, 1859, and was given burial in the Sisters' Plot near the mission.

"She edified us exceedingly by her patience and her submission to the Holy Will of God," the chronicler remarked conclusively.

Life at the mission settled down to an even tenor as the months moved along through late fall and early winter. Mademoiselle Elmire Guimond entered the Providence novitiate. Sister Agnes and Sister Pudent, the two newly professed sisters, rested briefly and then were assigned their new charges as mistresses of the boarding school and orphan girls respectively. The Sister Servant was bent on more business and more building—this time the expansion of facilities was for her "children of predilection," the orphan boys. Father Brouillet, home from his travels, busied himself with interests particularly proper to the man of God and gave a retreat to all the children of the mission, to the great delight of the nuns, at least. The spiritual wheel turned a full circle on the Feast of the Immaculate Conception with first Holy Communions, Confirmation, and the donning of the scapular of the Mother of God.

The crowning glory of the year 1859 came with the great day of Christmas. The Sister Servant was concerned to make it even more memorable than heretofore. She looked about the small cathedral and found it shabby beyond endurance. Scrub as she might, the rough floor of the sanctuary remained an affront to her eyes. The uncurtained windows were unlovely and the altar —how pitifully poor in ornamentation! She knew that His Lordship could not be called upon for money. She had tapped that source too many times already—for the sisters' convent, for the orphanages, for the episcopal residence, for the thousand and one small needs of the moment which would empty a far heavier purse than their bishop's. But as she wrestled with her problems, she became increasingly distressed that her Eucharistic Lord .Should be lodged so poorly.

Was there no one in Vancouver who had money? Actually, the only people of affluence there were the military folk. That was it! She would go to the fort. She smiled to herself thinking how often she had gone there before—to both General William Harney and Colonel George Wright. Her requests had always been courteously received. Well, there was nothing for it but to go again. They would give; she was sure of that. She was insistent enough as a beggar to know that it was easier for people to capitulate early, if only to get rid of her.

She wished that there were a better way, which would leave people glad that they had been generous. After all, they really - would be giving to the Lord Himself, and it was too bad that they could not get some enjoyment out of an act of religion. Her mind ran ahead to see herself going awkwardly from officer to officer, and from soldier to soldier. She knew that she was not a person to charm hearts—she with the blunt, uncouth speech and the heavy features. God had not given her grace of manner, but she could not reproach Him for that. He knew what was best for her. He had fortunately given her an understanding of beauty and charm and of what they could achieve for His service. For this insight she was grateful. That was one reason why she loved Sister Mary of the Precious Blood so much. God had trusted her with beauty. If God trusted the little sister so much, surely He intended that His gifts in her be used. So instead of herself taking up the collection at the garrison, she would send Sister Mary of the Precious Blood. The poor child would suffer, but she would not hesitate when she realized that out of her humiliations, God's house would emerge in a splendor befitting Him.

It was decided to take up a collection in the garrison. Sister Mary of the Precious Blood was named to have the charge of this collection. This was for our young sister a great act of self-denial. But how

THE BELL AND THE RIVER

great was the recompense for her abnegation when in three days she realized a total of $350.00. Immediately we bought a beautiful carpet for the sanctuary, a lamp, window curtains, chandeliers, and vases, etc., and had them all for Midnight Mass. The chapel (church) was resplendent.

The account is laconic enough, and perhaps Sister Mary of the Precious Blood could also take the experience for granted, after the event. Anyway, it was a glorious Christmas.

CHAPTER 16

A<small>MERICA</small> entered the fateful decade of the 1860's conscious of monstrous shadows lying across the broad land. The accumulated reasons for civil war were already at hand, needing only the lighted fuse of the overt act to set off a bitter and passionate struggle between the North and the South. It was not that war itself was inevitable' but only that men thought it so. Certainly the issues at stake had little immediate concern for the people of the Northwest whose chief interest in 1861 lay in the conquest of the wilderness and in the development of peaceful lines of communication and commerce. But the rancors of the East and South spilled westward to arouse the belligerence of those who had neither slaves to liberate nor states' rights to defend. As Americans they could scarcely be expected to refrain from joining sides in a war which aimed to change the definition of what being an American means.

Many an ardent spirit joined the regular armies of the North and South. Among them was the first governor of Washington Territory, Isaac Ingalls Stevens, who was killed in battle early in the war. Other notable military men were will known to the Northwest, and the news of their exploits drifted back to kindle interest in the battles and campaigns of the great struggle. General Ulysses S. Grant, General George B. McClellan, General George E. Pickett, and General Phil Sheridan had been stationed in the West and each had had some hand in its historical development. The regular army was called east, leaving Vancouver Bar racks with only a skeletal force until volunteer regiments authorized by the War Department were raised under Colonel George Wright. So the bugler's reveille continued to vie with the Angelus bell each morning, and at night his taps dropped in the darkness along the fields and rivers.

The Civil War did not greatly affect the life of Sister Joseph of the Sacred Heart or of the others at the Vancouver Providence. She gathered the children of her boarding school and her orphanages the more closely about her, and prepared to give them care and Christian upbringing to the best of her ability.

Young Sergeant John Rainey rode off confidently one day never to return, leaving his motherless five-year-old Jane and four-year-old Catherine at the Mission. There they remained brisk and busy with the things of childhood, unaware of the meaning of either war or bereavement. A daughter of Colonel George Wright and a daughter of Sergeant John Rainey became Sisters of Charity of Providence.

There, too, was Mary Agnes Gordon placed with the sisters for safekeeping. Her actress mother had given her child the frivolous name of "Cerita." "Little Cherry, indeed," the Sister Servant thought, when the girl needed a good solid saint's name to keep her unspoiled and innocent in the midst of all the froth of her mother's world. Well, baptism had remedied that bit of foolishness, to both the child's and the Sister Servant's satisfaction.

The waters of baptism flowed freely during those years, the church records being a mute witness to the fact that the children loved the sisters who cared for them. The children found it a simple step to God who so visibly managed all things well at the Providence. Even the names in the church register attest the presence of the sisters in the foreground of the children's lives. There is a generous sprinkling of Blandines and Praxedes, of Josephs and Vincents among those who came to the holy font, as well as the stately names of Philomene, Magdalena, Dorothea, Perpetua, Marguerita, and Marcelline right out of the Roman martyrology.

A name was not to be lightly bestowed, Sister Joseph felt. It had in it both supplication for the present and hope for a blessed eternity. So while she encouraged the half-breed Indian girls of the orphanage to learn the practical household arts of sewing, cooking, and cleaning, she rejoiced when they donned the melodious baptismal and confirmation names so loved by her own people. The world to which these girls would shortly return was at best a difficult one. She trained them diligently for their role as future wives and mothers, and then she pleaded with their name saints to find them husbands without delay.

Our first orphan girls are now very apt at work, I would love to find good husbands for them, because I much prefer to see them married young than to have them placed in families where their innocence is endangered. Once the half-breed girls leave us, they can be saved from danger only with the greatest difficulty.

Indeed life at the Providence was a succession of prayers, and of exhortations to prayer. Pray that the profusely blooming young orchard to the west of the church be blessed by rain and sun and spared from frost. Pray that the lettuce and onions, and then the peas and beans and squash, be worthy of Jimmie Wilks, Joey LaFramboise, Charlie LeDoux and all the small, nimblefooted crew from Saint Vincent's department who had planted and weeded with such care under the zealous prodding of the Sister Servant. Pray that God touch Colonel Wright's heart with generosity when he was approached regarding the lumber they so much needed for the new buildings. Pray that Mr. Joseph Petrain find a fertile piece of land for them along the lower river where they would have sufficient acreage for ample patato crop and for feed for stock. Pray for good Captain James Hardie whose wife and children were so ill. Pray for a good workman to help Damase Blanchet. Pray for their father and friend, the Vicar-General, who was so much occupied on their behalf. Pray for vocations. Pray . . . pray . . . pray. Pray to the heavenly queen, the Mother of God. Pray to the dear Sacred Heart of her Son, whom, alas, they had not honored as the Sister Servant wished or promised. Pray to Saint Roch to guard them from sickness. Pray to Saint Amable to save them from fire. Pray to good Saint Joseph who looked after all their interests. Pray . . . pray. . . pray.

With the resiliency of youth, the children prayed for now one intention, and then another, and the nuns were consoled at their growing piety and docility. The good God answered all the prayers, though sometimes not precisely as Sister Joseph requested.

Both orchard and garden yielded wonderful crops, and that was good because money was too scarce to be spent on fruit and vegetables. Nobody seemed to have much money because of the war.

Colonel Wright proved amenable regarding the building materials from the old Hudson's Bay fort. He deputed an officer to arrange that Sister Joseph and her workmen be allowed to take from the abandoned edifices of the Hudson's Bay Company the lumber they needed for additions and repairs at the Providence.

The last company officials had left Fort Vancouver for Victoria in the summer of 1860. The United States military people regretted neither their going nor the quick ruin which descended on their former habitations. The old buildings were a mute reminder of the once proud company which for so many years had successfully blocked American settlement in the Northwest. Colonel Wright was only too glad to have a tenable excuse for further depredations. His predecessor, General William S. Harney, would not have bothered to find excuse.

Sister Joseph of the Sacred Heart had arrived in Vancouver ten years after the Treaty of 1846 had struck a death blow to the Hudson's Bay holdings south of the forty-ninth parallel. She had never known the company in its heyday. She had, of course, been associated with a number of the company officials. Dr. H. A. Tuzo, the Hudson's Bay medical officer had encouraged the sisters in their works of mercy on behalf of former company servants and their children. In the late '50's Chief Traders Dugald MacTavish and James Allan Graham were good friends to the mission and Amy MacTavish was a boarder at the sisters' school. But whatever sentimental regard the Sister Servant had had toward the Honorable Company, and whatever respect she had held for its well-cultivated fields and orchards, she did not hesitate to make the most of Colonel Wright's permission. If she did not avail herself of this practical supply of lumber, others less scrupulous would do so without benefit of legality. By the logic of history, Hudson's Bay belonged to yesterday; fortunately, they had left behind them much which could be used at the sisters' convent and the orphan boys' new quarters. Two letters on the same day attest the fact that Sister Joseph did not delay nor scruple to make the most of a good thing:

Colonel Wright presents his respects to the Superioress, of the Sisters of Charity, and takes great pleasure in granting the request contained in the notes of the Superioress of this date.

Major Babbitt will be assigned to furnish the Superioress. with such lumber as may be necessary. Fort Vancouver, July 11, 1861.

Mother Joseph to Major Babbitt:

The Superioress of the Sisters of Charity presents her respects to Major Babbitt, and having received a favorable answer from Colonel Wright would be glad to know if she may send her workmen to fetch the lumber.

She would also request permission to have any other material which may be on the premises and which would be useful to her.

HOUSE OF PROVIDENCE, July 11, 1861

One doubts that the choice of lumber and accessories was left to Sister Joseph's workmen. She herself was too keen in the appraisal of wood to leave the task to her employees. The old buildings might present a picture of sagging timbers and general decay, but the Sister Servant knew that there was much that was sound if one was shrewd enough to recognize it. The Pariseau in her would know where to look. Hudson's Bay builders had used Douglas fir logs from the great fir stands immediately behind the river plain. They had built in the Canadian style with which Sister Joseph was surely familiar. It is not difficult to imagine her busily examining the old buildings inside the stockade, with young John Baptiste Blanchet, His Lordship's nephew, close at her heels. In rapid-fire French, she, no doubt, pointed out to this young man who was to become her able assistant in all her major building projects the sturdy, grooved uprights, the posts in the sills, the six-inch-thick, horizontal timber which formed the walls. Did "the other material on the premises" include small-paned windows, metal hinges for doors, bricks for the mission bake-oven? The grapevines which twined the crumbling piazza of the Chief Factor's house may have proved attractive, too, except that Sister Joseph would scarcely have waited five years for cuttings from those famous vines.

Being preoccupied with turning the occasion to the utmost profit, Sister Joseph did not regret the silver flag splashed with scarlet and gold no longer aloft above the southern stockade wall. Nor was she disturbed in her explorations by the memory of the majestic, white-haired giant, Dr. John McLoughlin, who had so Often looked out across this same grey-green Columbia to the Oregon foothills as he ruled the great fur empire with magnanimity and kingly dignity. The "white-headed eagle" had known how impermanent are the edifices of earthly greatness long before he was laid to rest in Saint John's Cemetery, Oregon City, in 1857. There was small probability that he would have disturbed the Sister Servant's search.

That old Hudson's Bay fort provided a rich yield for the House of Providence is confirmed by the chronicles. A note of jubilation and accomplishment creeps into the account:

We bless Divine Providence for this latest benevolence; indeed we thank God whole-heartedly for His prodigality toward us. Vacation passed to the sound of hammers. Shortly, the annex was completed. The sisters themselves did the painting. When the pupils returned, the sisters took possession of a pretty little community room, an office for the sister superior, and a novitiate.

Things were certainly going their way.

His Lordship had promised to pay the workmen, if the sisters would furnish the construction materials. He proved as good as his word and paid $232.00.

· · · · · · · · ·

Sister Joseph believed that it was Our Lady who answered their prayers for vocations. With the perceptive delicacy which the Mother of Christ exercised in the Gospel scenes, it came to pass that within the space of a month they had a new and attractive room for the novitiate, a new novice mistress, and three new postulants. Sister Blandine, now five years professed, succeeded

Sister Praxedes as the mistress of novices. With the entrance of American girls who knew no French, the language requirement was of prime importance. So to twenty-three-year-old Sister Blandine who spoke English with ease, was confided the religious formation of Maria Sullivan, Anastasia Wall, and Nancy Crate.

Maria Sullivan, whose religious name was Sister Mary Augustine, was the daughter of Mrs. Maria Sullivan of Portland. As the owner of extensive property on the east side of the Willamette River, in the area subsequently called Sullivan's Gulch, Mrs. Sullivan was a generous benefactor to the sisters and an active co-worker with Sister Joseph of the Sacred Heart. It was with a full and grateful heart that the Sister Servant welcomed the daughter of her friend to Providence. Another good friend, Anastasia Wall, who became Sister Philomene of Jesus, was Dr. David Wall's young sister. The third postulant, Nancy Crate, later Sister Mary John Baptist, was one of the girls from the boarding school. Her father, Mr. Frederick William Crate, had come from London in 1849 as a millwright in the service of the Hudson's Bay Company, and had remained at Mill Plain after the company had withdrawn from Vancouver.

Sister Joseph viewed the entrance of these three fine recruits as the seal of God's approval on her labors. Here was guaranty for the future. Here, too, was the spur for a deeper spirituality and greater assiduity in prayer, in spite of the complexity of material things which crowded in on her life. Under no circumstances must she give scandal to God's little ones.

She knew too well that only by the grace of God would she be kept from that disaster. By her unremitting prayer she must bind God to her need of Him in this matter. It was the old, old conflict. The irrepressible impulse of her nature to get things done, the burning activity which blinded her towards the sensibilities of those who were slow, betrayed all her good intentions. "The good which I will, that I do not; but the evil which I will not, that I do."

At the time of the yearly retreat in August 1861, she had sought counsel of Father Urban Grassi, S.J., and 'had been admonished by him to learn the art of moderation.

"I shall reform my life, 0 Lord! I shall reform my life," she wrote in her retreat resolutions, without in the least knowing how reform could be accomplished. How should the eagle unlearn the art of soaring? But the matter was serious, and evidently others were as unhappy with her as she was with herself. She wrote to Mother Philomene sadly: "I notice in rereading your last letter that you are not pleased with me. Alas, this is one of the bitter fruits of my garden which I must often pluck with tears."

And to her beloved Monseigneur Bourget she spoke of her inadequacy and inner confusion: "I am frightened of the title of foundress which is imposed upon me, along with the responsibility of forming young sisters for our works. I fear that the example I set before them will live as long as the Institute lives. What a tragic thing, my Lord, should the seed of a bad spirit be left by me to grow among them."

Their own kindly bishop, His Lordship of Nisqually, evidently heard echoes of the small discontents and frictions. He, too, wrote the venerable Bishop of Montreal:

There are little miseries which plague my community of religious. Sister Joseph is very pious, zealous, and all afire for the good works of Providence, but she is also too hasty. She is censured for not giving correction prudently. She offends by making reprimands at unfavorable times. Her manner opens a wound anew instead of healing it. Thus she makes her sisters suffer, though I am sure her intentions are very good.

Small wonder that the Sister Servant clung with all the ardour of her generous nature to the living heart of Christ. It was not that she dramatized herself as a misunderstood religious. She would have been the first to acknowledge that others understood her only too well and were just in their criticism of her blunt and forthright manner. Religious devotion was not for her an escape from unpleasant reality. It was rather the sanctuary where all things became whole again though she herself remained the weak and imperfect creature in the presence of the God of all Perfection and Beauty. On the anniversary of her Holy Habit she wrote to Mother Philomene:

Seventeen years ago today I was clothed in the Holy Habit of religion. What delights from the Divine Bridegroom have been hidden under this humble garb! What graces and favors! At the same time that happiness inundates my soul, I must bewail the unfaithfulness which humiliates me. But truly, Mother, it is too much to speak of crosses and sacrifices in religious life when a quarter hour spent with our sweet Spouse compensates for years of sorrow or regret.

That her griefs were quickly behind her is shown in the same letter when she spoke of the joy she had in realizing a longplanned project. At the time she was named for Oregon, in 1856, she had promised herself that she would erect an altar to the Sacred Heart out of gratitude for having been chosen as a missionary. Money was not lightly to be spent in the Oregon country, and not all her piety would allow her the luxury of an altar to the Sacred Heart when the mission so sorely needed such things as beds, mattresses, washtubs, and cooking utensils. Once again the military at Fort Vancouver came to her aid.

Captain James Hardie's family had frequently been commended to the prayers of the sisters and the orphans, and had been cared for during their illness by the Sister Servant and the other sisters. The little boy, Arthur Donald Hardie, died in the spring of 1861. Mrs. Hardie gradually recovered her health under Sister Joseph's solicitous care. In gratitude Captain Hardie wrote her:

REVEREND MOTHER,

Your goodness has made me desirous of doing something for you in recognition of the attentive care the sisters have given my family. There came to me the thought that a new altar of the Sacred Heart of Jesus in place of the old one would give you pleasure. If it is agreeable I shall have one made immediately.

If it is agreeable . . . How often she had puzzled over her dilemma. That she had had no authorization from her superiors for such an obligation, and that community custom prescribed that its devotion par excellence was that to Our Lady of Sorrows had not deterred her from making commitments. She had not been above bargaining with God about the Vancouver Providence. He of Infinite Majesty had met her terms, and she had been uneasy about her unfulfilled promise. Now through her. generous friend, God Himself was taking the matter out of her hands. She wrote with satisfaction to Mother Philomene, making it clear that the whole matter now rested on a different basis.

I consider this mission (Providence, Vancouver) as the result of the fulfillment of my promise to the Sacred Heart of Jesus, not in the perfection of its success, but in the ascendancy over the difficulties we have had to surmount. I assure you, dear Mother, that on receiving the letter of this good officer, Captain Hardie, I reflected that Our Lord imposes on me the obligation of building His altar, because we must, in justice, comply with the intentions of the donor.

One wonders if the good Sister Servant had anything to do with planting the idea in Captain Hardie's mind. The whole Vancouver community shared her gratification in the success of the bit of artifice, if such it was.

As you may well believe, the gift was accepted with tears. Shortly after, our old Cathedral took on a new air, being made beautiful by the new altar. Always the sweet Heart of Jesus will be honored here through us. This is our apostolate. Christ's loving heart will be the *alpha* and the *omega* of all our enterprises, the beginning and end of all our works.

No sooner was the altar of the Sacred Heart erected than the sisters found their own hearts widening to enfold another group of neglected persons. Again the chronicles tell the story:

In the course of the spring, Marie Comito, a Catholic woman, was placed under our care when she gave evidence of growing insanity; we received her hoping that she would become well. One of us remained with her at all times. But she became so furious that the city authorities placed her in prison under the surveillance of a gaoler. There was the poor woman under the supervision of a man who had neither morals nor principles of any kind. We were much afflicted at this condition of things. In compassion and lively anxiety for the poor creature, we determined to devote two small lodgings near the boys' orphanage to housing the mentally deranged. Wishing in this to follow the example of our dear Mother House where this beautiful service had so primary and dear a place, we undertook the care of the insane. Sister Praxedes, our good assistant superior, who had worked at Longue Pointe for several years, was given the care of the inmates and their quarters. These latter were blessed under the name of Saint John of God.

In 1861-62, there were two mental patients; in 1862-63, there were eight; and by 1866, some twenty-five persons were cared for, first at the small buildings on the mission grounds, and then later at more spacious quarters on Eighth Street directly west of the military reserve. Sister Joseph was able to obtain from the territorial government of Washington a contract which paid the sisters $8.00 a week for the lodging, board, washing, medical attendance, and care of each insane patient. The governor of Washington Territory, Mr. William Pickering, visited the house on Eighth Street and was "kindly disposed in our regard," according to the Sister Servant's report to Father Brouillet.

She had hoped, in the traditions of her community, that out of the small beginnings a great and permanent work would grow. She envisaged a splendid hospital for the insane which would be able to house all such unfortunates. In the mid-nineteenth century, there were few inclined to show either pity or charity toward the poor bereft creatures who more often than not were the object of laughter and cruelty. It would have been hard to find a more wretched or mistreated group in the brash, raw society of the Northwest. Yet she saw in every sick body and clouded mind the suffering Christ she loved and yearned over. She was shaken with grief and vexation when the turn of events made it necessary for her to relinquish the care of the insane.

That all was not well with the contract, the Sister Servant discerned almost from the beginning. Like all direct and artless folk who have learned the value of money through industry and economy, she was suspicious of the paper money which the government of the United States was issuing as "greenbacks." The understanding was that the sisters be paid in *coin*, since this was the only kind of legal tender Sister Joseph trusted. A dollar that was worth only sixty cents was a contradiction in terms to her. Judge Edward Wyche, who had drawn up the contract, assured her that there was no necessity to insert a clause demanding payment in hard money.

The good judge must surely have known that since greenbacks

were legal tender, payment for any debt had to be accepted in greenbacks if the debtor offered them. He probably either hoped for the best or thought he could strike a bargain later. He did not understand the tenacity of the Sister Servant's will. When the Territory of Washington paid its debt finally in 1865, it was some $4,000.00 short of the original understanding because of discounts in money values. Sister Joseph promptly receipted the bill for half payment only and wrote a sharp note of protest.

Governor Pickering, who had seemed so kindly disposed three years ago, now refused to renew the contract. The care of the insane was handed over to a good Republican cohort whose bid was higher than that of the sisters. Sister Joseph understood American politics as little as she understood paper money. She was indignantly affronted at the treatment both she and her poor pitiful charges had received. The governor, on his side, probably reasoned that since Catholics usually voted the Democratic ticket, they were responsible for the paper money in circulation. After all, the Democrats had backed the South, and the South had caused the war which caused the paper money.

Judge Wyche was again drawn into the fray, and His Excellency the Governor was sent the following letter in late 1866.

If a citizen of the Pacific Coast paid one of his creditors with Legal Tender without allowing discounts (for devaluation) he would be published in the newspapers as a Swindler. You may remember that the contract for the Insane as drawn up and presented to your Excellency was accepted by you for payment on a coin basis to be remitted quarterly. At great inconvenience to the Sisters, who have been obliged to borrow money at a high rate of interest, you have withheld payments for long intervals. The Sisters have carried out their part of the contract to the letter. They are presenting their petition to the coming legislature for all back pay, amounting to $4,000.00. 1 am confident that you will submit their petition to the members of the House with the most favorable recommendations.   JUDGE E. WYCHE

Sister Joseph had no sanguine expectations regarding the governor's favor, but she did believe in the power of prayer. Once again Heaven was assaulted by petition. "Ask and you shall receive," Our Lord had said. The Sister Servant kept Him reminded of His promise. In January of the following year, the territorial legislature passed the bill awarding $4,000-00 with interest to Sister Joseph of the Sacred Heart.

The money came in handy, to be sure. The House of Providence had been refused credit that winter. But though the temporal wants of their institution were assuaged and though her faith had been justified, the Sister Servant felt no sense of victory. At best, it was a rear-guard action. Saint John of God, that house on Eighth Street, which had given such fine promise now stood empty. What would her beloved Mother Gamelin have done with the whole matter? Wherein had she, Sister Joseph, mismanaged the affair of the insane to such a degree that they had been removed from her care?

She could answer neither question objectively, but she was convinced that her own complacency, her tactless and feverish haste in well-doing, were somehow at the root of her failure. The House of Providence in Vancouver would bear the scars of her defects. She would have been daunted had she not been the daughter of Joseph Pariseau; from him she had learned some thirty years ago that flaws in the grain of the wood add to its beauty when it is properly sanded and polished. She must learn to face her own weakness and live with it, knowing that power is made perfect in infirmity–knowing too that all goodness is from God.

With a few improvements, the house on Eighth Street could be used as a new Saint Joseph Hospital.

CHAPTER 17

THE PROW of the *Owyhee* cut through the smooth, green water of the Columbia. In the wake of the riverboat there was an aftermath of pale froth. Sister Joseph of the Sacred Heart stood with Sister Catherine on the foredeck, surveying the Oregon and Washington shores to right and left. They enjoyed the morning sun which was but now beginning to warm the clear air. For both of them this was their second trip to the Walla Walla country and beyond.

It was late July, 1866. The two sisters had been up in the cool dawn to board the train at the Dalles–that Dalles-Celilo portage train which, along with the Cascade Railroad, was once hailed by a grateful public as "harbinger of civilization."

By now the Sister Servant had a comfortable knowledge of the river route, and she was sincerely pleased at the material developments which were being made in this land she had come to love so well. That she had been able to embark on the *New World* yesterday morning on her own doorstep in Vancouver, reach the Lower Cascades at eleven o'clock, board the elegant, buff-colored coaches there for the Upper Cascades at one o'clock, transfer to the sidewheeler *Oneonta* at two o'clock, and arrive at the Dalles in the early evening was impressive progress, Sister Joseph thought. The whole long journey to the Dalles had been accomplished in comparative ease and safety in one day. There was still a great distance ahead and it would not all be as easy as that on the river; but they would plan all that as soon as they reached Walla Walla, and God would take care of the outcome. In the meantime they could enjoy the comparative luxury which their $40.00 tickets allowed them.

It was a strange country once they left the Dalles. The giant firs along the two shores were displaced by spruce and pine as the land became turbulent with rumbled rock formations. Then the earth flattened from a line of bluffs along the river. The trees disappeared except for occasional clumps of willow and poplar. Great wastes stretched endlessly to the north and south without a sign of life. The air was dry and hot, but not oppressive. The *Owyhee* pushed ahead at fair speed all through the long day, as the sun moved up overhead and then dropped slowly behind them.

There was leisure to pass the time of day with the good, bluff captain, Thomas Stump, and to have him point out first the mouth of the Deschutes River and then the John Day. Above all, there was time to hear of his recent exploit in taking the *Okanogan* from the upper river over the Tumwater Falls at Celilo. He knew all the Columbia's sunken perils and tricky currents. He also knew the Idaho gold-mining country to which they were going. He had carried thousands of miners and their equipment up the Snake River, and he had brought back many a weary argonaut owning only the clothes he had on. There were rich strikes lately in the Lewiston-Orofino area, and he had transported a good deal of gold on some of the trips. He thought the nuns would do well on their begging expedition. It was too bad that they were not making the entire trip by steamer, though it was only to be expected they go by way of Walla Walla to see the sisters there. Times were better now than they had been a couple of years back, and there was a lot of traffic between Portland and Walla Walla. It was unfortunate that the latter city was so far from the river. Sister Joseph listened alertly to the Captain's observations. There was much to learn from the rivermen.

When not conversing with the captain and the passengers, the Sister Servant tried to pray. At home there was so little time for quiet prayer. Now that she had this interval of tranquillity, she found that her mind was so geared to headlong urgency that sustained reflection on spiritual things was difficult.

The river itself had a way of distracting her. The Columbia caught at her thoughts and whirled them along with its smooth, irresistible current. While in the mission orchard or in the gardens with the boys of the orphanage busy around her, she had only to raise her eyes to see the great silent river there below them. It was a constant background for her life and work. The Columbia had brought her to Oregon in 1856; it had also seen here on her way home to Saint Catherine Street, Montreal, and to Ile Jésus in 1863.

Sister Joseph let her thoughts slip peacefully into the remembrance of that visit. On the seventh anniversary of the original departure for Oregon, she had again crossed the threshold of the Asile and knelt in its beautiful and beloved chapel to renew her vows and her dedication to the Sacred Heart of Christ. Once more she had held in her arms Sister Martin, that dear Julie so closely bound to her by ties of blood and affection. She had mingled with her superiors and sisters of the Mother House and had been transported out of herself in the happiness of being with them again. She had seen Monseigneur Bourget and had had a blessing from his frail, tremulous hands. She had gone to Saint Martin de Laval and Saint Elzear to visit her own people, returning to them as she had left them twenty years before, through the heavy snows of winter. Seeing them again with the eyes of a stranger, she had somehow understood herself better. There had come to her the comforting knowledge that in the end God would have His way with all the Pariseaux. He would bring them all home, eternally home, after He had tempered their strength and redressed their weaknesses. Surely this was the meaning of life.

The passionate ache in her heart at the absence of her father from his place at the head of the table had been assuaged at this insight into God's design for her and hers. She had been able to lean on faith and to find strength to withstand all inordinate grieving. And as she heard again across the wintry fields the deep-throated refrain of "Great Bourdon" in Saint Martin's bell-tower, pouring out its ancient reminder to worship, she had heard also in the recesses of her mind the bells of Vancouver on the Columbia. They, too, spoke of worship. They proclaimed the adoration of a wide and generous heart which is at home everywhere because God is everywhere. Surprisingly, she had realized at Saint Elzear that she could be lonesome for Vancouver as well as for Montreal. Truly, home is where the heart is. She had not left home when she came to the world along the Columbia. She had only widened its boundaries.

How often she had crossed this great river to visit Portland and the Sisters of the Holy Names. She well remembered their simple gratitude for the sacks of vegetables and fruit she had brought them shortly after their arrival in the fall of 1859. Indeed their gratitude was so obvious that she had known that there was little else in the house for food that day.

The Vancouver Providence had had little enough to spare in those days but that little she had happily shared with the dear sisters of Longueuil. She made it a practice to visit them at least once a week, and whenever some feast day warranted it, she and Sister Blandine stayed overnight with them. Then several of the Holy Names would reciprocate by returning with them to Vancouver the next day. In time, Captain Turnbull had made it easier for the two communities by giving them passes on his riverboat, and now they need not be nagged by their consciences for being unduly lavish with their meager funds. She herself had never scrupled, because both groups enjoyed the visits so much. Had not our Lord Himself said that bread alone is not enough?

What cheerful times they had together. How many evenings spent in the wonderful games of their youth, "Sur le Pont d'Avignon" and "La Chanson des Fleurs" until the community room rang with their laughter! She had found it pleasant to renew her friendship with Mother Mary Veronica and Mother Theresa, the two good friends she had known since her postulancy. She smiled to remember how circumspect they had all been in those days near Viger Place. She was glad to report in her letters to Monseigneur in Montreal, as well as to her own superiors, that the relationships between the two communities were amicable and neighborly.

Thanks be to the Lord, the Holy Name Sisters were prospering now, and they, like the Sisters of Providence, were finding a greater apostolate than they had personnel for its full accomplishment. The boarding school at Saint Mary's attracted students from the whole Columbia River area through which she was now passing, as did her own orphanage and boarding school. She had frequently reminded her own sisters that it was but right that the rates at Saint Mary's were higher than theirs in Vancouver because the Holy Name sisters were specially trained, whereas her own community had been instructed by Monseigneur to be the last and the least in all things.

God knew how little there was for Providence to go on. Her presence on the *Owyhee* on this trip was due to the desperate financial straits of the mission. All their economy, all their unremitting industry had not been able to tide them over their grim need for money. So now she and Sister Catherine were off to the mines so that the Portland and Vancouver merchants would once more extend them credit. She had brought Sister Catherine because she believed that her Irish wit would be an effective complement to her own importunity. She herself did not take a "No" easily, but Sister Catherine could get a donation without the "No" ever being born in the heart of the prospective giver. After many journeys together the two of them were used to each other's company. They were the ones who had gone to Walla Walla in 1863 before the school had been accepted there.

Sister Catherine had been professed with Julie, Sister Joseph's beloved Sister Martin, and belonged to one of the later groups whom their superiors had sent to Oregon. Some twenty-nine sisters had come to the West in Vancouver since December 1856. Four had gone on to the Rocky Mountain foundation immediately, leaving thirty-two now on hand for the Vancouver Providence and its allied houses of Steilacoom and Walla Walla.

The Sister Servant's heart still ached for the one no longer there. Little Sister John Baptist who had been their own Nancy Crate, was now their first intercessor in Heaven. Two years ago she had been laid to rest beyond the garden in the northeast corner of the mission grounds, barely a month before she had pronounced her vows. Sister Joseph had known that she was sick unto death during the last months of her novitiate, but the child had been so eager to make her vows that none of them had had the heart to refuse her. She had died at six o'clock in the evening of September 21, 1864, as the Angelus bell was inviting to prayer the world along the river. On her faltering lips had been the words, "Jesus, Mary, my good Mother, take me."

The impressive funeral two days later, with His Grace of Oregon City and His Lordship of Nisqually present, along with the entire family of Providence and half the city of Vancouver, had not lifted the grief which lay on the Sister Servant's heart. She was still remembering the gay and beautiful child whom Mr. Frederick Crate had brought to her door in 1858. She and Sister Blandine had given the resolute name of John the Baptist to their Nancy, hoping that she would be their precursor before the throne of the Most High.

Looking now at the endlessly flowing river, Sister Joseph wondered how much of the time allotted as her own portion had joined the vast sea of eternity. It was a sobering thought. She hoped that for her' too, this world would end with the bells of Saint James pealing the glories of our Lady. But what a foolish thought to be concerned with dying when there was obviously still so much living to do. This journey on the *Owyhee* had to do with the quick and not the dead. To the rough, flesh-and-blood miners whose hearts she hoped would not be so hard as to deny her the alms she sought for her orphans, to the good people she would have to rely upon at various places in the long journey to Lewiston and Orofino and beyond, she would have to be very much alive. She must succeed, too, if the House of Providence was to be tided over this present emergency.

The works in Vancouver had expanded until Sister Joseph now had a hundred children to feed and shelter, not to mention the sisters, a half-dozen old people, and the forty patients at Saint Joseph's Hospital. Now that the house on Eighth Street had been vacated by the insane, it must be renovated for the patients. This present time was the fitting occasion for a new hospital. She needed money for current debts as well as for the new ones which she must contract.

She could not afford to let herself dwell on the drudgery of these endless begging tours, nor on the long days away from Mass and Holy Communion. Instead, she must make virtues of the necessities under which she and her companion traveled. Besides, she despised self-pity in all its forms. Had she not freely offered herself for this work? Had she not herself proposed this journey? That she no longer felt the exhilaration of youth at a new experience was no good reason to be less aware of God's generous care of her. To be quite honest with herself, she did not suffer as much as many another would have on these expeditions. She had a strong and vigorous body which even in middle age did not easily tire. She had always been content with simple things. Creature comforts meant little to her. She liked pitting her will against a task; she liked the satisfaction which came with its accomplishment; moreover, she liked to dwell on the freedom which this begging tour, if successful, would give her. She would pay the debts and then she would improve the house on Eighth Street. She would put in strong staircases and good balustrades. She would fit out a well-stocked apothecary shop. She would see that there was a cheerful dining room for convalescents. Above all, she would furnish a hospital chapel, believing as she did that the best care for man's ailing body was that which also ministered to his soul.

While her mind was busy with plans for the new Saint Joseph's, the long hours on the *Owyhee* passed quickly enough. The fierce afternoon sun turned the Columbia into an expanse of molten gold, then dipped behind the brown hills. New colors washed over the land-beige, heather, turquoise blue, mauve, and purple. The river became serenely green again. After evening prayers said quietly on deck the two nuns made their way to the crowded luxury of the cabin with which the kind captain had provided them.

Wallula was reached next morning at ten o'clock. From there on the journey was by stage to Walla Walla. By late morning, the two sisters were being jostled and jolted along the deeply rutted road. Through the dust and the heat of the day, with a merciless sun overhead, they moved across a land devoid of all vegetation except for low growths of sagebrush and bunch grass. Then far ahead they could see the Blue Mountains and their foothills shimmering through the haze. Finally they came to a green valley and cultivated fields of grain and hay. By five o'clock they were in Walla Walla and under the welcome shade of the alder, birch, and poplar trees which line the city's streets.

The stage turned in before an impressive red brick building on the edge of the town. Before they had alighted, the nuns of Saint Vincent Academy were in the driveway to greet them. The dust and grime, the fatigues of the long journey were quickly forgotten as their dear sisters made them welcome.

Sister Mary of the Nativity, Sister Columban, and Sister Paul Miki had been in Vancouver only once since the opening of the mission in February, 1864, and looking on their eager faces now Sister Joseph understood the hunger they had endured for the companionship of their sisters.

Relaxing in their native tongue they were now gay together. First, there were prayers of thanksgiving in the humble oratory. Then there came food and endless chatter of the Vancouver Providence, of the latest news from the Steilacoom foundation, of Montreal and home. They visited the house and the church. Their good friend, the Vicar-General, Abbé Brouillet, was absent on one of his frequent trips, but they must view this whole property which his vigorous will had produced by dint of determination and toil.

Abbé Brouillet had remained their friend, but the Sister Servant knew that he was still likely to lash out in criticism of her plans and policies. She understood the Abbe' and had a wholesome respect for his zeal and his ability. Indeed, the reasons for occasional clashes were probably due to the fact that these pioneers were too much alike. Both were tireless and strong-willed, and neither could be easily rebuffed when intent on achieving a purpose conceived to be good and proper.

The Abbé believed, as she did, that the best interests of the Church in the Northwest would be served by the long- range policy of education. So many of their own people were confirmed in evil living and a shameful faithlessness that hopes for the future

lay only with their children. In the face of their own meager preparation and their poverty, the missionaries must courageously undertake the building and maintenance of schools. Others doubt-
less could do the task better than they, but others had not done it,
and Our Lord was looking to them. Along with schools, would go
those other reclaiming works, like the care of the sick and the aged.
Abbé Brouillet was busy even now in the beginnings of hospital
work in Walla Walla.

Sister Joseph marveled at what had been accomplished. The
building in which the nuns were presently lodged, had been erected in 1863-64. The Sister Servant remembered sharply those difficult days at the outset when Abbé Brouillet had been kindled to
explosive wrath against them all.

The Abbé had been in and out of Walla Walla for twenty-five
years and had watched the town grow from a Hudson's Bay post
to a thriving American town. As it showed promise of becoming
a metropolis as a transportation center and farming community,
he was eager to promote the growth of the Church there. He had
asked and obtained the promise of sisters in 1863. He had raised
some $2,000.00 in Walla Walla for the building of a school, only
to learn when his plans were well under way that his whole scheme
was jeopardized. Father Charles Vary's mission at Steilacoom had
absorbed the sisters who would have gone to Walla Walla.

At the time, the Sister Servant was in Montreal, but the letters which Abbé Brouillet wrote caught up with her there and still
crackled with rage and disappointment. It was an impasse which
would plague the Sisters of Providence often. In their desire to
Christianize the Western land, they would allow themselves to
be drawn into commitments which their numbers did not war-
rant. In this instance, the cause was, as usual, good, and both clerics were too eloquent in their own interests to be withstood by
the poor nuns. Sister Praxedes had been acting superior in place
of Sister Joseph of the Sacred Heart, and she had not had sufficient experience to hold out against the zeal of Father Charles
Vary. The Sister Servant could not blame her. The time had not
been too distant when Abbé Brouillet had argued fluently for a

foundation in the Puget Sound country. His Lordship of Nisqually, too, had favored the Steilacoom foundation. But however desirable this beautiful mission on the far reaches of the Sound, there still were not enough sisters in 1863. Sister Catherine and Sister Mary of the Precious Blood, both so sadly needed because of their language qualifications, had been sent to aid Father Vary, and Abbé Brouillet had felt himself badly used indeed. In the end he was pacified. He had written the Vancouver sisters on November 8,1863:

Should you have to inconvenience yourselves and even make your establishment in Vancouver suffer, you cannot in honor and in conscience refuse me. On your word I have taken on engagements with the people in Walla Walla, and the conditions proposed being fulfilled by them, I am held to fulfill my engagements. Now the conditions which you propose to me, you know as well as I, cannot be withdrawn honorably or conscientiously.

By December 1863, he was again reassured and busy about the never-ending business of raising money:

Our bazaar will begin this evening and I am confident that the prayers of your children will have effect, for it could not be presented under better auspices. It is the affair of the entire city. Everyone speaks of it and everybody lends a hand. . . .

Your house is standing and ready to be shingled. It is truly a beautiful house, the largest in the city, and built in the old-country style, strong and solid. If the bazaar is a success, the sisters should prepare to move in soon; if it is a failure, they will have to wait until I can see clear in my business which at this writing is in a veritable chaos.

Early in the new year he had written Sister Joseph of the Sacred Heart who was still in Montreal:

Good Mother Joseph: Walla Walla's big day has arrived. Three of your sisters are leaving tomorrow morning to open their school at that place. They are Sister Mary of the Nativity, Sister Columban and Sister Paul Miki. They will be accompanied by an orphan, Miss Rose Pellan. I shall have the happiness of accompanying them myself, and of installing them in their new home. . . . the work of Providence evidently. Your expectations and mine have not gone awry.

The people of Walla Walla showed what they could do. They procured $2,000 for us of which $1,200 was paid in subscriptions, and $800 was clear profit from our bazaar, besides $400 promised and not yet paid. . . .

To respond to the wishes of everybody I had to build on a larger scale and more beautifully than you desired. The house is 46 feet by 26 feet, two and a half stories high, with a whitewashed lean-to shed for kitchen. The outside is finished. There is yet much work to be done on the interior, on the second floor and the rooms for the sisters. The rest is a large room without wainscoting, sufficiently prepared, however, to hold classes for day pupils during the summer. Once finished the house will accommodate day scholars and about thirty boarders. Everyone is looking forward to the arrival of the sisters. I shall be very much surprised if they open school with fewer than forty pupils.

Father Brouillet's expectations were fully justified. The citizens of Walla Walla opened their hearts to the sisters with sincere cordiality. The Sister Servant had received the same generous welcome in 1863, and still remembered how the people of their own race had flocked to the Frenchtown house which Mr. jean Marie Abadi had turned over to them at the old Saint Rose Mission. It had been on that preliminary visit that Mr. Joseph Barron had sold them the three city blocks of land, complete with a little brook crossing it, all for the sum of one dollar! The property lay at the edge of the town, and it was there that Father Brouillet had built the school and the new little church.

From the beginning the school had been well patronized, having had between sixty and eighty pupils the first year. Surprisingly, many of their best friends in the town were Jewish people, and a fair number of their students were of that race.

Best known of all their benefactors in those days as well as in those coming later was Madame Alicia Thomas. She was a wealthy Catholic who never tired of helping the sisters by sending them gifts of food and furnishings, by her kindly counsel, and by her steadfast defense of their efforts and accomplishments.

Remembering Madame Thomas' friendship, the Sister Servant resolved to visit her before leaving on the Idaho trip. The begging tour would not be any via *crucis*, but it would certainly not be pleasant.

CHAPTER 18

THE DETAILS of this harrowing journey can best be told in Mother Joseph's own words as she later wrote them in the chronicles of that year.

After placing our journey under the protection of Saint Joseph, we left Walla Walla for Idaho City. We were given the friendliest of welcomes by the Reverend Fathers Toussaint Mespellier and André Poulin. This was a meeting of old friends. These kindly priests introduced us into Christian families and gave us every instruction possible for the success of our guest. Hitherto we had traveled mainly by boat; from now on we went by stage coach.

In Idaho City and in the mines of that locality we collected the amazing sum of $3,000.00.

During the five or six weeks of our begging tour in Idaho we were received most cordially. Indeed, we were the object of the sincere sympathy of even infidels and Protestants, who marveled at our daring, and commended our perseverance. The miners came to meet us and, in order to make our passage through the mines easier, went with us by easy stages from one digging to another.

Encouraged by these good offices, we made up our minds to visit our sisters at Saint Ignatius Mission and set out forthwith for the territory of Montana. Spent with fatigue we arrived at Missoula in September. We rested for a few days there at the hotel conducted by some Catholic people. We then resumed the work of collecting funds in the mines to the south. We met with considerable coolness here, yet succeeded in obtaining $2,000.00. Many of the miners showed themselves to be very generous. Of the five thousand dollars of our collection, we spent five hundred dollars for the expenses of the journey from Vancouver to Saint Ignatius Mission.

Imagine the surprise and the happiness of our four solitaries of the Rocky Mountain country, Sister Mary of the Infant Jesus, Sister Paul Miki, Sister Edward, and Sister Remi. On seeing us, the poor nuns were overwhelmed with joy. Though this mission belongs to the vicariate of Vancouver, this was the first official visitation by a superior since this house had been founded two years earlier. It is unnecessary to say that during our eight days with them we received their most delicate attention. But all too soon these days of repose came to an end and we had to leave them.

This time we were to travel neither by boat nor by stagecoach; only on horseback could we get through the dark forests that lay between us and our own lower Columbia country. To spare us further expense, the sisters at Saint Ignatius loaned us their saddles and riding habits. The Jesuit Fathers furnished us with horses. In the last days of September our little caravan set out. It was composed of Father Louis Saint-Onge, an Indian named Sapiel from the mission, Father Joseph Giorda, S.J., who went with us as far as Missoula, and Sister Catherine and myself. Following our cavalcade were two pack horses with provisions and a tent. So equipped. we pushed ahead into primeval forests and rugged mountain ravines. Except for meeting a few miners now and then, our solitude was unbroken.

Each night we were concerned with the business of making camp. One thing was sure—we all had good appetites. Every evening we would hasten to locate the three things indispensable for a good camp—water, grass, and trees. At a favorable spot we would dismount, and in the twinkling of an eye, every one of us would be busy at the necessary tasks. Father Saint-Onge went hunting for game, Sapiel cared for the horses and collected faggots, and we sisters took charge of the cooking. Very shortly all would be around the kettle, each with his bowl, doing credit to the stew.

Nothing is more congenial than a meal around the camp fire, with each one recounting a story while waiting for the *crêpe* to be made or the meat to broil. After a cheerful supper and a short, fervent evening prayer, each one would wrap up in a blanket, taking saddle or pack for a pillow. The tent was assigned as shelter for Sister Catherine and me. Refreshed after such slumber we would begin again next morning with breakfast at the campfire; then after packing

our belongings we were on our way once more until dark. After this
fashion we spent eighteen long days and nights out of doors.

As I have said, nothing is more pleasant than such evenings when
the weather is fine. But we arose one morning to find that the sun was
not shining and the sky was overcast. However, we had to be on our
way. We ate breakfast in haste and set out. Presently it began to rain.
After several hours it not only rained but it stormed. When our caravan
halted for the night, building a camp was a challenge. By that time we
were wet to the bone. Finally we did succeed in getting a small fire going inside the tent, which had been set up with great difficulty. Then
we resigned ourselves to lying down in the mud as near to the fire as
possible. A few evenings later a great tree fell two or three paces from
the tent in which we were sleeping. You can understand how fervent
was our *Te Deum*.

Toward the middle of our journey, we spent several days in a particularly dense forest. We' had been following a narrow trail which barely
kept us from getting lost. When we were simply spent with fatigue we
found ourselves between two mountain ranges which lie between the
Coeur d'Alene Mission and the Flathead Mission. There was scarcely
room to camp. We had a good supper on venison which Father Saint-
Onge had killed during the day. We then said an earnest evening prayer
and had just wrapped ourselves in our blankets when a terrifying howl
frightened us almost out of our wits. Hurriedly Father Saint-Onge took
his revolver and Sapiel seized his knife. The Indian quickly cut firewood
to start a blaze around the camp. They knew that wolves ordinarily do
not pass the line of fire, and that generally they do not attack singly but
call out to each other as a signal for attack. The first terrifying call was
answered in the distance by another and then another . . . and then on
every side. A half-hour after that first howl, we were surrounded by half
a hundred of these furious beasts. Our horses were tethered inside the
line of fire. I cannot describe the fright of those poor animals.

The spot on which our camp was built had been burned over
a few years before so that the trees were very dry. And now the fire
which had been meant to keep the wolves at bay began. to threaten
us as well. A burning forest seemed to surround us. Great branches
fell to the ground. This dreadful scene was made worse by the howl
of the wolves now redoubled. We battled burning cinders and blind-
ing smoke as best we could, but only prayer saved us. Some of the
provisions burned, our tent caught fire several times, and our saddles

were damaged. But finally the night of horror passed, and with daylight the wolves left. Although the trees had been too damp for a widespread forest fire, our peril had been very real. We offered humble thanksgiving to Almightly God for having delivered us and protected us in the midst of all danger.

As we were preparing to break camp, we heard the beat of horses' hooves trampling the trail nearby. Before we could move, we were surrounded by a troop of mounted Indian warriors. They were in warpaint and ghastly to behold. Our fear was soon dispelled, however, because as soon as they saw our crosses and recognized Father Saint-Onge, they offered their hands in token of friendship and respect. In spite of their determination to be off on a scalping expedition, they treated us well. We gave them some food and were relieved to have them leave us peaceably.

There we were, still in the depths of the interminable forest, in the midst of which the old Mission of the Coeur d'Alenes had been established. Toward evening of another day, we found ourselves on the bank of a small river and prepared to camp there. The horses were put some fifty feet away in an enclosure of fallen trees. They were left untethered in this corral. While raising the tent Father Saint-Onge saw some tracks which aroused his suspicion. He called, Sapiel who told him these were the prints of a grizzly bear, known to the Indians as the most dangerous animal in the forest. But what was there to do? It was too late to go farther. They decided to say nothing of our danger but to keep watch throughout the night. Their only weapons, a six-shooter and an ax, were inadequate against such an enemy. They gathered wood and immediately after supper made a large fire because they knew that bears fear fire, and approach only if driven by hunger. Knowing nothing about this threat to our safety, Sister Catherine and I slept peacefully within the tent while our guides acted as sentinels. Thanks to the dear Heart of Jesus, the night passed without incident. Early in the morning Sapiel went to look after the horses. What was his dismay to see a large grizzly bear attacking one of the horses. When the bear saw Sapiel, he jumped the logs of the corral and made for the Indian. Sapiel took to his heels with the bear in pursuit. Twice the animal struck at him with claws outspread, but by a supreme effort the man evaded the attack. Suddenly the bear was distracted by the sound of bells. A pack train of mules loaded with merchandise came in sight and the cries of the Mexicans leading the mules and those of Father Saint-Onge put the bear to flight. Poor Sapiel in his fright had been leading the bear right into our camp! What the consequences might have been, God alone knows. Once more we thanked the Lord for this new deliverance.

Another incident took place on this journey, but not wishing to alarm us further Father Saint-Onge did not tell us about it until we had reached home. One night this good priest was awakened by a sensation of cold and felt something glide across his body. He knew at once that it was a rattlesnake, and had enough presence of mind to lie perfectly still that the reptile might settle down to sleep. After what seemed hours, he sprang to his feet with a bound so that the serpent was forced to fall. It crawled away leaving Father Saint- Onge unnerved and shaken.

Finally on October 16 we arrived in Vancouver, safe but fatigued by our long ride on horseback, grateful for the success of our quest.

Later as she read this account of that memorable journey, Sister Joseph marveled at how dull her words had made it. Few women before her could have traveled as much of this northwest wilderness, and surely she and Sister Catherine were the first sisters to have done this. In some ten weeks' time they had traversed a half-dozen areas distinct in character and climate, each with its own beauty, its particular perils, and its special generosities.

She remembered the hot, dusty approaches to the Grande Ronde country along the old Oregon road to Boise and Idaho City, and she remembered gratefully the cool reassurance of the Blue Mountains on the trip back. She remembered the sandy wastes along the Snake River and the wild, reckless current of the Clearwater on the way to Lewiston. That Orofino country had been good to them. She had no clear recollection of the ugly mining towns other than that they had given Sister Catherine and herself richly of their hospitality and their gold.

Then, there was the Mission Valley in the Flathead country. How could she describe the clear air, the exhilaration, and the peace of the mountain meadowland? She understood now why our Lord had gone so often to the mountains for prayer. See, too, had felt that there the Heavenly Father was accessible to her need and her supplication. She had come away from Saint Ignatius Mission with her faith in God's Providence renewed and strengthened, so that in spite of her human fright she had been able to believe that the terrifying circumstances of the fearful journey through the Bitterroots were God's arrangements. His power and His glory were manifest; and above all, His goodness prevailed. Now as she remembered those days through the thick forests she was conscious of a certain satisfaction. They had pitted their wills against the forces of nature. The enemy had been clearly seen and fought openly. There had been times since when she had known a subtler foe.

Principalities and powers had cloaked themselves in darkness, and she was no longer sure how the battle was going. Part of the trouble had always been her own inability to put in words those things which were real and important to her. She had a tendency to let facts speak for themselves. And her communications were blunt where they should have been persuasive.

She saw so clearly the importance and the growing scope of their work in Vancouver that she was likely to be impatient with people who were over-cautious or slow. Now was the time to consolidate all the scattered beginnings. Now was the time to build, build, build. It would never be easier. All that the sisters had begun in the West was being jeopardized by the uncertainty besetting the Mission Claim, and there was only one way to meet that threat head on. They must use the new property outside the disputed area and build there. Morever, they must build impressively because what they were to erect must show forth the glory of God. If they themselves believed in the Kingdom of God here in the Northwest, they must give expression to that belief in brick and stone. They had already given evidence that they were willing to serve God in the person of the poor and the helpless. Now, if God so willed, they must give the work permanence.

Before the arrival of the sisters in Vancouver in 1856, His Lordship of Nisqually had already filed with the American authorities a claim to the section of land surrounding the old Saint James Church. Around this claim a historic, legal battle had already begun to brew when Sister Joseph realized the need for a better site for her Western Providence. In the long years of contention between the United States government and the Hudson's Bay Company no decisive action could be taken in Vancouver. But the town grew, and with its grew the tangle of conflicting claims by the United States Military Reservation, the City of Vancouver, the estate of Amos Short, and the Roman Catholic Mission. For fifty years feelings ran high on this subject and were frequently fed by the fuel of differences in religion and nationality. In the 1850's it had seemed reasonably clear that the plat west of the Military Reserve would become recognized as the townsite and that this area would eventually develop into the city of Vancouver.

On January 23, 1857; the City of Vancouver was incorporated by an enactment of the Washington State legislature, even though the area of the Townsite Claim was also claimed by other parties. On this Townsite Claim the Sisters of Charity of Providence had acquired one-half of block 33 on Eighth and Reserve streets. Here was located first the hospital for the insane, and after 1866, Saint Joseph Hospital. But even as early as 1861 Mother Joseph had moved ahead to buy additional property on the Vancouver Townsite plat.

Lying directly north of the hospital location was a timbered area facing the military reserve to the east. It was a beautiful piece of property which topped a gentle rise of land above the river. In 1861 it was still a tangled wilderness with giant Douglas firs swaying dark, blue-green boughs overhead and, below, masses of ferns and underbrush.

Through Mr. Predmore, a French Canadian formerly employed by the Hudson's Bay Company, two more blocks came into Mother Joseph's possession. The previous owner, having built cabins on this property and occupied it for two years, gave Mother Joseph a quitclaim deed for the sum of $325. During the summer of 1862, under siimilar conditions Mr. D. J. Thornton took up two adjoining blocks bordering on the military reserve road and sold his claim to Mother Joseph for the same amount. Now there were four city blocks cleared of timber and fenced in, each two hundred feet square, with the intersecting streets. As early as 1867 she had petitioned the city council of Vancouver to be allowed the use of that portion of the streets intersecting the property owned by the Sisters of Charity of Providence between Tenth and Twelfth streets. With a sizable majority against her, no move could be made to break ground.

CHAPTER 19

Aᴍᴇʀɪᴄᴀ, in 1866, was developing very rapidly despite the tangle of reconstruction. Americans still reeled from the impact of brother pitted against brother–and the wounds still lay open. Heavy war debts, the struggle of readjustment, and flagrant political corruption strained the moral fiber of the country. Four million slaves had to find a place in the white man's world; thousands of plantation owners, lacking labor and the means of acquiring labor, faced depreciated lands. The uncertainty of the West had barred many from taking advantage of the Homestead Act of four years back, for only the few had ever succeeded in cultivating the land and establishing homes in the face of floods, blizzards, droughts, and Indian hazards.

But communication and transportation developments, climaxed in the railroads, were beginning to sprawl across the country. Government subsidies and extravagant grants of acreage promoted the steel lines while literally pouring millions into the pockets of a few.

Miners forming the vanguard, the migration of the 1860's brought to the West the ambitious, the restless ' and the discon. tented. Small mining towns cropped up wherever gold dust circulated. Up and down the Columbia, streamers carried droves of miners headed for the Cariboo, the Snake River Valley, and the Salmon River Valley. Wagon trains from the East spilled thousands of prospectors and greenhorns across the Western country.

The Providence community on the north bank of the Columbia profited by the gold stream through contributions of the miners to the projects of charity. For many years the sisters toured the mining towns collecting money for current expenses, and using the balance to finance a hospital, or orphan asylum, or an Indian mission.

. . . .

Father Junger's soutane draped over her arm, and in her hand a small wooden box of nails, Sister Joseph of the Sacred Heart stepped briskly away from the sacristy of Saint James Church across the small yard toward the convent, the early November wind whipping her cape and ruffling her apron. It was a cold wind . . . rustling among the firs, bending the cedar tops, and scurrying the rich hemlock cones about her feet. Vancouver winters gave much warning in advance. Frost-crisp mornings, cold intermittent rains, gray overcast skies, and chill, penetrating winds sent the early settler to check his wood supply and appraise his provisions. Sister Joseph remembered that tomorrow she must give the roofs of her seven scattered houses a thorough going over, just to be sure. Ten years of pioneering had taught her to take nothing for granted. Ten years had taught her to read many signs in the river, the skies, and the forests that hemmed in the little settlement.

Her pioneer intuition told her that a living could not be grabbed from this country. The patience of the dependent planter, the diligence of the homemaker, and the convictions of the missionary had to go into the soil of this land before the land would give back wealth and security. To Sister Joseph this was not a few acres to drain of abundance and then desert as had been the fate of the ghost cities along the bonanza trails. She was here to stay; she would never leave. This work of Providence was not a thing confined to time.

She paused, her eye running the length and breadth of the four hundred square feet of the Mission Compound that represented her ten years' harvest. This was her Providence Asile, but someday it would be transplanted and all these works so lovingly entrusted to her would be drawn together in one large building.

But away with this musing ... There was immediate work to be done, and first of all, the chaplain's soutane which needed attention. The clergy were always to be Sister Joseph's prime concern. The missionary priesthood found a staunch benefactor in Sister Joseph of the Sacred Heart, who had time to tend their needs. Many of them in their declining years were to seek out her hospitals to die in that same care of Providence. Every small need of a priest was, in her eyes, a major need. Even up to the year before her death, when a brain tumor had almost destroyed her sight, she had written to Mother Mary Antoinette:

There is no one here to take up this work . . . Will you have a coadjutrix sister learn to make soutanes, and cut them by measurement? I did not learn this. Sister Vincent de Paul and I have filled this need and done much work together. We are now at the close of our careers and there is no one to replace us. Is it not a disgrace to find ourselves incapable of rendering this service to the clergy?

As Sister Joseph reached the door of the convent, her thoughts were cut by the excited voice of Sister Blandine. It was a telegram—from New York! The message was brief but it set the community in a whirl.

Mother Philomene and her group of travelers
will arrive in Vancouver December 7.

Sister Joseph studied the words. There was no doubt in her mind but that more sisters were coming to help them.

How the past decade had changed the face of the country! Flashing messages from east to west in twenty-four hours had comparatively simplified the complex structure of life in the West. To think of the time when it had been a matter of weeks, even months, before news had penetrated the far corners of the country.

Twenty-four hours . . . Sister Joseph mused, and as she so often found herself doing these past months, her thoughts turned to the sisters in Chile. What might a telegram have done to change the plight of that bewildered group whose wanderings along the Pacific Coast had been so indecisive. If communications with Montreal had been possible within a mere twenty-four hours, surely their determination would not have given way to faltering and fatigue. Speculation . . . yes, there had been much of that during these last few years when subtle enemies had threatened to reduce the mission to failure. But she, Sister Joseph, had clung to the Montreal Mother House despite the period of loneliness and gloom experienced by the five when they had received no word from the Mother House until five months after their arrival at Fort Vancouver.

Every letter to Monseigneur Bourget and to the Superior General had been a renewal of Allegiance to the community. Every move to be made in the new mission had been first presented to the community for its blessing. Distance often breeds independence, and particularly was that true of life during this period of pioneer initiative. Sister Joseph was a woman with marvelous powers of vision and endurance. In many instances it would have been much easier for her to have relied on her own judgment; it would have been quicker. Things moved slowly between Montreal and Vancouver. But Bishop Bourget's mandate of October 30, 1856, was not confined to mere paper; she was soon to have the eye and ear of authority. . . . That would be so much more effective than her poor rambling letters. Already even, community burdens seemed to ease, and the huge problems of an hour ago began to dwindle.

The ensuing days were spent scouring and setting the houses in order. Long hours were employed in preparing accounts, enumerating needs, and illustrating plans for the proposed buildings. Sister Joseph was to give an account, the records of her work. Would the superiors find the Providence of the Holy Angels and its four foundations thriving in this diocese of Nisqually? There had been times, God knows, when it had not shown signs of great interior life. She had tried to build, but had it not been sometimes too vigorously and perhaps upon shifting ground? Had not her obsession to expand the works introduced disturbing elements?

Just five years ago she had written Bishop Bourget of shortcomings, of her desire that one of the higher superiors visit the new mission "to correct the irregularities of my administration." The Bishop of Montreal had written:

Be always of one heart and one mind among yourselves, doing all in your power to settle within your family circle the little difficulties that might arise to trouble your peace and happiness. Believe your sisters and yourself to be the least able, most imperfect of all communities, then all will go better and better . . . .

. . . .

December seventh finally arrived. The seventy orphans, scrubbed, and shining, had received detailed instructions as to how to comport themselves when the moment arrived-in fact, from the time that the steamer whistle sounded.

But no ship arrived. Throughout the day Sister Joseph, with two of the orphans, walked down to the landing in hopes of sighting the steamer. Night came. The brush along the river bank faded away. The river was quiet, its current swift, with the black waters eddying and lashing the wharf. This great river to the West looked peaceful, but the treacherous Columbia bar did not allow people to dismiss lightly the fact of overdue steamers. Sister Joseph turned back to the Compound, disappointed.

The next morning, while the community Mass was being celebrated in the Cathedral, the travelers arrived. Besides their beloved Mother Philomene, in the group were His Grace, Francis Norbert Blanchet and His Lordship, Augustine Magloire Blanchet, returning from a Council of Bishops held in Baltimore, Sister Praxedes of Providence, absent for the past eighteen months, and seven missionary sisters.

At ten o'clock that same day the Bishop of Nisqually celebrated a solemn Pontifical Mass as Holy Mother Church's most profound expression of gratitude to Divine Providence for the fruition of His designs during the past epoch of the Nisqually diocese.

Days with their cherished visitors were filled with recollections of their homeland and the recounting of experiences in their adopted land. The winter months were less dismal. There was the joyful feast of Christmas; there was the golden feast of Epiphany surrounded by community customs of warmth and love.

Visiting the small cluster of buildings, Mother Philomene noted all to be in keeping with the foundation spirit of the

Community. With charming simplicity, Sister Joseph presented each orphan to the Superior General, commenting, no doubt, with a patronizing pat on the child's head. Had Mother Gamelin herself visited this mission, she would have been quick to see the poverty, and would have openly commended Sister Joseph, just as had Mother Philomene, for the charity, zeal, and courage so manifest in this Western arm of Providence.

It was at the close of her visit of the Providence of the Holy Angels that Mother Philomene announced to the assembled community the General Council's election of Mother Praxedes of Providence as Mother Vicar of the Providence of Vancouver to succeed Sister Joseph of the Sacred Heart, now appointed bursar for the western missions. There was a deep silence throughout the community.

The silence in Sister Joseph's heart was the most profound. A lesser woman might have quailed or writhed at what could have been interpreted as a pronouncement on an administration that had failed, one that had placed in jeopardy the future of the community in the West, one that—and she was aware of it without rancor—had been oftentimes misconstrued. As crucial as was the present with heavy debts hanging fire, and establishments insecure, her release seemed a sign that another hand at the helm could be no greater risk than the course along which Sister Joseph of the Sacred Heart was directing the group.

She was a Pariseau, strong-willed, impetuous, and energetic. Prudence and sympathy had often been lacking in her governing. She was now being relieved of responsibility. There was no personal disappointment for God knew she had never wanted nor relished the position given her by Monseigneur Bourget. Two weeks after arrival at Vancouver, she had confided to Mother Caron her fears upon being named superior.

". . . to be charged with the guidance of others, to govern a house, to train young sisters with my inexperience, my disagreeable disposition, my ignorance; all these thoughts come crowding upon me and crush me. . . ."

The words of Joseph Pariseau came to her—the words which had sealed discussion of the Papineau affair . . .

". . . the voice is the voice of God speaking. . . .
It is for good children to listen and obey."

Lovingly she embraced her co-founder, co-worker, and now her Mother Vicar. Mother Praxedes of Providence had been schooled in the life and virtues of Mother Gamelin, under whose direction she had lived for six years. In 1856 when she had been chosen to go to the West, she had said, "I am not good for such. You may take me and I will do what I can." *Do what I can . . .* that she had definitely done. Her mature outlook on the religious life had been a great help to Sister Joseph from the very beginning. These two women were now to continue side by side, governing and financing, moulding souls and erecting buildings, nurturing the spiritual growth of the community and establishing missions wherein the spiritual life might find a channel to reach out to others in nursing, consoling, teaching, and–loving.

The appointment of bursar was no small recognition of Sister Joseph's executive acumen and wise judgment, for at the time the missions were oppressed by debt, especially the Providence of the Holy Angels, which, in fact, was in a state bordering on bankruptcy. The future of Mother Gamelin's daughters here along the Columbia was reliant on the quiet wisdom of Mother Praxedes and the undaunted vision of Sister Joseph of the Sacred Heart.

Having visited Saint Joseph Hospital, traveled to Steilacoom, to Walla Walla, and also to Tulalip to consider the possibility of answering the plea of Father Casimir Chirouse, O.M.I. for sisters to conduct an Indian school, Mother Philomene began preparations for a visit of the Saint Ignatius Mission in July, 1867.

A few weeks before, two sisters, Sister Catherine and Sister Pudent, had volunteered to go on a begging tour to the mines, a venture which promised hardship and entailed regret at leaving the mission during their Mother's stay in Vancouver. But the only solution to the urgent and immediate need of funds was a collection.

Sister Joseph of the Sacred Heart had been the first to step forward offering herself for the collection trip. Her chagrin at passing on to the new Mother Vicar such a huge financial burden impelled her to shoulder the responsibility of wiping out the debt.

Mother Philomene refused her offer. This Sister Joseph, for her number of forty-three years, had aged beyond them. The past decade had been marked with more vicissitudes, anxieties, and problems than the ordinary woman could meet in a lifetime. She had coped with floods in 1861 when the mighty Columbia, swollen and raging, had destroyed the potato and grain crops, leaving no provisions to see through the winter a personnel of one hundred fifty; under the direction of the Bishop, Father Louis Vary had managed to collect $527.75 to sustain the impoverished community. In 1864 she had known the tragedy of losing two mental patients by fire. She had staunchly defended the legal rights of the community in the face of intrigue in 1866; she had triumphed. Suppressing her family pride, she had canvassed the familiar Canadian dioceses of Montreal, Quebec, and Three Rivers, in behalf of her Western missions. She had risked her life in the treacherous tours to the mining settlements of Idaho. Her achievements read like a litany, caught up by the response, *Divine Providence . . . be forever adored, loved, and thanked.*

Mother Philomene considered how right Sister Joseph's father had been when he had entrusted Esther Pariseau to Mother Gamelin in 1843: "Madame, you will find her able to give you valuable assistance . . . she can plan and supervise the work of others . . . she will someday make a very good superior."

Plans underwent adjustment in July when word from Montreal advised Mother Philomene to cancel her proposed trip to Saint Ignatius, Montana, and return to the Mother House as soon as possible. On October seventh, just one week before the departure of Mother Philomene, Sister Catherine and Sister Pudent returned from their collection tour, fatigued but well satisfied with the three thousand dollars to pacify temporarily Sister Joseph's persistent creditors.

In the company of Father Louis Saint-Onge, whom they had met at Walla Walla, the travelers on horseback, with provisions carried by four pack mules, had begun their long trek over hot, dry prairies, inching along mountain paths paved with soft mud, where thawing snow swelled the creeks and washed the trails. Sometimes they had bound together fallen trees to provide a crossing of raging streams. Swamps had, in one instance, submerged, Sister Catherine to her shoulders in mud. They had finally reached Missoula and from there traveled on to Saint Ignatius Mission, forty miles farther. Here they had spent eight days with their sisters, resting and mending their torn, soiled clothing. Father Remigius de Ryker, a Montana missionary, had accompanied the sisters into the mining towns, where they had collected their huge sum.

For Mother Philomene, ten months of visiting the West ended on October fifteenth. On the eve of her departure, the sisters had tried to show their gratitude, delegating Sister Joseph of the Sacred Heart to speak their sentiments. It was a theme which was to ring out down through the wide development of Providence in the West, and one that would evince the closely knit spirit of the Sisters of Providence, who despite scattered geographical boundaries, could unite always in one allegiance to her who stood in Mother Gamelin's place.

. . . and we solemnly declare that we wish to be of one mind with our Mother House. And since the tree is known by its fruit, we wish to prove by our works and by our good understanding the vigor of the sap that sustains the humble branch which the hand of Divine Providence has planted in this vast territory. We will console your motherly heart by our respect and submission to the one who, vested with a part of your authority, will exercise her influence over all the houses of the Vicariate.

With a large farewell group of orphans, sisters, and friends on shore, Mother Philomene boarded the steamer for Portland. From that port she was to sail on the San Francisco-bound *Sierra Nevada* in company with Reverend Aegidius Junger, Sister Columban, and six sisters of the Holy Names and of Saint Ann.

There were last-minute messages, long looks, and sustained waving of hands until the steamer disappeared from sight. The Vancouver community turned back to their home. It would be seven long years before another official visitor in the person of Mother Caron would stand on the banks of the Columbia. Mother Joseph walked slowly back to the Compound in company with

Mother Praxedes. There was no need to speak; their thoughts must have been identical. There was no self-pity. They'd bargained for all this. When Bishop Prince had blessed them in 1856, his sentiments had been theirs.

"Go, my daughters, to make the Holy Trinity honored. You are happy to make a sacrifice in favor of that poor, forsaken land. Were there but one soul to be saved, you should not hesitate."

. . . .

Two weeks later Mother Joseph of the Sacred Heart wrote to Monseigneur Bourget, who, Mother Joseph was certain, had been instrumental in sending Mother Philomene to the West:

Each year has been stamped with your paternal and pastoral solicitude. I do not hesitate to say that the spread of the faith in Oregon and our vast territory of Washington in great part owes its progress to your intrepid devotedness. If the annals make no mention of it, the echoes of the mountains proclaim it, to Him Who knows all.

CHAPTER 20

BELCHING sparks, wheezing and rattling, the Central Pacific finally reached San Francisco where four Sisters of Providence, Vancouver-bound, alighted after a trip of twenty days by rail. With its gaudily painted coaches, dangerously swinging kerosene lamps, and tobacco-spotted wood stoves, this first transcontinental train of 1869 was no streamliner. Its recent race across dry valleys and precipitous mountain country to connect with the Union Pacific– a race baited by extravagant land grants and government bonds– had steel-tied the East and the West, making a strong empire of America's thirty-eight million people.

To the little community living on the rim of the country, Sister Mary of the Blessed Sacrament, Sister Peter of Alcantara, Sister Mary Dorothy, and Sister Pacific gave a first-hand account of prairie expanse, rugged mountain terrain, fertile valleys, and hot deserts. During the past thirteen years the sisters of the western community had left their own country to become a part of this land. But what did they really know of it? With its coastal cities they were only vaguely acquainted; with its inland cities they were, for the most part, unfamiliar. Along the Pacific and Atlantic coasts they had sailed; they had seen the treacherous gaps where mighty rivers tore into the sea, but little did they know of the country drained by these powerful forces. Their America was this place men called Vancouver, building on the north banks of the Columbia.

Excitedly the missionaries told of all they had seen–herds of buffalo roaming across prairie land and deer scampering over grass-tufted plains. From the small, grimy windows they had watched cowboys hemming the herds of long- horned cattle. They had seen scattered Indian encampments where tribal members in blankets, feathers, and paint had crept out of their tepees to peer at the strange steel creature cutting through their lands. They had seen much; they had heard much, too. There had been talk among the passengers that the Indian troubles were cropping up throughout the West. Tribes were moving restlessly; in some places fresh conflicts had broken out.

Between 1865 and 1880 America paid heavily for the imprudent invasion of the red man's domain. Twenty-two million dollars was a high price to pay for confining the Indian to a few acres of barren soil. The Indian saw his great lands and even his "federal protected" acres dwindle; he saw abuse, waste, and contagion. During these years shrewd leaders such as Chief Joseph, Red Cloud, and Sitting Bull stood between whipped tribes and the white aggressors. One incident representative and predictive of where all this was leading was that of the Sioux uprising in June 1876, when General George A. Custer's detachment of two hundred and seventy-seven men was massacred under the command of Sitting Bull.

Along the mining roads even now the Cheyenne were harrying the settlements and attacking the stagecoaches; the Apache and the Navajo were grimly fighting in the canyon and desert country. The typical attitude of the Indian was expressed by Too-hul-hul-sute, the Nez Percé orator:

> The Great Spirit Chief made the world as it is and as He wanted it, and He made part of it for us to live upon. I do not see where you get the authority to say that we should not live where He placed us. . . .

Too late America discovered the truth, that a people cannot be whipped into subjection.

Reports of the plight of the Indians reminded the sisters of the reason for their being in this remote corner of the country. It was for the welfare of the Indian as well as for that of the white man that they had so eagerly left Montreal in 1856; thus far the work with the Indian had not been extensive.

In answer to Father Pierre DeSmet's plea, a group had gone to the Saint Ignatius Mission in 1864, to teach the Pend d'Oreille tribes. Directly from Montreal, Sister Mary of the Infant Jesus, Sister Mary Edward, and Sister Remi had come to Vancouver and after one month's preparation had left for Walla Walla where Sister Paul Miki had joined them.

The harrowing account of their seven-hundred-mile journey to that missionary post described the inconveniences of four hundred miles in the saddle, battling windstorms, and rainstorms. Escorted to the shore of the Coeur d'Alene Lake by canoe and raft. Nor was that the only danger. It demanded grit and determination to cross the Bitterroot Mountains.

"Where ya headed?" shouted the miners who met them on the narrow mountain passes.

"To Saint Ignatius Mission."

"You are the first white women to cross these mountains. You can never live in such a place. No white woman can live there," they warned.

But on the missionaries went, wading through rivers and skirting treacherous ravines. Arriving at Saint Ignatius at the end of eight weeks, they found additional difficulties. Under the direction of Father Urban Grassi, they began to study the complexities of the Indian tongue. It was the age- old lesson of becoming all things to all men . . . Of the four sisters, the most proficient as a conversationalist with the Indians was Sister Mary of the Infant Jesus, the Sister Servant. She never tried to learn English; her adopted country was the land of the Indian; she gave herself completely to this cause.

Victims of exploitation, the Indians, none too happy with their living space, found sympathetic response in the Sisters of Providence. Although Sister Joseph's resources were inadequate and her funds meager, she begged help for the sisters who set out to found missions. Sister Blandine's enthusiasm for the Indians was channeled into the cause of the Snohomish tribe on the Puget Sound reservation of Tulalip in 1868. Another five years and the sisters had settled at Colville, setting up their school, Providence of the Sacred Heart, to teach the red man that, although he had lost his lands, he must yet save his soul.

The apostolate widened by 1878 to include the Immaculate Conception Indian School in DeSmet, Idaho. As early as 1870 the chief of the tribe, Selstice, had written Sister Catherine at Walla Walla, pleading for *women blackrobes*. On a begging tour in 1866 Sister had mingled with the tribe, and the good Chief had not forgotten. Repaying the visit he and eight of his men in tribal dress visited Walla Walla in 1870, asking if they might enter the house of *the chief of the women blackrobes*. The sisters were most gracious and apparently quite charmed the Chief. A letter from him arrived not many days later.

Our hearts were full of joy when you passed through our country. Now I want you to come and live with us and teach our girls. Our Fathers, the Blackrobes, take care of our boys and we are glad; but our girls are orphans. They are ignorant and they will always be that way unless you come and take care of them. When I went to see you, you made me so welcome that I could see how well you like the Indians; now I want you to ask the chief of the women blackrobes to give us sisters. We will build a house for them and we will help them. We will do all they tell us. I beg the Great Spirit to fill your heart with mercy for the poor Coeur d'Alene girls. Our Fathers, the Blackrobes, teach us that the Big Chief on High gives plenty for a little charity to others. So the reward for the women blackrobes will be very great if they come to open the eyes and the hearts of our poor girls! Yes, I hope the Great Spirit will touch your heart and open your ears to our prayers. Pray for me and for all my children.

SELSTICE
Chief of the Coeur d'Alenes

The good chief kept his promise. When Sister Mary Hyacinth, Sister Constance, and Sister Mary Francis established themselves in DeSmet, they found great generosity among the Indians. Often the Indians paid them friendly calls or simply came, knocked at the door, and before any words could be exchanged, pressed some gift of meat or flour into the sisters' arms. Sometimes the Indians explained their gifts in their own childlike way, "Our hearts told us that you needed it."

The Indian was a unique pupil; he was the child of the forest, the plain, and the river. His innate sense of the reality of the Supernatural gave him the ascendency over the white man. To the Indians the forest talked, the mountains instilled wisdom, and the rivers murmured counsel. The awareness of life all about him, and at the same time, the consciousness of his inability to cope with the many forces of nature, bred in him humility and simplicity. That spirit fertilized the missionary ground.

But the missionary had to develop a like awareness, a deep understanding of the Indian's outlook, and above all, he had to know how to point to the Great Spirit through the things of nature. He had to know how to use nature to symbolize the truths of God, the soul, and eternity. Teaching was not easy. The clutch of environment, the coldness of prejudice among the elders of the tribe, the irreparable damage of the white man's example—these were factors which gave no guaranty that today's lessons would be remembered tomorrow. The Sermon on the Mount could barely penetrate in the face of the white man's blatant misdeeds. The missionary had to practice patience and maintain great purity of life, so as not to give the lie to his words; strong faith, deep trust, and unswerving love were essentials. His integrity was the platform of his words, the rock which made the words firm and enduring.

As years passed, people were to forget the heroism of the Indian missionaries. In ages of well-equipped schools, systematized teacher training, and education for Catholic action, it would become quite easy to dismiss the early Indian apostolate as a good thing, an emergency, a philanthropic venture. A country that progresses rapidly easily forgets its beginnings. The names of those men and women who spent their lives among the Indians have, by comparison with other historical figures, passed into oblivion. Even the accounts of the Indian apostolate of the Sisters of Providence are scant; little is known of what passed in those missions, and yet, what an adventure-filled life for women who were, humanly speaking, often ill-prepared. They had no grasp of pedagogical principles; they boasted no linguistic skill; often they were totally unfamiliar with the locality as well as the country in which they taught. But they had a mission directed by obedience for the glory of the infant Church in America or in Canada. They knew how to give themselves and how to endure in the achieving.

These Indian missions and eight others which eventually came under the direction of the Sisters of Providence were not all longlived, and many of them were marked with the seal of God's approval-the cross. The sisters who cared for the Indian suffered from inadequate housing, poor organization, insufficient finances, and gross misunderstandings. However, hardships vitalized the roots of the community for Monseigneur Bourget had often told the sisters that if crosses were ever wanting to the Institute then the ruin of the community would be imminent.

. . . .

In November of 1869 the community received an unpleasant jolt in the form of a notice addressed to His Lordship, Bishop A. M. A. Blanchet, ordering the Mission Compound to vacate the premises in the military reserve within sixty days. Intending to take an adamant stand on this issue, His Lordship promptly set to work negotiating with Washington D.C., demanding the price of the Mission Claim before he would make any move. A commission having been appointed by the War Department to investigate the Mission Claim, matters quieted down for a while. On March 3, 1870, another notification was served the Catholic Mission of Saint James; it was to vacate the military reserve of Fort Vancouver, by order of the Adjutant General, U.S.A. and Headquarters, Department of the Columbia, Portland, Oregon, and to do so within ninety days!

The command filled the community with consternation. The future suddenly darkened-the sisters facing eviction with two hundred homeless persons on their hands. Sister Joseph's fear was a sword. She saw fourteen years of stinting, planning, and laboring wiped out in a moment! Indeed, the Lord was severely testing her courage and trust. The fear did not, however, freeze action. She made visits to the little buildings, urging the orphans to pray . . . joining in the prayers of the old people, helping the sick to beseech Divine Providence. The sisters earnestly begged the Sacred Heart for protection.

Meanwhile, His Lordship contacted Abbé Brouillet who was at the time in Washington, D.C., representing the Mission Claim. Messages were sent, the citizens heatedly backing His Lordship. Four hours after the Bishop's first message of protest the telegram came.

Order for Removal has been suspended.
by order of SECRETARY BELKNAP

The eviction threat was a further prod to Sister Joseph to forward her building plans for the House of Providence. Surely, this incident furnished strong support for the big venture. However, one had to be practical about some things; she had no money, and even with the greatest faith, you had to have a little. Hadn't the Bishop of Boise, the Right Reverend Louis Lootens, invited her to make a collection tour of his diocese to help finance her charities?

. . . .

Fireweed spires had begun to climb and blackberry leaves to creep through the smothering salal when Sister Joseph of the Sacred Heart and Sister Joseph of Arimathea set out on a threemonth begging tour of the Idaho mining fields. With Reverend Amable Archambeault as guide, the two nuns traveled on horseback, sleeping in makeshift tents under the open skies and living on a meager fare of pancakes and dry crusts.

Throughout the gold-boom towns of Silver City, Granite Creek, Pioneer City, and Centerville they walked, through these towns and many others which had rocketed to fame overnight. In Idaho City they begged where men gathered in saloons still discussing the year- old execution of Sim Walters, the brash murderer of a wealthy rancher. Murders were common talk, and Governor Ballard's list of hangings was of considerable length. John Early carried them by stagecoach between Boise and Silver City where

Indian uprisings were constant threats. Through sagebrush foot-hills and dry cliff country, the sisters guided their horses, grateful for the presence of Father Archambeault. They were jostled amid the traffic of those mushroom towns, along with packtrains and freight wagons that wallowed in the muddy streets, dumping car-goes of goods unceremoniously in front of shacks. They brushed by knots of miners who lolled on the shamble steps of the *Idaho World*, brewing over Editor Henry Street's latest partisan slant.

The mining towns which were strung out north of Boise were booming settlements with an air of recklessness and daring. But beneath the daredevil exterior, there were many hearts and minds bent on justice. From their diggings they liberally contributed to the two sisters who represented institutions that were safeguards of that justice. But there were also unscrupulous individuals who could flash a pistol or flourish a bowie-knife at will.

One morning the sisters and Father stopped at a log cabin res-taurant in Lone Creek. No sooner had they ordered their break-fast when two swarthy-looking men entered the room and sat down opposite the sisters. Their intent staring and subtle ques-tioning alerted the sisters to the probable intentions of the two fellows. That same evening the two suspects reappeared. This was repeated; often on the streets Sister Joseph noticed that they were being followed by the same two men.

Late one afternoon, as the sisters were returning from visiting the mines, one of the men, with a nonchalant air boldly swag-gered up to Sister Joseph.

"Ain't you 'fraid to travel this way?" he simpered, eyeing the bag which hung on her arm.

Shrewd Sister Joseph replied, "Surely, you don't think we keep with us the money we are collecting? What are express offices for?"

Shrugging their shoulders, the two men turned and sauntered off, while the missionaries quickened their pace in the opposite direction. A few days later they discovered that the two fellows were in the town jail on the charge of murdering a man for his nuggets. The sisters immediately directed their steps toward the first express office as they left Lone Creek.. There they deposited their collection of $2,600. Years later Sister Joseph mentioned their great devotion to their Guardian Angels during the mining tours.

Mother Joseph's life was stocked with similar manifestations of the hand of Providence. Her reliance on the protective power of God lay deep in her spiritual fiber. It was not a bubble on the surface of her living which burst at the slightest provocation. It was a quiet, strong God-assurance that made her fearless in acting, knowing that doing things for His glory never cluttered the vision of man.

Monseigneur Bourget never regretted having sent Sister Joseph of the Sacred Heart to the West. Early in her religious life he had discerned the makings of a great woman. Her letters to him revealed great simplicity and humble obedience; his letters to her, paternal pride and loving solicitude.

> The detailed recital of your works fills me with joy and happiness, as I always include myself in your good works and holy undertakings. . . . Could I experience a greater joy than that of knowing that those whom religion has given the way of perfection, and that it pleases the Lord to accept their labors, their trials, their hardships, and their nightwatchings. . . . Courage, therefore. Let the past be a lesson for the future.

> . . . . I feel that I am nearing the end. May I sleep the sleep of the just, while my daughters in Christ fill the world with the good odor of their religious virtues, above all, with the exquisite perfume of that simplicity, humility, and charity which St. Vincent de Paul has bequeathed unto them as a priceless heritage. . . .

It was on the occasion of his golden jubilee of ordination to the priesthood that Monseigneur Bourget granted permission to reopen the Western novitiate, which had been closed in 1864. As novitiate quarters, Mother Joseph constructed a small annex to Saint Joseph Hospital on Eighth Street.

· · · · · · · · ·

After five years of waiting for the City Council to grant permission to connect their property for the purpose of building the House of Providence, the sisters were favored by the passage of

Ordinance 76 on July 7, 1873. A ten-acre plot of land was theirs on which to build, with all intersecting streets closed to enable them to centralize. It was the dream come true, the answer to many months of prayer . . . the realization of the hopes of the little Providence of the West.

The General Council in Montreal, however, remained conservative, withholding permission to go ahead with the actual construction. The Providence of the Holy Angels was deep in debt. Anyone would predict danger in such a huge enterprise when she realized the simple fact that with the passing years the works of the House of Providence had multiplied, while the income remained more or less stationary. While Montreal considered, Mother Joseph, with her architect, John B. Blanchet, planned the building. Everything was ready to move when the moment of permission should arrive.

Divine Providence intervened in May of 1873 when Mother Caron, Superior General, visited Vancouver. This holy woman, one of the first foundresses of the. Institute, was highly esteemed by Monseigneur Bourget, who in the same year wrote to His Lordship of Nisqually:

"Mother Caron is so humble, so charitable, so good and devoted that all her undertakings are marked with untold success."

It was this same Mother Caron who had sent the band of five westward in 1856. She had, together with Monseigneur Bourget, planted the Western mission; she was now the one whose consent to the building of the House of Providence was to give shape and impetus to the future growth of Providence.

Mother Caron visited the seven small buildings, noted their inadequacy, and aware of the fact that they stood on disputed land, saw as did Mother Joseph, the need of immediate construction. Carefully and minutely she examined the accounts of Providence of the Holy Angels, consulted Bishop Blanchet, the Mother Vicar, and the bursar. Her conclusion was emphatic; there must be no further delay.

With the proposed grounds inspected and the position of the building decided, ground was broken in June. Besides His Lordship and Father Aegidius Junger, Mother Caron, Mother Praxedes and Mother Joseph of the Sacred Heart participating in the ceremony, there were also the orphans, each lifting a shovelful of dirt.

The treasury of the little community showed only $11,400, while four times that was needed to finance the structure. Mother Joseph felt and heard the strong opposition among the sisters. If it had not been for Mother Caron's insistence, she might have hesitated. . . . After all, that had been her flaw all along—action without enough deliberation. At least, it had seemed to be that way, and yet, were she to relive the problems of the past seventeen years, the decisions would follow the same pattern. But there was Mother Caron waving aside all protest. "Go ahead with confidence. Divine Providence will never fail you as long as you never withdraw from the beautiful simplicity which should be the ornament of religious houses."

Naturally speaking, it did take courage to build at a time when the United States was gripped in a depression. Frenzied railroad construction and the consequent tying up of great amounts of capital, which at that time yielded no adequate returns on investment, had collapsed five thousand commercial houses. A half-million laborers were idle. The face of the country was not a happy one. It was all too easy to point to those misfortunes and then wince at this venture of a treasury which contained only one-fourth the money to see it through. The little community had no get-rich-quick strategy on which to rely. It had no finance magnates, but it did have a woman who drew with confidence from the rich treasures of Providence; she always found that her credit was in good standing there.

. . . .

"*. . . they are mothers for orphans, teachers for abandoned children, physicians for the sick, dispensers of relief for the needy, and consolers of every kind of affliction. . . .*"

Mother Joseph drew herself up to attention. That was Father Junger's voice winding up the sermon on this day of the laying of the cornerstone, September 21, 1873. Mother Joseph's eyes wandered out over the crowd . . . familiar faces, many of them others not known, but friends, all of them. There were many people, she knew, who had come that morning from Portland on the Carrie. Officers from the garrison mingled with the people; the orphans were grouped on one side near the sisters. In the midst of them sat Mother Caron. Mother Joseph had hurried up the workers so as to have this ceremony before Mother's return to Montreal, and they had made it—just three days before sailing time.

The afternoon sun was warm. Mother Joseph hoped Father Junger wouldn't keep these good people much longer.

"What thanks shall we offer them, what gratitude shall we bestow on them? But as their humility refuses praise . . ."

The words drifted off . . . Mother Joseph's distractions poured in upon her again. If only Monseigneur Bourget could be here . . . and Mother Gamelin. They were the two who should lay this cornerstone—and all the sisters now serving on the scattered missions . . .

". . . we can wish them success and say: Increase, O family, blessed by heaven and beloved of mankind; increase to . . ."

Blessed by heaven . . . how true, thought Mother Joseph. To the people standing here this afternoon that was probably mere eloquence of expression, but for the sisters who stood here and for those who lay in the Mission Compound, this was the story of their lives in the mission country. Now what was it that the good father was saying?

". . . be the consolation of the world at large, the universal refuge of the distressed, the antidote of all the miseries which afflict poor human nature. . . "

Mother Joseph recalled the little Saint John of God Asylum which had stood on Eighth Street, with its twenty- five patients. How she has loved that work which has its source in Mother Gamelin's humble planting. The loss of the mental patients in 1867 had deeply grieved her.

Let us all bless and thank Divine Providence who thus favors us by the erection of such an institution in our midst. Let us assist and help the erection and sustenance of it as far as our means allow . . .

Yes, God had favored them and He would continue to favor them. Father Junger had asked the people to support the new foundation, and yet Mother Joseph knew that never would there step forth a millionaire to cancel their debts, or cover the cost of the building. That was not the way of God with the Sisters of Providence. The little community on the banks of the Columbia would struggle from one year to the next and would never falter because its foundations were God.

. . . in the words of the prophet, "And now, O Lord, bless the house of thy servants, that it may be forever before Thee, because Thou, O Lord, has spoken it, and with Thy blessing let the house of Thy servants be blessed forever."

Forever . . . the world had a ring to it and sent Mother Joseph's thoughts ahead down through the years. This House of Providence would forever sing the praises of Divine Providence. It was not a matter of non-crumbling walls, but a matter of sending its spirit out into all parts of the West through the sisters who would always be mindful of the cost of winning the West and would let themselves be moulded in that spirit. The walls of this house were to hallow the years and hold the memories of those who would here be schooled in His love, vow their allegiance to Christ in poverty, chastity, and obedience, and, perhaps spend their declining years here.

The crowd was moving. Mother Joseph stepped aside as the people in solemn procession, one by one, struck the stone and left near it an offering. *God bless this stone*, Mother Joseph prayed. *Be Thou the cornerstone.*

Following the final ceremony of Solemn Benediction, words of congratulations filled Mother Joseph's ears. "It's a fine monument to the West . . . no doubt that it will be the most magnificent structure this side of the Mississippi. . . ."

Mother Joseph looked out from the side of the new building. It was well chosen. Its location on the brow of the hill gave a commanding view of town and river. But all this was just the beginning. Now to build. . . .She was well aware of the meager funds in her keeping.

The sun was edging toward the cloud bank beyond the Columbia. A slight breeze had come up as Mother Joseph turned toward the Mission Compound. The words of Father Junger followed her. . . . *Bless the house of Thy servants that it may be forever before Thee . . .*

CHAPTER 21

BRACKEN was turning a dull brown at the base of the Douglas firs when Mother Joseph moved the sisters, the boarders, and the orphans into the House of Providence on Tenth and Reserve streets in 1874. But the transfer did not solve her difficulties—not all of them, at least, for the immediate future bore not the semblance of a promise of any material security. A debt of twenty thousand dollars would be hard to shake off. Mother Joseph could not say it aloud, but she admitted it to herself—the building could not possibly be completed for another ten years. Any further attempts now would be haphazard ones and this building had to give witnesses. . . . His home would have to wait; the parlor could serve as the chapel. That's the way Saint Joseph would have done it, she felt.

Saint Joseph, confidant of Mother Joseph of the Sacred Heart, president of the Providence corporation, was having his share of glory in this new building, thanks to Doctor David Wall. The six-foot statue in the niche above the façade was a credit to him.

The moderate temperature of September and October soon chilled into the grim grayness of November. Brooding rains clung to the tall cedars, quivered, and throughout the nights slowly dripped to the earth. Stiff northwest winds battered the walls and clung to the comers of the building, their penetrating cold warning the community of an early winter—another problem.

Mother Joseph considered the situation. The wood stoves which she had found satisfactory in the seven small houses certainly made no impression in this three-storied building. The sisters could probably endure the inconvenience, but the orphans presented a picture that pained Mother Joseph. They were utterly helpless in hiding their discomfort or in conserving their warmth. Throughout the night they whimpered and coughed in dormitories which could not be heated simply because there were not enough stoves.

Was this it? Was this the moment that was to climax her imprudence? Had she erected an impressive building with commodious rooms only to find its inmates lacking the bare essentials? Roof they had, but the body required something more. A debt of $20,000 had a way of standing squarely in the path of providing.

It was Mother Praxedes' wise judgment that turned to prayer, with everyone beseeching the Sacred Heart to show a way out and to preserve the one hundred orphans from sickness. Divine Providence would point out a way; of that Mother Joseph was sure, even though at the moment she was deeply perplexed. Man must use what God has given him to complement the strategy of faith.

Late into the night Mother Joseph pored over the accounts until her eyes no longer saw anything but only the stark recording of debt—$20,000. They were being put to the test—the whole community—and God help her to clear the debt while still preserving harmony and peace. A continual status of financial insecurity could easily, though subtly, shift the goals of a religious. Financial insecurity could so easily breed a wrong emphasis on life's material aspect. And who was to stand accused at the hour of reckoning but the person who, though surveying the dangers and knowing so well the limitations of man, nevertheless plunged into an enterprise. Yes, but certainly under the protection of the Sacred Heart. It must always be this way. The school of Mother Gamelin had long ago exorcised the spirit of complacent independence.

A personal awareness of individual responsibility in shouldering common debts in order to allay the cost of growth was a characteristic of the entire community in those early days of

Providence in the West. So it was with this twenty-thousand-dollar debt. The sacrifices and planning which spearheaded the payment of it boasted an esprit de corps that made any obstacle surmountable.

For quick results Mother Joseph resolved to put on a bazaar that would interest and attract the townspeople. The hamlets along the Columbia were generous donors as well as patrons. Results often netted as much as $1,000.00.

In the annals we read that on one of the numerous collection tours along the Columbia a farmer had donated a cow for a bazaar. The freight hand at The Dalles was approached by the donor.

"I don't know how to label this cow."

"Where is it going?"

"To Mother Joseph in Vancouver."

"Well, put the tag around her horn–FOR MOTHER JOSEPH. Everybody knows the old Mother. She'll get it. The old *Undine* has carried a lot of freight for her."

The cow came straight through and was raffled for as much as $250.

Just the previous year Sister Agnes and a novice (later Sister Mary Conrad) had canvassed the Puget Sound region, traveling by canoe, by tugboat, by stage-, and very often on foot. Indians had often befriended the sisters, not only paddling them down the Sound in their canoes, but also inviting them to share their fire, food, and lodging.

The two sisters had begged for their charities in Port Townsend, Port Blakely, Port Madison, Port Ludlow, and Seattle, small towns which jutted out from the jagged, timbered coastline spotted with lumber camps in full operation to supply the goldmining-boom city of San Francisco. Seattle . . . whose foundation had been laid in a mother's tears, the energetic little colony which was leaping ahead in population and industries, possessed an indomitable spirit. Wooden shacks leaned out over its waterfront, but beyond there were signs of more permanent construction. When the two missionaries returned to Vancouver they placed in Mother Joseph's hands $1,800.

Into South America the begging tour had been carried by

Sister Peter of Alcantara and Sister Oliver. As a compensation for the hardships of that journey, the sisters had some delightful moments of reunion with the Sisters of Providence of the Chile foundation of 1852. Mother Bernard Morin had not only granted them a guide but had also substantially contributed to their cause. Their eleven months had been most productive; they had collected some six thousand dollars! Sister Oliver, fatigued by the long, arduous trip, was replaced by Mother Joseph of the Sacred Heart for further begging in British Columbia.

Realizing the hazardous aspects of the mission into British Columbia, and aware of the absolute need for a parallel of prayer and activity, Mother Joseph solicited the prayers of the Carmelites of Montreal. She knelt at the feet of the daughters of Saint Teresa, that heroic nun who had traveled the length and breadth of Spain founding her missions.

. . . it is with greatest confidence I come to recommend our dear missions to your holy prayers; also do I recommend the success of a collection begun under the protection of Saint Joseph to obtain funds to pay the debt on our building. . . . We are obliged not only to supply sisters to care for the orphans, to instruct the ignorant, and to nurse the sick, but we must also build, and from day to day maintain, feed, and clothe our adopted children.

The fervent writings of your seraphic Mother have many times inspired me with courage in the difficulties of our humble foundation; although our objective is different from yours, yet we have the same purpose in mind, to give glory to God. It was her confidence in Saint Joseph that prompted me to ask you to become a partner in our work, so that I and my companion may return to our convent with the necessary resources to carry our charities on for the glory of our holy religion and the honor of our good father, Saint Joseph, under whose powerful patronage this mission was founded. Since you are inheritors of the power which your holy Mother exercised on his paternal heart, he will not refuse your petitions in our behalf. . . .

This was the spirit of Mother Gamelin—constant reliance on prayer, with the contemplative spirit so perfectly wedded to the active life. It was the secret of Mother Joseph's achievements.

Bishop Charles J. Seghers in Victoria and Bishop Louis d'Herbomez, O.M.I., in New Westminster graciously granted permission to the two sisters to take up a collection in their dioceses. Bishop d'Herbomez had withheld no truth regarding the nature of their proposed trip up the Frazer River to the Cariboo mining region. "I hope," he said to the sisters, "you will be well received wherever you pass; yet I beg God to give each of you a dozen Guardian Angels to protect you from all the dangers to which you will surely be exposed." Encouraged by this frankly realistic prayer and farewell, the sisters began their three-hundred-mile trek to the goldfields of the Cariboo.

So this was the Fraser . . . Sister Joseph had heard of it from the miners in the Idaho camps. Some had boasted of their tussling with the river; some had fabulous tales of the inexhaustible gold which lay deep down, close to bedrock. But there had been some experiences which the miners had refused to talk about. No, the Fraser wasn't a friendly river. It had the name of being the most treacherous body of water on the North American continent. Still, from this crest on which lay the port of New Westminster, the river seemed to have lost its fury.

Mother Joseph's thoughts during that trip into the Cariboo diggings were mostly fastened on the river. How it reminded her of the Eastern waterway of her early life, the Saint Lawrence, that they resembled each other, but in that they were so different, and yet so extremely important to the country. The Saint Lawrence was docile, mannered, and easily navigated; the Fraser was untamed, unmanageable, and yet to be coped with. The Fraser was the West! It had the obstinacy, the impetuosity, and the daring that were so characteristic of the region. Her life, she mused, seemed always to follow the river. . . .

The perilous journey into the Cariboo included three days of riding the stormy waters of the Fraser, and four days of ramshackle coaches careening along narrow roads which were mere furrows in the sides of perpendicular cliffs. The dizzy flow of the river, caught up in a mad whirl of rock and water, seemed everlastingly gouging out the foundation of the hills. The coaches groaned and creaked as they wormed their way through closely packed mountain terrain, where peaks towered six and seven thousand feet high. Horses whinnied and cringed at the steep descents and narrow winding trails in this aptly labeled "horse-killing country." During most of the trip Mother Joseph and Sister Peter could only look at one another, not daring to speak, keeping their eyes toward the mountain side of the passes, veering away from the sheer canyons on the other side where death edged so closly.

Reaching the Saint Joseph Mission where Father McGucken, O.M.I. was stationed, the sisters rested briefly before setting out for the mines. The quartz and placer operations were no hindrance to Mother Joseph. Up the sheer sides of rocky cliffs or down into the black grimy, subterranean passages she managed to reach the miners. After three weeks among the prospectors, the two nuns returned home, stopping in the Puget Sound area for a final collection in their grand begging tour. On October 31, 1875, they arrived at Vancouver, swelling the treasury and reducing the debt of the new building by $10,000!

Throughout the years, very rarely did financial complications freeze all mission expansion. In 1863, there had been repeated requests by His Grace, Most Reverend Francis Norbert Blanchet, the Archbishop of Oregon City, for the Sisters of Providence to found a hospital in Portland. Assuming a responsibility of such huge proportions at a time when the community was trying desperately to staff the Indian missions had been impossible. However, on July 19, 1874, when a group of associates of the Saint Vincent de Paul Society knocked at the doors of the community offering to the sisters a group of houses in Portland, provided the sisters would build a hospital on the donated land, Mother Joseph found it very hard to turn aside from this proposal. It was the feast of Saint Vincent de Paul; she saw in it God's loving Providence. Negotiations moved quickly and within twenty-four hours Mother Joseph of the Sacred Heart sat at her drafting table, planning the construction of the new hospital which would naturally bear the title of Saint Vincent Hospital. Within one year, the new building was opened and blessed by His Grace.

. . . .

Since 1856 devotion to the Sacred Heart had been uppermost in the life of Mother Joseph and her Western community. Monseigneur Bourget had told the five foundresses:

You will have for Sister Servant, Sister Joseph, who will henceforth bear the name of Sister Joseph of the Sacred Heart, *so that you may always remember that it will be through the Divine Heart of Jesus that the new foundation will labor successfully for the propagation of the faith. . . .*

It had been a solemn prophecy and the ensuing years were to bear out its truth. Repeatedly, Mother Joseph had promised a prominent place in the first foundation for the honoring of the Sacred Heart. Partial fulfillment had been realized in Captain James Hardie's gift of the altar in the Cathedral. But now with the erection of the main building of the House of Providence, she knew something more should be done.

And so it was! In December of 1874, the sisters received a beautiful oil painting of the Sacred Heart from Reverend Father Zetherin Resther, S.J. The picture had been intended for his sister, Sister Peter Claver, as a gift to the new Saint Vincent Hospital. When Mother Joseph saw how beautifully it fitted into the niche between the Sorrowful Virgin and the tabernacle of the main altar of the House of Providence chapel, she pleaded to be allowed to keep it. She was so convinced that the whole incident was a definite design of Providence that the other parties involved felt niggardly giving even a thought to an opposed action.

Mother Joseph wrote to Monseigneur Bourget:

The arrival of the magnificent oil painting, sent by the Reverend Father Resther, S.J., was to me *a guarantee of the protection of the Sacred Heart,* and the picture came just in time to *restore our faith. . . .*

She wrote to Father Resther:

Oh, I have the greatest confidence that your worthy superiors who are truly devoted to the Sacred Heart as yourself will permit you to seek other contributions from people of good will so that *in Vancouver as well as Portland the Sacred Heart may be known, loved and Honored.*

Sister Peter Claver wrote to her brother:

Please understand well that Sister Joseph's petition is not made to get you into any trouble. Don't do a thing about it unless you can easily do so. I did not dare to encourage her to write to you. On the contrary, I told her you could not do anything in the matter; but neither could I prevent her. *I should have feared to dim the glory of the Sacred Heart had I done so.*

Everything had worked out in perfect timing since the chapel, though unfinished, was to be blessed in the spring!

Joys and sorrows tumbled out in rapid succession in those years of financial crises. There had been the satisfaction of extending the Providence works to Yakima in 1875 and to Cowlitz in the foundation of the Saint Francis Xavier Mission.

Born of grim hardship, the struggling community at Yakima City limped along for several years. Political bickering, prejudice, and indifference moved Mother Amable, Superior General, to consider closing the Mission, but the entreaties of a few kept it open. Sister Blandine of the Holy Angels, superior of the Saint Joseph Mission, lamented the condition to Sister Joseph in the fall of 1876.

As things are now, I do not see how it will be possible to continue the mission for the whites in Yakima. There are no resources to maintain a school where all the people are about to depart to make a fortune elsewhere. There is no money in circulation and it is too great a risk to make a loan of several dollars with no guarantees.

It is my impression that the time has not come for these people to have the sisters here. But I leave this question to others with greater foresigh. . . . Apart from the many physical inconveniences here, the deprivation of the Blessed Sacrament, of a resident priest, and of daily Mass are the real trials we endure . . . I am here like a fish out of water, and I sigh for the day when an Indian mission will open to take me out of this place.

But in spite of the despondency of Sister Blandine, the mission continued, moving to North Yakima in 1887.

There was also the sorrow caused by the Columbia River floods of 1876, which destroyed the crops on the river farm. Mother Joseph found her treasury drained, her debts unpaid, and the personnel facing stark poverty. The Carmelite reformer's complaint to Christ about His treatment of His friends might well have applied here. But Mother Joseph remained firm. In the face of a crop loss, she was often heard to say, "My good father Saint Joseph and Divine Providence will supply our needs."

Her sources of income were three-the tuition fee, the monthly collection in the barracks, and the annual bazaar. Of course, there were the begging tours into the mines, but these were not regular and were considered only in emergencies. The generous support given her by the soldiers was always to be relied upon. In fact, it became customary for Mother Joseph to be notified by the commanding officer when the paymaster was due to arrive; she was reminded to have a sister at the fort to solicit financial help for the House of Providence.

With the passing of each crisis, Mother Joseph found her faith in Divine Providence strengthened. Monseigneur Bourget had told her more than once–

It seems to me that you should not lose courage in the difficult trials of life, for experience has shown you more than once that we are never better off than when we have apparently reached the limit of our resources.... I have never heard it said that you were forced to eat grass; and yet, before leaving for Oregon, you had resolved to do even that, if necessary.

Her sufferings and hardships she often confided to Father Junger. Paternally he advised and consoled her:

We see only our miseries, our contradictions and the disarrangement of our plans, but God sees the good that these contradictions will bring about ... Keep up your courage and do all for the glory of God And he will bless the little you receive, which may reach the hundredfold.

Father Aegidius Junger, after twelve years of being chaplain to the sisters, was named in March of 1876 to assist the enfeebled Bishop of Nisqually. Father Louis de G. Schram replaced him. Mother Joseph was sure that Father Junger's holiness and executive ability definitely set him in line for eventually filling the bishopric.

But there was in the humble priest no ambitious trait or desire for such an office. He wrote to Mother Joseph:

I am well satisfied with my present position. I have only one desire to retire into some religious solitude to prepare my soul for eternity. But I must not think of retirement. I shall try to work out my salvation amidst the dangers daily encountered by a secular priest.

He often had told Mother Joseph, "Each trial brings a blessing on your establishment." Trials . . . there were many of them. The bursar of Holy Angels decided that there was no alternative but to assume the role of beggar once more. Unable to pay the interest, and with the building in an unfinished state, she wrote to the hierarchy for a letter of approbation for another begging tour.

. . . .

In midsummer Mother Joseph set out with Sister Mary Augustine to collect throughout the mining camps of eastern Oregon, southern Idaho, and Colorado. Detailed accounts filled the abundant correspondence of the veteran beggar. As concerned as she was to finish the collection in a limited time, still she wrote of attending to the needs of the clergy in the small, scattered Idaho and Oregon parishes. Tailoring a new cassock, mending Church linens and vestments, embroidering a new tabernacle veil, and supplying furniture for poverty-marked rectories—all these claimed the attention of Mother Joseph.

At Boise Father Toussaint Mesplie, the genial little priest whose life among the Indians had been fraught with such dangers, entertained them for a few hours and acquainted them with the mining areas, suggesting routes and procedures for collections among soldiers as well as among the miners.

It was while they were traveling to Denver by stagecoach that the two sisters had an experience which Sister Mary Augustine was never to forget. As for Mother Joseph of the Sacred Heart, it was just one more on a long list of events.

As they were riding along rough mountain roads, the coach jerked to an abrupt halt. The four horses were seized by masked men who thrust guns through the windows, with laconic command to pile out and drag their baggage and belongings with them. With pistols leveled at them, the passengers lost no time stumbling out of the coach. As Mother Joseph dropped her bag at the side of the road with the others, she mumbled to the petrified passengers, Pray . . . pray . . . pray!

The baggage collected into one pile, the travelers were told to climb back into the coach. Mother Joseph lagged behind, watching the bandits who had already begun to pilfer the luggage.

"Mr. . . . Mr. . . ."

Breathless whispers came warningly from the passengers who did not savor being shot, "Be quiet. Please be quiet!"

"Mr. . . . , my boy," Mother Joseph called a little louder. One of the bandits in the midst of the rifling jerked back, surprised.

"My boy, that black bag. Please give me that black bag."

While the passengers didn't dare breathe, the bandit queried, "Which?"

"That one—the black one to your right . . ."

"This?" He pointed to a small black satchel.

"No, no," she shook her head.

Finally he lifted a rather ample-sized carpetbag. Mother Joseph nodded. "Yes, yes, my boy. Give it to me."

Still apparently astounded at the audacity of the nun, the bandit carried the bag over to her and dropped it at her feet.

"Thank you. Gold bless you, my boy," came Mother Joseph's courteous nod.

The looting of the other bags continued. Completing the raid, the two men rode off, leaving the passengers to gather up the bags. The coach moved on toward Denver without further incident. Mother Joseph winked at Sister Mary Augustine whose gasping was still audible, and confidently patted her bag. Two hundred dollars still safe among her clothing!

As the days shortened and the long, cold nights set in, the placer mining operations began to shut down. By the time the first thin, white coat had slipped over the hillsides, the miners had already loaded their ponies and abandoned camp. The two nuns planned their trip to the East where they could continue their collections.

The remainder of the begging tour dragged out through sixteen months. With waves of strikes washing through the country and labor in open denouncement of the corruption of capitalism, the sisters realized that begging would not be wise at this time, neither in the United States nor in Canada.

The waiting months were well used. Ever on the alert to learn and perfect their skills, with an eye to benefiting her Western missions, Mother Joseph molded wax images of the Infant Jesus. She had the open mind and open hands which found it good to take hold of wood, clay, or wax and give shape to the image in her mind. At fifty-five, with fingers agile, nimble, and sensitive to beauty, she was as eager a pupil as she had been in the days at Saint Elzear. She was keen to discern beauty of line, and simplicity of design. Throughout her religious life she always encouraged the young sisters to learn as many skills as they could, to develop all their talents to capacity, so that the community might give just that much more glory to God. It was always the good of the community and the good of her sisters that prompted Mother Joseph to dedicate her own energies and to encourage others to do likewise.

Contacting Stanislaus Pariseau, she gave him orders for the construction of a wool-carding machine and a spinning wheel for her to send to her, Western missions. Stanislaus was astounded, no doubt, at the specific details which accompanied the order, but just as he had followed the injunctions of his sister in the cause of the *Younger Sons of Liberty,* so now he executed her plans. He not only filled her order, but also provided hand carders for individual use and a weaving machine for making rag carpets. All of these Mother Joseph later established in the House of Providence.

While purchasing supplies in New York for the various departments of the Vancouver Mission, Mother Joseph bought something which she had had in mind for many years. In a letter to Mother Praxedes, she explained the nature of the shipment:

Mr. Blanchet will tell you I sent a bell. It seemed to me, dear Mother, I could not pass by Troy without procuring this glory for our Immaculate Mother. It was the twenty-first anniversary of our foundation, December eighth. May the ceremony of its christening bring you in donations the price we paid for it.

Now Providence from east coast to west coast would ring out in honor of the Immaculate Conception and Redemption of mankind. Clear and vibrant, the bell would always remind men along the Columbia that their plenitude was due to the Incarnation of the Son of God. The bell would vie with the river in reminding them that God's condescension and His cherishing of them, through His loving Providence, is everlasting. . . .

It was nearing the spring of the year when the steamer *Vancouver* moved up the Columbia and edged into port. Twenty months' absence was a long time; Mother Joseph was glad to be home again. As soon as she had greeted the sisters, she busied herself with opening the boxes containing all her treasures. Among other things there was a bust of Monseigneur Bourget, and there was a wax figure to contain the relics of a martyr. Excitement ran high, and as Mother Joseph looked around at the sisters, pleased with their reactions her thoughts momentarily wandered. It was good to be home with those you loved, and who loved you.

The noticeable absence of Sister Mary of the Precious Blood filled her with sadness. She had not ceased to ache over that loss of which Mother Praxedes had written in October. She had only to step outside to see across the grounds the burial mound of her companion foundress. She had been the first of the five to go. . . and Mother Joseph missed her. Thoughts darted back to that young girl of such striking beauty, who at the age of eighteen was perfectly surrendered to God; who could accept the West . . . "Oh, it does not matter where I may be sent, just so I can become a religious." Twenty-one years of teaching youth, of forming young people to the virtues and ideals which seemed to come so natural to herself, had laid a marvelous foundation for the schools to be directed in the future by the Sisters of Providence.

When typhoid fever struck, Sister Mary knew she would not live through it. Her lips moved in constant prayer for the community in which she had come to know Christ so intimately. Eight days of suffering were the culmination of twenty-one years of religious teaching. Few women, Sister Joseph thought, would ever have the novitiate that Sister Mary of the Precious Blood had. . . . She had been surely tested and, God knows, she had not been found wanting.

What about the other four? When would it be? She, Mother Joseph, had always clung to life; death seemed alien, and yet, there were occasions when she yearned for that completion of time, that flowering of life. Providence was growing and these sisters would carry on, while her name would become a memory, but a part, definitely a part of this West. What was it that His Lordship had said in a letter sent her while she was in Montreal—

Your community holds a prominent place among others. It was scarcely born ere it spread its branches afar, showing its elders what they too should do. The little community in Vancouver seems to be well spiritually . . . perfect union . . . which is an unequivocal sign of union and peace with God.

Union and peace . . . and how much she needed to develop that spirit in herself, "lest having preached to others I myself become a castaway . . ." Crosses of misunderstanding, jealousies, and criticisms seemed to meet her at every turn. She lived under superiors and with sisters who seemed to be God's Providence in her sanctification—by the hard way. She had written to Mother Praxedes in the midst of one of these mental sufferings.

. . . The accomplishment of a work for the glory of the Sacred Heart is sovereignly displeasing to the devil and if he can frustrate it, he will do so. *Shall we abandon all for these little straw crosses?* I assure you, I would rather receive my superior from the hand of God than choose one of my liking even if I were given the choice . . . *The only important thing for me is to do the work of God; the rest is nothing.* Pray for me . . .

In April Mother Joseph made her retreat under the Reverend Joseph Cataldo, S.J. She felt satisfaction after the $5,000 collection trip, but fatigue, also . . .

CHAPTER 22

IN 1878 the aging Bishop Bourget sent messages to the quickly spreading Providence of the West, urging prudence, unity, religious regularity, study and practice of the rule, charity, and esteem for ecclesiastical dignitaries. There must be no spirit of individualism among the sisters, no one person rising for applause or seeking personal glory. The new mission of Providence Hospital in Seattle, together with those soon to follow, was the result of concerted effort.

"I am the Way, the Truth, and the Life." These words held the important lesson for every Sister of Providence as she took care to see that her spiritual growth was well in advance of the material growth of the community. It was a must, therefore, that she put on the mind of Christ; and where could she become better attuned to that than in the reading and study of the *Imitation of Christ and the New Testament?*

Mother Joseph pondered the truth of growth. Providence had began to build, indeed, but it was wise, periodically to test the foundation. Corrosive elements could so easily infiltrate to undermine the plans of the builder. It was so easy to impede Providence and still be loud in protestations of all being to His honor and glory. Deception had a way of clinging to ambition like a fungus. Yes, one had to test the foundation. Building by religious communities must always be a two-way plan, a thing that had to do with two kinds of growth.

Just preceding the twenty-fifth year of jubilee in the West,

235

Mother Joseph's energies were divided between Walla Walla and Astoria. The sisters at Saint Vincent Academy had finally arrived at an impasse. They no longer could accommodate in space of time their numerous patients, a service which they had combined with their teaching for the past fifteen years. Mother Joseph set to planning Saint Mary Hospital, a separate unit with its own local administration. As for Astoria, that, too, was a need and the building was pressed by an urgency toward completion before the fishing season began, diverting the attention of the people and withdrawing financial support which was definitely needed to transform the old Arragoni Hotel in a refuge for the sick.

In the year of jubilee, Mother Joseph of the Sacred Heart received a letter from the four aged, foundress companions of Mother Gamelin-Sister Mary of the Immaculate Conception, Sister Mary of Seven Dolors, Sister Caron, and Sister Zotique. Maternally, they appraised the progress of the Western foundations. It was, indeed, Mother Gamelin's spirit in contact with her daughters.

> Everything in your establishment in Fort Vancouver bears the stamp of Divine Providence. In your history is revealed the work of the Lord who created all things out of nothing; who chose the weak to confound the views of human wisdom; in effect, in order to accomplish the designs of charity He chose you, the humble daughter of this little congregation, for the foundation stone of the spiritual edifice destined to second the apostolic work of His ministers to a people yet living in darkness.
>
> In responding to the call of Our Lord, you ascended the mountain of Calvary.
>
> . . . we form these ardent wishes: that you may always walk in the way of perfection; . . . that the spirit of the world may never dim the luster of your purity and your charity; that you may always be but one heart and one soul.

Mother Joseph gratefully responded to those devoted mothers who had seen her and her four companions depart in 1856, and who had followed the journey and growth with prayers. She had long ago come to the realization that it is not the planter who causes the seed to grow; it is God beseeched by His loved ones. Cherishing in her heart the words of the foundresses, "Through those insurmountable difficulties an amiable Providence has guided your way," Mother Joseph wrote a reply which contained the usual lament of incompetence and guilt for the many spiritual losses to the sisters.

"God has performed providential mircales in our favor. But what has He not the right to expect from an old pioneer?"

She begged them to redouble their prayers that ". . . the tears that follow my pen will not be sterile."

. . . .

Following fast on the observance of the silver jubilee of Providence in the West came renewed and intensive effort to complete the chapel of the House of Providence within a year. Mother Joseph resolutely closed her account book and decided that it was now or never. The money which she had been able to set aside for the project, little though it was, she attributed to a number of successful bazaars and begging trips. Twenty-five years in Vancouver—and the Eucharistic Lord had waited. Besides' one never got caught up. Smooth waters were not found in this country. The fire that destroyed Saint Joseph's Hospital three years before had drained the treasury. Struggling missions were asking for help. When would it be otherwise?

But there was time for resolution, and that was all. In midwinter Vancouver received word that a fire at DeSmet had burned down the convent and boarding school. Laying aside ledgers and tools, Mother Joseph hastened to the frantic little community. Although the catastrophe was doubly tragic in view of the convent's having been built only two years earlier, Mother Joseph did not stand long weeping over the ashes; before she returned to Vancouver she had finished sketching plans for a new convent.

During the year 1882 she personally directed and helped to build the chapel of the House of Providence. The hired labor received hourly directives and inspection from this woman who had planned every feature of the construction, and who, furthermore, knew the precise manner in which she wished every piece of work to be performed.

Although she was eager to complete the chapel within her fixed time limit, still there was no impetuosity to motivate haste, resulting in slipshod work. In a letter of May 6, 1882, she remarked that, although she had geared herself to finish the chapel by the feast of Our Lady of Sorrows, nevertheless, the season had not been "favorable for mixing good mortar."

Architect, contractor, and builder, she was determined that this chapel should be the finest that Providence had ever erected. The woodcarving was to be precise and artistic; she did most of it herself. Everything placed in the chapel must be devotional, raising the mind and heart to God whose temple it was. The Pieta which she planned to place above the picture of the Sacred Heart must be a "large one, with good expression; we want it to do good to our people, who understand only what they see." There must be unity, with the lines of the four side altars and miniature sanctuaries converging on the handcarved main altar where Christ was enthroned. And, of course, up above the main altar, to the right, was the long-vowed altar to the Sacred Heart. Surely, He would be pleased. Eventually, some six or seven years later, Mother Joseph was to add to the Sacred Heart altar a gold heart with nine small angel heads symbolic of the adoring choirs.

Night after night as Mother Joseph knelt before the altar, half-planning and half-praying, she was impressed by the chapel's dominant note of compassion. There was the appealing picture of the Sacred Heart embracing the symbolic lamb of errant human nature, and above it was the statue representing the maternal sorrowing of Mary. But had not Christ's compassion climaxed in giving this Virgin Mother to mankind? The chapel, she reflected, was a tribute to the compassion of the God-man for people like herself who had experienced so much mercy, understanding, and care.

The devotions to the Sorrowful Mother and to the Sacred Heart had perfectly blended in her life. Now the two were beautifully represented in this chapel—the resolving of a problem, surely, that had so often perplexed her; but with her spiritual maturity gained through suffering, the two had now perfectly coalesced.

Between the completion of one phase of the work in the chapel and the beginning of another, Mother Joseph made hurried trips to Seattle to measure additions for the rapidly growing Providence Hospital. The Georgetown county farm project of 1877 which had evolved into Providence Hospital at the Moss residence on Fifth Avenue and Madison Street was spreading out, even more so since judge Orange Jacob, Seattle's mayor, had sold his adjacent land to the persistent Mother Joseph.

· · · · · · · ·

Mother Joseph of the Sacred Heart would never forget January 25, 1883. The chapel, the finest work that her mind and hands could produce, was officially and solemnly dedicated to the worship of God. The Pontifical High Mass, the prayerful offering of the building to the Builder, the plaintive chanting of the *Miserere*—were all manifestations of her profound interior joy. Well might this be her *Nunc dimittis.*

The enshrinement of the relics of Saint Victor had a prominent part in the ceremonies of the day. Placed within the lifelike wax figure which she had moulded five years ago, they were borne in a glass casket to the side of the chapel and placed under the altar of Saint Joseph. Both the living in heaven and the living on earth had a rightful share in this temple's worship.

Saint Paul's admonition to Timothy often encouraged Mother Joseph in the midst of her interminable striving.

"Dearly beloved . . . fight the good fight of faith; lay hold on eternal life, whereunto, thou art called. . . ."

The triumphant palm was to be won, but the struggle must be constant. There would probably be no final quick blow of the sword; suffering now seemed so drawn out, so testing to the heart and soul. But the basic love-was that not the purchase money of the martyrs? Saint Victor, pray for us . . .

The dedication year had only half run out when sorrow touched the heart of Mother Joseph of the Sacred Heart, as well as a great portion of the Northwest. It had to do with the passing of a figure whose life and works had been so intimately bound up with the life and works of Providence. The name of Archbishop Francis Norbert Blanchet, who died in Saint Vincent's Hospital in 1883, called up a host of memories for Mother Joseph, memories that had to do with a resolving of vocation, and a forging of the will to action. His many years of laboring in the Northwest had revolutionized the cause of Christ in this land. What would now follow would forever look back to his unfaltering zeal.

As his successor, Archbishop Charles J. Seghers, who was auxiliary with right of succession, so eloquently expressed, "He was the apostle of the coast . . . The seed that was sown here and grew into a large, lofty tree, was sown by his hand; to him under God we owe the flourishing condition of Christianity in this country."

When the beloved archbishop had retired to Saint Vincent's Hospital, Portland, Oregon, he succinctly reviewed his missionary role:

We came to this country accompanied by the late Modeste Demers, the first bishop of Vancouver Island, in 1838, to preach the true Gospel for the first time; and where then we saw nothing but "darkness and the shadow of death," we have now flourishing dioceses and vicariates, prosperous missions, a zealous clergy, fervent communities, and a Catholic people of whom we expect great works and noble deeds. Forget not your old and loving spiritual father; forgive him his mistakes and shortcomings; pray for him that his sins may be forgiven and forgotten when he will be called on to give an account of his stewardship . . .

On July 10, with the sisters assembled for annual retreat at the House of Providence, a solemn service in the chapel commemorated the greatness, holiness, and zeal of the prelate and interceded for him with the Almighty. Occupying a throne in the sanctuary, His Lordship, A.M.A. Blanchet, openly shed tears at the loss of a brother whose partnership in the West had doubled their ties of kin.

Within a year the death of the Reverend J.B.A. Brouillet in Washington, D.C., robbed the community of another staunch friend and benefactor. Mother Joseph reflected that the Sisters of Providence would always remain indebted to this energetic figure whose penetrating vision and diplomatic skill had given security and duration to their Indian schools. Through him, government funds had been allotted them, and protection of their interests assured. From the Indian Bureau in Washington, Father Brouillet had ever remained alert to the red man's plight.

His bureau had been the outcome of a situation in which the Catholic missionaries had found their work being supplanted by the unfriendliness of the Administration of the Commission on Indian Affairs. President Grant's Indian policy of giving all the Indian agencies to "such religious denominations as had heretofore established missions among the Indians," placed many Catholic Indian tribes under non-Catholic control. With controversy continually being whipped up through false propaganda, and the missionaries handicapped in not being able to be always on hand to refute malicious contentions, in 1874 the two prelates of the Northwest had decided to place in Washington, D.C., an authorized representative of the Catholic Indian Missions of Washington.

Mother Joseph's letters to Father Brouillet had always been filled with accounts of the schools, the farm, the cost of maintaining the houses through hard winters and depressions, floods, starving cattle, new crops, and cost of purchases.

I give you these details, good Father, because you are deeply interested in all that pertains to the welfare of Providence . . . Please pray that God may be glorified.

That God may be glorified . . . The desire obsessed Mother Joseph during the years of rapid mission expansion as she became increasingly aware of the fewness of years remaining to her. The missions had made considerable progress despite adversities, and had it not been due to the abiding protection of the Sacred Heart? He had become in a very special manner the Protector of her houses by the erection of the Vicariate of the Sacred Heart in 1884, and seven years later, by the formation of the Province of the Sacred Heart.

The achievements which had marked the years, however, had often fallen short of what she desired. Her keen eye detected blemishes for which she always blamed herself. After the visit to the missions by the Ecclesiastical Superior of the Institute, Mother Joseph received a letter from him appraising the spirit of the Province of the Sacred Heart. She had previously written him, asking him to point out the shortcomings of her province.

Although you did not reprimand us, we have not the temerity to believe that you found us perfect nor our administration; notwithstanding the desire that we have always had to work for the greater glory of God and the propagation of the faith . . . It would be presumption to believe we have not made blunders.

The Very Reverend Canon J. Alfred Archambault had visited all the Providence missions of the Northwest, endeavoring to spur the sisters on to greater holiness, and in some of the missions, as Colville, Coeur d'Alene, and Saint Ignatius, to lessen the friction between the sisters and the Jesuit Fathers. Bitter differences had arisen through misunderstandings and the conflict of diverse personalities. In a letter to Mother Joseph he touched on this matter as well as on another item which grieved her even more.

There were wrongs on both sides; that is admitted by all and they seem now to be disposed to make good as much as possible. We understand that without charity and without union we cannot labor efficaciously to consolidate the work begun and continued through so many sacrifices.   . . . .

A religious charged with responsibility in a community must ask herself at every moment, will such an action or such a decision, or such a work ... turn to the greater glory of the Master? Could it be, perhaps, that without knowing it, I place the good of God after my own, or after that of my community?

When visiting the many houses of the Province of Nisqually which you conduct, I was impressed by the fact that in several it appeared to me that the *sisters seemed preoccupied with temporal affairs and dominated by an exaggerated fear for the future* . . . an injustice and ingratitude toward Him, Who up to the present, has conducted you by the hand and has really spoiled you by His numberless blessings.

From whence comes this marked difference between the Province of Nisqually and that of Montana which is also carrying a debt?

Nevertheless, in Montana there prevails a calm and perfect confidence in Divine Providence. At times, while speaking to me about finances of a nature to cause worry, the sisters did so in a tone dominated by a thought which indicated that God would provide for the conservation and consolidation of His work. *I leave it to you to examine this fact and to look for the explanation of it.*

The bluntness of the remarks must have cut Mother Joseph of the Sacred Heart who at seventy-one years of age was forced to admit that during the birth and growth of Providence in the West she had been its principal guide. Throughout the years her positions had been of such a nature that she had either conducted all the affairs of the Western community, or drawn out its boundaries, advised missions, and laid foundations. There it was—the old demon, Action! Her reply to Father Archambault was selfaccusatory.

Father, it is true; I have extended to my sisters that spirit of servitude. I thank God that the new provinces are not affected by this servile spirit. *Continue to pray for me, so that I may make reparation for the damage to the community* . . . I feel that your letter contained a special grace. I believe that the good God has seen all and knows the sincere desire we had to advance His kingdom in these infidel regions. He will, in His merciful Providence, regulate our affairs. *We should have prayed more and with greater vigilence considered our resources.*

CHAPTER 23

"THANK GOD for this venerable jubilarian. No one can measure the sacrifices she has made, the difficulties of travel she has undertaken, the physical fatigue that has been here in the strenuous labors of erecting the many mission monuments . . . She has never weakened in her zeal to spread the faith of Jesus Christ. She has done more to advance Christianity on these Pacific shores than have many priests in the diocese. Her abilities, her charity have done more for the cause of Christ and His ministers than could be compiled in one volume, were they all written . . ."

"You have said enough—please! interrupted Mother Joseph.

"Not yet . . ." Bishop Junger continued. . . .

The speech had followed his reception program in Mother Joseph's honor, celebrating her fiftieth year of religious life. As Bishop Junger had ceremoniously pontificated at the Mass in the crowded chapel, the thoughts of a half-century had flooded the mind and heart of the pioneer nun. They had to do with the warm sunlight of the Ile Jésus . . . the heaviness of a day in September with the sickening reality of quicklime . . . the damp fog of an early November morning . . . the voice of Monseigneur: ". . . accept this foundation for the greater honor of His Divine Majesty . . ." . . . the nausea of homesickness . . . the shrinking of the body from the demands of the soul . . . and the firm voice of His Lordship, "We considered . . . the care of the poor and the sick . . . contribute greatly to the formation of families . . ." Throughout Father Cronin's eloquent sermon about energetic labor of God's glory, of steadfast service in His cause, the jubilarian saw beyond the chapel walls, out past the wooded barracks, beyond the Columbia, and those mountains.

It had been hard; she would never deny that, although she would never regret it. One doesn't struggle for almost four decades in the West and sum it all up as easy. *Esther Pariseau* had come along with her when she had left the Mother House for the unknown West. She had clung to Mother Joseph. And still one couldn't say that the failures were the failures of Esther Pariseau and the successes were the successes of Mother Joseph of the Sacred Heart. They were all one and who to say which was which . . . The foundation which the Builder had chosen to lay for the Western Providence was not clay-free. It had been a struggle, from within and from without.

The chair on the epistle side of the altar where Bishop Blanchet had been wont to sit was conspicuously vacant. His death just seven years before had turned another chapter in the West and Mother Joseph of the Sacred Heart was not so sure that it would not be the last one for her. Seventy-two years were quite factual. They left no room for fancy.

She looked up out of her reverie and for a moment she saw it all once more. . . . Monseigneur was standing there . . . he was questioning them, and her own voice, vibrant with the daring of youth, speaking of ". . . chastity, poverty, obedience, and . . . to serve the poor for the rest of my life." And the Pariseaux, all gathering around their first fruits to the Lord, and Julie embracing her and hopefully whispering in her ear what she felt she would do. Julie . . . No one would ever know the cost of leaving her. Every visit to Montreal had been an occasion of joy, to visit to exchange thoughts and hopes, and to kneel together in prayer. But even Julie was gone. The Lord had so arranged, in His gentle Providence, that they should be together for those last hours. One month after Mother Joseph had arrived in Montreal, Julie had died.

There had been so many detachments to be cultivated, detachments of all kinds. Her correspondence during the past ten years had given evidence of the internal conflict which had plunged her into barren desolation. Saints have had much to say of the purgation of the soul and of the slow, tedious process by which the spirit is moulded in the unitive way. The mastery of one's soul within the scope of faith and fortitude is a grim achievement. One is forced to walk when impelled to fly; one is condemned to waver when urged to run; one is forced to stand when one's whole being cries out for the need of doing. Ile darkness of the soul is grave; the light is a distant thing.

Obstinacy, which God seems to have left with Mother Joseph as a "sting of the flesh," often blocked her immediate understanding and acceptance of community innovations. Traditional ties were strong in this woman who had stood beside Mother Gamelin in the beginning years of the community. She loved her institute and cherished its progress, but frequently personalities loomed up and Mother Joseph lost sight of the total good. The words of Mother Mary Antoinette in 1894 were blunt but sincere:

> "You are suffering and you must suffer more, although
> we would love to fill your soul with consolation . . ."

Mother Joseph's suffering was silent. She used it to perfect her spiritual life, to become an ardent mendicant at the throne of God's mercy.

To Mother Mary Antoinette she wrote after Reverend Alfred Archambault's visit to the West:

He told me he could see in the works accomplished in the West the effects of Divine Providence, the Finger of God. What more could I desire? There now remains for me only to prepare for eternity, to submerge all in the ocean of Divine Mercy.

This woman who knew the use of tools, the feel of good material, and the marks of an honest tradesman so often complained to God that she had bungled the structure of her spiritual life. In 1894 she humbly confessed to Father Archambault:

A word from you will help, I know to elevate my intellect, which clings to earthly things. It is very necessary, for my poor heart is hungry and longs for the heavenly; but a long life spent in the worries of material things has left me little aptitude for the contemplation of things eternal.

For some time the mystery of my Redemption has singularly attracted me, and accompanies nearly all my thoughts. As I disengage my mind from temporal cares, the adorable Trinity, planning the Redemption, takes its place, and the holy communication with the Immaculate Virgin becoming the Mother of God and my Mother ravishes my soul and fills me with hope. Then the union, the heart-to-heart talks with the God-man, the God-spouse, inebriates me. But these few considerations must be a foretaste of the great things to be meditated and contemplated by the religious soul.

Many of the jubilee festivities were held in the new west wing of the House of Providence. In 1874, when the building had been occupied, there were many who considered it far too large for practical purposes. In 1889 it was already too small to accommodate the works despite the sizable write-up by the *Vancouver Independent*: ". . . a gigantic structure . . . probably the largest brick building in the State of Washington, being three stories high and covering about two acres of ground."

Through the planning and workmanship of Mother Joseph and through the financial backing of the superiors of the Western missions, an extension of one hundred feet had been added in 1891. Throughout the three-day jubilee celebration Mother Joseph was applauded by all for an unparalleled record. Every program presented kept catching up the threads of her life. How Mother Praxedes' presence would have added to these memories. Her death six years ago had left a deep sorrow in the heart of every Sister of Providence in the West. Always ready to listen, console, and advise, her quiet, maternal wisdom had lent stability to the community during the first days in the West, had helped to sustain it through the crucial, growing period.

Just a few days ago Mother Joseph had visited her grave in the Saint James Acres, the new cemetery to which eight years, before the bodies of the sisters who had been buried in DeSmet, Walla Walla, Steilacoom, the Mission Compound, and on the convent grounds had been transferred. Two of her party of 1856 lay in the reserved area near the beautiful crucifixion group, Sister Mary of the Precious Blood and Sister Praxedes of Providence. Mother Joseph had prayed by their graves which lay in the shadow of the lovely crucifix which she herself had carved out of the fir sapling brought from Montreal many years ago. But today Mother Praxedes' absence was especially felt. To Mother Joseph it seemed selfish to be hearing all this eulogizing when it hadn't been merely through her efforts that the community had reached such stature, or that she had lived to see this day.

But the past was called up, and it thrilled her heart. Grief and material losses during the last decade had marked each year in a more definite degree than previously, or was it that she simply could not cope with them as efficiently as she had in her younger days?

The death of Bishop Bourget had left an emptiness in her heart. Mother Amable's letter of 1885 had expressed the magnitude of the community's loss:

> "He was our father, our support, our light—
> since the birth of our humble community."

No one knew that so well as did the beloved Mother Gamelin now dead these many years, and surely, next to her, no one knew so well as did Mother Joseph of the Sacred Heart.

That loss had no sooner struck than it was followed by the death of His Lordship, A.M.A. Blanchet, in February 1887, the passing of a man whose hand had nurtured the growth of Providence and had seen it rise to spread to distant places. His last years at Saint Joseph Hospital had been a seal of benediction on the community. In the midst of the jubilee festivities Mother Joseph felt loneliness. . . .

As the celebrations lengthened out, the pioneer nun often found herself reviewing the last decade of mission growth. Providence was growing, and thus far, her age had been no obstacle to building. It seemed only yesterday that she and Sister Joseph of Arimathea had traveled to Spokane to build Sacred Heart Hospital, Spokane . . . a site of boom prosperity springing up on the dynamic ore of the Coeur d'Alenes. It had seemed a good place to build. Sitting in the *California House*, with the ceaseless ebb and flow of local affairs drumming in their ears, she had explained to Sister Joseph of Arimathea the great advantage of opening a hospital in what was then known as the "metropolis of Eastern. Washington." Its 7,000 population was certain to triple within two or three years; Mother Joseph knew the signs. This was the place to build.

She and her companion had resided in a rough shack near the land purchased for the hospital. It hadn't been comfortable. She remembered many a night when they had used oilcloth coverings to protect themselves from the rain. While Mother Joseph planned the building, good Sister Joseph of Arimathea had made regular trips to the mining camps to solicit contributions.

Before Sacred Heart Hospital had opened in January 1887, Mother Joseph had also traveled to New Westminster to sketch plans for Saint Mary Hospital, to be built on a gift tract of land from Bishop Louis d'Herbomez, O.M.I.

Nor was that all. The little farming community of Sprague was clamoring for a school to serve its growing needs. On December 28, 1886, Saint Joseph Academy had been erected by the pastor, Reverend Aloysius Meuwese. Mother Joseph accepted the mission and remodeled the house for the Sisters of Providence by including a chapel of her own design.

In 1881 Mother Joseph had seen the erection of Providence Saint Amable School in the capital city of Olympia. It had always been the wish of Abbé John Baptist Brouillet that the sisters establish themselves in that Puget Sound city whose educational tone and cultural atmosphere were so conducive to the apostolate of teaching. The school had been the special 25th anniversary foundation made by Mother Amable in her official visit to the West, in answer to the request of Reverend Charles Claessens, pastor. But soon the city was desirous of having a hospital.

Although the land was a gift, the problems of personnel and equipment presented a barrier; however, when she had learned that the Methodist Church was a rival in her apostolate, she lost no time in securing permission from Montreal. The building was erected on the site of the present Capitol buildings. During its construction 1886-87, Mother Benedict Joseph, the first superior of Saint Peter Hospital, toured the logging camps for donations.

In the janitor's shack at the academy, the first patient was lodged.

In 1890 Mother Joseph had traveled to the northernmost shores of Puget Sound, to Port Townsend, the waterfront community of a rich, new country. There on the heights, Saint John's Hospital was built, looking down on blue waters and over a harbor dotted with handsome square riggers.

In the same year she had erected Saint Eugene Indian School in Kootenay, British Columbia, and then one year later, in 1891, she had traveled to eastern Washington to found Saint Elizabeth Hospital in the fast-growing city of Yakima at the request of Reverend Joseph Caruana, S.J. Since 1875 the sisters at Saint Joseph Academy had been nursing in the homes, but now the government was asking for a definite institution for the care of ailing government and city employees who had been engaged in irrigation work. Two years later, there was a new Saint Ignatius Hospital in Colfax.

Thus Providence was spreading out to quiet valleys, raucous waterfronts, pompous capital cities, and thriving industrial centers. Successful they would be in God's good time. She had long ago learned to wait on His designs.

The business of erecting and financing missions had not been her sole concern. Besides crucial depressions and widespread strikes, throughout the country, there had been the constant menace of fires, floods, and epidemics.

Diphtheria had struck down many of the orphans in 1890. Throughout many nights Mother Joseph had sat by the bed of a feverish child. There had been some hours for thought and prayer which had effected in her an ever greater spirit of calm reliance in the face of human helplessness. Doctor David Wall's efficiency and devotedness had brought the epidemic under control.

Three years later it was smallpox which ravaged Portland and Vancouver. Mother Joseph feared for her orphans. It was in February that she received a frantic message from Saint Vincent Hospital, Portland, Oregon. The superior, after secretly nursing a diseased patient who had been unwittingly admitted to the hospital, was infected herself. What was to be done? Would a quarantine be declared? Would their doors be closed?

Mother Joseph placed her concern for the orphans in the Sacred

Heart; she sent a message to bring Sister Mary Conrad to Vancouver just as soon as possible. Hurriedly she swept and prepared the attic of the laundry for the patient. When the five o'clock ferry moored the next morning, Sister Mary Conrad was taken ashore and rushed to the room prepared for her at the House of Providence. There she remained for six weeks in isolation. It was Mother Joseph who, under cover of darkness each night, supplied all the needs of the patient and her nurse. The Sacred Heart had protected them; no other case appeared among the sisters or the orphans.

This last year 1895 was one that Mother Joseph loved to review. Compensation for all the fatigue, sickness, and suffering had been here in the visit of Mother Mary Antoinette, assistant general and directress of education in the community, who came to instruct the teachers of the western provinces, shape school policy, and revise the curriculum.

Mother Joseph knew that the narrowed course of studies had handicapped the sisters and lessened the prestige of their schools. After the pupils had made their first Holy Communion, they were obliged to enter public schools for the completion of their education. Mother Mary Antoinette insisted on revising the course of studies. Certain features of the public school courses were to be incorporated in their new curriculum. Formidable opposition by Father Louis de G. Schram to what he feared might become tantamount to base compromise, and more, almost a soiling of the Faith, did not intimidate Mother Mary Antoinette. She tenaciously adhered to educational principle, eventually convincing the good Father, who was extremely kind and devoted, that algebra, astronomy, and geography were not attacks on the Faith.

Mother Joseph admired the conviction and vision of Mother Mary Antoinette. This was a great contribution to the Faith here in the West. To mould the intellect to a keenness that made truth acceptable was a strong drive toward the security of the Faith—and out of that religious security and certitude what great things could be done for God here in this country! The pioneer nun envisioned in a strong teaching system a power house for religious recruits.

Mother Mary Antoinette had laid down system and organization for the teaching profession. It had been a crying need which Mother Joseph had often expressed in her letters to the Mother House in Montreal. The teachers needed directives and clearly defined goals; otherwise the Providence schools in the West were sorely jeopardized. To standardize the system and guard its objectives, Mother Mary Antoinette appointed two directresses of studies, Sister Mary Wilfrid in Washington and Sister Aristide in Montana.

Besides teaching, there had been other concerns during the past few months. In fact, just last month, the new Saint Vincent Hospital in Portland had been dedicated amid general acclaim. It was a unique transformation from the 1875 wooden structure. Mother Joseph nodded her head in approval as she recalled the boast, "Pride of Portland." It had the finest improvements and modernized equipment that she could afford. She and Sister Mary Theresa, superior, had traveled to the East, inspecting nursing centers and interviewing hospital administrators. The desirable' features had been pooled and channeled into the beautiful Saint Vincent Hospital.

. . . .

As Mother Joseph knelt at Holy Mass the morning following the jubilee activities, her gratitude found adequate expression only through the words of the Psalmist—

> *To thee, O God, my God, I will give praise upon*
> *the harp; why art thou sad, O my soul, and why dost*
> *thou disquiet me?*

> *Hope in God, for I will still give praise to Him:*
> *the salvation of my countenance and my God.*

CHAPTER 24

As THE late autumn days of 1895 pressed on toward the turn of the year, Mother Joseph's growing concern was Bishop Junger's health. Since the spring when she had invited him to occupy the apartments of the late Bishop Blanchet at Saint Joseph Hospital, he had failed noticeably. His face had become wan and haggard; his step, halting. Although Bright's disease was proving a heavy cross, he was determined to carry out his regular pastoral duties. Right now he was up in the Puget Sound region visiting the string of missions along that far-flung expansion of forest and water.

Mother Joseph was not surprised to note the utter exhaustion of the Bishop on his return to Vancouver on December 14. She saw to it that every care was lavished upon this prelate who had been a benefactor of the Providence missions for the past thirtyone years. But on December 26 he suddenly became critically ill. With scarcely enough time to summon Doctor Wall and Father Schram, but with Mother Joseph of the Sacred Heart by his side, the second Bishop of Nisqually died.

The sorrow at his loss was somewhat assuaged when the announcement of the espiscopal successor was made several months later. Mother Joseph was overjoyed. It was to be her "Eddie," the young man whose vocation she had nurtured from the time he was eight until the day he entered the Grand Seminary at Montreal. She knew his family well. Often when shopping in Portland, she had stopped over at the O'Dea home. When the

Saint Vincent Hospital was in the process of erection, it was Eddie who on the dark winter evenings had accompanied Mother Joseph on her inspection tour after the workers had gone home.

The young boy had fidgeted with the lantern as he had confided to Mother Joseph the desire that he had for the priesthood. It was she who had encouraged and advised him. There was so much that a minister of God could do in this Northwest to lift men's aspirations.

Now the announcement that Father Edward J. O'Dea of Saint Patrick's Church in Portland was to be raised to the episcopacy absorbed the thoughts and activities of Mother Joseph as she prepared episcopal robes, embroidered silver slippers, and detailed plans for the great day, September 8, 1896, the consecration date of the third Bishop of Nisqually.

Mother Joseph's last years were reminiscent of traveler making last-minute preparations, filled with anticipation, and yet lingering over the memories of the years that had passed. The seething activity which had surrounded her whole life slackened very little during the last years of that life. Her correspondence was filled with itemized lists of things to be done—houses to be erected, laundries to be renovated, chapels to be redecorated, and clerical garb to be mended.

But other than this "lingering," there seems to be no other reason for her last visit to Montreal in February of 1898. Other trips had been keyed with urgency, marked by numerous material needs for her missions, but this sixth trip to her homeland was her last glimpse of the Mother House . . .

The financial donations, the souvenirs and gifts which she brought home fifteen months later seemed to indicate begging tours. And yet, reluctant to reveal the sentiments of a woman of seventy-five who knew time was running out, her letters showed a restraint and a loneliness. One wonders whether the roads of the Saint Elzear countryside were retraced. In a letter to Vancouver she wrote, "I live in my room. I prefer it to all the beauties of Montreal and the country . . . " There was, despite the solitude, a spiritual restlessness.

When she received word of Father Schram's death in 1898,

Mother Joseph mourned for days. The litany of departed friends, benefactors to her body and soul, was indeed lengthening. Those names she remembered in her evening prayer, when from out the trusting loneliness of her soul she prayed, *De profundis clamavi ad te Domine, Domine exaudi vocem meam.*

When she returned to Vancouver in the late spring, Mother Joseph's spirit seemed rejuvenated. There was the customary air of awe and surprise as she unpacked her boxes. There were chapel linens, a book bindery, a printing press, a mold for Saint Joseph statues, a wardrobe for His Lordship, the Infant of Prague, and materials of lustrous texture for tabernacle veils. Even the unsightly head of Saint Joseph in the chapel hadn't been overlooked. A new head she had moulded in Montreal, to correct what she had always considered a flaw. Not many hours after her return, sounds of the "beheading" issued from behind the screen before the side altar. Groans, sighs, and repentant ejaculations occasionally interrupted the rasping of the saw, admitting the obvious indignity of the act.

Mother Joseph's skill at statuary and waxwork was remarked far outside her family circle. In her basement workshop Mother produced exquisite figures of the Infant Jesus, delicate of feature and line, which are found in many of the Providence foundations —even to this present day

Lightly shorn in not too conspicuous places, Johnnie Steffan"s hair supplied the beautiful golden curls for the wax Infants. Johnnie, together with his sisters, had been placed in the orphanage when he was three years old. At six, his hair was more abundantly cropped to adorn the life- sized wax figure of Saint Lucien in Saint James Cathedral. Despite the copious tears shed by his devoted sisters, Mother Joseph had decided that Johnnie had been a girl long enough.

In the summer of 1899 Mother Joseph was forced to plan, scrape, and beg to procure sufficient funds to keep up the repairs, to furnish the needs of the orphanage during the summer months, and to renovate the chapel. It had long been her wish to install electric lights, lay hardwood floors, and paint the walls and the altar.

During the month of July and August many of the sisters begged throughout the Snake River Valley and the Klickitat country. Besides, right across the street in the military reserve, the 2,600 encamped soldiers who awaited passage to combat duty in Manila, generously contributed to Mother Joseph's fund, and in return for their kindness, she supplied them with fresh vegetables from the farm.

Even during the A.P.A. uprising when a law had been passed prohibiting any solicitors from entering the military reserve, the colonel in charge of the post had emphatically told his men; "The Sisters of Providence are exempted and it is my intention that they will always be well treated here." In fact, this same officer gave orders to his men that in case of any fire or other disaster at the convent, they were to assist without any formal command.

Why this kindly regard for the Sisters of Providence? Might it not be traced back to the first years of the foundation in the West when the sisters had found the unfortunate sitting on their doorstep before there was even a roof for their own heads. Mother Joseph had laid a firm foundation for the social works. No individual was ever barred from her charity or brushed off in the direction of some other benefactor. Night vigils with the sick in their homes, soliciting the services of the garrison doctors for the suffering who could not pay the fees of the local doctors, personal nursing of victims with contagious diseases—all of these constituted her inheritance which was the poor.

In 1891 when the Sisters of the Precious Blood had come to Oregon from Saint Hyacinth, Canada, Mother Joseph had immediately adopted the community and made their needs her concern. The Portland inhabitants had maintained an indifferent attitude toward a cloistered community, neglecting to give them the alms which were their very subsistence. To the poverty-stricken community Mother Joseph sent wagonloads of vegetables and fruit every month. In later years the Sisters of the Precious Blood were to refer to Mother Joseph as their "Providence." With the special permission of their Bishop, the sisters were even permitted to leave their cloister to visit Vancouver where Mother Joseph taught them the art of moulding wax figures, crucifixes, and statues, whereby they could have an assurance of earning bread for their religious family.

. . . .

At the turn of the century Mother Joseph was diligently employed in designing and embroidering a tabernacle veil to be placed in the Cathedral of Montreal, a gift to Archbishop Paul Bruchesi in gratitude to God for Canon Alfred Archambault's recently obtaining the definitive approbation of the Daughters of Charity Servants of the Poor, known as the Sisters of Charity of Providence. To the archbishop she wrote in February:

To me this humble gift is that much more precious since I am indebted to our Mother Foundress for the first lessons which I received in this sort of work. Be not surprised, my Lord, to find in the whole the stamp of advanced age. When one is seventy-seven the fingers lose their suppleness. I would love to believe that Mother Gamelin from high heaven will look with pleasure on this small ornament placed on the tabernacle of the cathedral of Montreal as the result of her zeal to initiate her sisters in all sorts of industries to obtain the means of relieving her dear poor in need.

But my Lord, it is not my intention to write a panegyric of this strong woman whom God gave to the Institute of Providence as Mother. I desire only to express to your Lordship my joy in belonging to the great religious family of Mother Gamelin. Would that it were in my power to tell you my gratitude to God for having prolonged my years until this day when it is given me to hear the homage that is rendered to her memory and her merits. Shall it also be my consolation to see the cause of her beatification introduced jointly with that of our holy Founder, Bishop Bourget? Oh, what an ineffable joy it would be for us all, for me in particular. Then could I say my Nunc dimittis. Until that day I must labor with all my strength to extend the works of charity according to the spirit which they bequeathed to us, and which today makes their glory and highest eulogy.

It was during this centenary year of the birth of Mother Gamelin that Mother Joseph of the Sacred Heart erected her last mission. At the repeated pleas of Bishop Augustine Dontenwill,

O.M.I., the General Council decided to grant this foundation as a centenary offering. Mother Joseph received a wire to proceed to New Westminster to select a suitable location with sufficient acreage for an orphanage. The land purchase, despite prejudice and ill will, was so providentially transacted, and the other building complexities so neatly disposed of that the sisters unanimously asked Mother Joseph to petition Mother Mary Antoinette for the title of Providence Orphanage.

I will be godmother. I ask you, Mother, to grant the favor of this beautiful name, Providence Orphanage. It is probably the last child I will have the honor of holding over the baptismal font—in this instance to honor the memory of our venerable Mother Gamelin in her splendid example of devotion to Divine Providence which we find in almost every page of her beautiful life.

Although this was the last building planned and supervised by the pioneer mother, nevertheless, it in no way lacked expert craftsmanship nor artistic detail. Every evening after the workers went home, Mother Joseph made a meticulous inspection of the day's work, climbing ladders to test the beams or prying under flooring to check the foundation. She was always known as a taskmaster when building was the job on hand. It had to be well done; there was no such thing as tawdry or mediocre construction. She had been known to disassemble brick chimneys not built according to specifications, and to reconstruct them herself from the foundation, to the amazement of the workers who returned the next day.

Her precision and finesse lent a permanency to everything she built, so that in 1953 she was to win the acclaim of the American Institute of Architects as the Pacific Northwest's first architect.

It was this permanency in construction, this stability, which she likewise cherished in the Institute of which she was a member. At every stage of its progress, Mother Joseph rejoiced. When on November 21, the decree of approbation was read aloud, the official sanction of the Holy See on the growing family of Mother Gamelin and Monseigneur Bourget, she, humbly kneeling with the rest of the community, rejoiced, saying, "At last Rome has spoken!"

The modifications issued by Mother Mary Antoinette following the approbation decree were received by Mother Joseph in a marvelous spirit of faith and filial obedience. Among other points were included the five years of temporary vows, the fusion of the tertiary sisters with the community, and the admission of the young professed to the community immediately following pronouncement of their vows. Mother Joseph manifested no surprise nor displeasure. "The few changes which you have made do not surprise me. On the contrary, they seem to be the natural consequence in the guidance of the Institute as yet in its formation period." The Rule was holy. Christ's authority had no gaps; it had been delegated–Rome, Montreal, the missions of Providence. "What now remains for us to do, but to embrace it (the Rule) with all our hearts and put it into practice with respect and the greatest possible perfection!"

In an age of individualism so characteristic of the nineteenth and twentieth centuries, the lesson of Mother Joseph's harmonious coupling of initiative with reverence for tradition stands out in bold relief. Her personal acquaintance with the founders was no doubt the support for tradition, while the democratic spirit of faith and expansion rested on her mission to a pioneer, enterprising Northwest where an opportunity overlooked was often a future lost.

While in Montreal at the close of Mother Mary Godfrey's term as superior general, Mother Joseph wrote to her superior in Vancouver:

What sorrow for all when the moment arrives for the strong woman, Mother Godfrey, to be discharged! She directed the Institute with wisdom and caused our works to expand in the way of justice. I say justice, for it is justice to our holy founders to nourish, to develop, to increase the works they had in view at the time of our foundation.

She knew of no "comfortable" way to nourish the works of Mother Gamelin. Had not Monseigneur Bourget said that they as daughters of the Mother of Sorrows must find their rightful places with her at the foot of the cross? Writing to Mother Cecile, assistant general, in 1897, she said:

Oh, if I were young! We would do much good on a mission where there would be misery, and where it would be necessary to make sacrifices. Nowadays we look for too much comfort in this land which offers so much . . .

It was this spirit which shaped her outlook on mission foundations. Overwork, financial worries, depleted personnel usually were then, as now, the major factors in maintaining conservatism in considering a new mission. Mother Joseph never considered these as points of negative value, but she did maintain that pointing up only these was not the complete picture. The Son of God had other things to say about evangelical labor, and these should be also considered by religious doing His work. Hardheaded practicality allowed no room for reliance on Divine Providence, but were they not *Sisters of Providence?*

When the acceptance of a hospital in Oakland, California, was proposed, Mother Joseph expressed her opinions on the subject in a letter to Mother Mary Antoinette in 1901.

. . . I have no intention of making my opinion prevail, for you are enlightened; to me belongs submission. Before God I have only this to say, that for the sisters of the Oregon Province, it will not be without sacrifices that they open this mission.

You know that by the grace of God our sisters are capable and very devoted in the care of the sick and understand the direction of a hospital. Our Saint Vincent's today is the admiration of all visitors. . . . At present our sisters of Portland have six novices who will make their vows in a year . . .

. . . *if in making a foundation we wait until we do not have to deny ourselves, we shall never take on a new work, for we shall never be without work.* In one of my visits to Montreal, Monseigneur Bourget said: "Your sisters complain that they have so much work; so much the better; if that is their only subject for complaint, all will go well." The Catholic influence which dominates the city seems to me the advantage of a mission in Oakland. It will furnish us with good English-speaking subjects, and they are so much needed.

I believe, dear Mother, that our holy Founder and our venerated Mother Gamelin have cast an eye of approval on the selections which have marked the foundations you have made to mark the centenary. You have shown preference toward the poorest and most self-denying. How often I heard Monseigneur Bourget say, "Serve the poor by preference, but do not neglect the, rich, because their souls are often more neglected than those of the poor." We often discover this in our large hospitals. So it is, dear Mother. Do not refuse Oakland . . . No doubt in Oakland everything will not look too rosy, but as in other places, Providence will provide.

In March, 1901, Mother Joseph of the Sacred Heart put aside all thoughts of repairs and debts, and under the direction of Reverend A. A. Ragaru, S.J., entered her last retreat.

CHAPTER 25

O<small>NE MONTH</small> after her retreat, Mother Joseph of the Sacred Heart wrote of her spiritual life and her physical sufferings to Mother Mary Antoinette:

What a delight is mine, Mother, to belong to a religious family which is so well organized. All this has been accomplished in my old age when I am at the vestibule of heaven where I shall find all those who have begotten us in religion. And I must tell you this, since a good daughter conceals nothing from her mother. Jesus favors me beyond anything I can express. Please tell our worthy Father Superior (Father Archambault) that his wish for the union of my soul with Our Lord is being accomplished. *Now more than ever I enjoy that total abandonment of my interests into His divine hands.* I do not know what that good father will say of this fusion of hearts and of tender reproaches of the Divine Spouse who presents Himself laden with riches and spiritual gifts ready, to share them with me abundantly as spouse with spouse when I but make myself attentive to the outpourings of His Heart.

You know that I made my retreat. At the outset, scarcely was I in the presence of the Blessed Sacrament when, without expecting it, I was drawn into one of those heart to heart embraces, and was so submerged that I thought I would melt with love. I thanked Him, and then said to myself—Why should I not renew this act each time I am before the tabernacle? I must avow, Mother, that ever since my entry into religious life, I have made it a habit to pause before the chapel door whenever I pass it, and beg our Lord to him me in His Divine Heart, and send a ray of light into mine. He has given me more than a ray; He has given me a flame, and made fruitful my striving for union. In order not to abuse His kindness, to the best of my ability each time, I ask His pardon for the past and beg the grace to serve Him better in the future.

I rendered an account of my conscience to the retreat master, and when I mentioned that despite this state of things I am neither a soul of prayer nor of mortification nor of silence, he told me not to dwell on what I am, but to strive to perform all my actions, prayers in a spirit of reparation, because reparation supposes sacrifice. *And sacrifice is so good for me.*

I try to profit by the sufferings occasioned by the loss of my eye; I do not say this to complain, but they are acute, day and night. The doctor finds the cause rather obscure. They can do nothing for my right eye; but up to the present, they have succeeded in preserving the sight of the left eye, at least sufficient for use, as this letter tells you. All the right side of my face is swollen, inflamed, and painful. I expect that this will finish in ulceration.

If God wants it to be so, why should I not want it? To date it has not prevented me from doing a little work. I realize that this trial is an excellent means of acquiring conformity to the Will of God, to obtain which is all I ask. Although the operation on the glands seems to have been a complete success, this flare-up may be the recurrence of the disease. There must be something to detach me from this life, which in my seventy-ninth year is still very dear to me.

Mother Joseph's first reference to her physical sufferings had been in December of 1900. At that time she had a premonition of paralysis, as the pain in her face was so intense.

Do not be alarmed, Mother. That is what God wants. Otherwise, my health is good, and I am able to work almost as well as in my young days, perhaps too much, and not enough at my sanctification. . . .

To Father Alfred Archambault she wrote her understanding of this cross:

May the good God grant me the grace to accept this trial as a proof of His love. I am not generous enough to purify my conscience by mortification. He does it Himself, purifying it by corporal suffering, which I scarcely had known before this sickness. . . . As to the sacrifice of my life, I hope to make it with a good heart when it pleases the Divine Spouse to come for me.

The winter of 1901 was spent in the infirmary where Mother Joseph quieted her activity and passed the hours in prayer. Around her bed she often gathered a few orphans to pray with her. Always so aware of the limited duration of attentive prayer in little ones, she kept beside her bed a small box of candy as a treat for those who prayed the rosary with her.

The orphans always loved Mother Joseph of the Sacred Heart. Very rarely had she been seen working on the grounds or on the farm without an orphan tagging along. Frequently, in the days when she was in active service, she would go to fetch two or three orphans, take them up to the chapel, and lead the Way of the Cross, flanked by the little tots who stood in awe of this big sister who could do so many things and tell so many nice stories. It had been Mother Joseph's means of obtaining very urgent needs. And as she would crowd down the aisle with the children milling about her, she would say aloud for their benefit, "Sixth station: Veronica wipes the face of Jesus with her handkerchief and He gives her His picture."

Her little friends loved her. She could laugh with them and enjoy their pranks. Her famous sabots, which Mother Joseph kept on the porch in readiness for rainy weather trips around the ground, afforded the children many games and capers. They would take turns shuffling in them; up and down they would clatter on the porch. And when hazelnut time came, they used the shoes to crack the nuts. . . .

And now their thin voices stammered along without Mother Joseph's firm voice. They missed her out in the yard. Wasn't she ever going to get up and tend the farm again, and work in the carpenter shop?

. . . .

The recollection of the sufferings which had marked the early days of the foundation emerged from the letter which she received from Sister Blandine of the Holy Angels, her companion of foundation, now a patient at the Mother House.

Whatever be your painful sufferings every day I beg our Lord by the intercession of Our Mother of Sorrows, that He will put into your heart a part of that sublime fiat of resignation and patience, of which

He has given so touching an example in His sorrowful passion.
. . . dear Mother Joseph, you should be well advanced in your
preparation. A grand jubilee, the remarkable surrendering of your
accounts in Canada and Vancouver–all this says enough, in your favor;
you are not unprepared for the big journey.

While awaiting our reunion in heaven let us pray for one another.
Pardon all of my past and believe my sincere affection . . .

Yet, the crosses of the past seemed as nothing in comparison
with her present affliction. She had been young then; she had
been able to lose herself in work. Her energy then had seemed as
ever-flowing and inexhaustible as the undaunted Columbia River.
But now there was so little strength to accept the Cross. Father
Ragaru's letter she kept close to her, for the advice was timely and
outlined, her last scope of action for the Sacred Heart:

"With your suffering eye look kindly on Him who allows you to
suffer. You gain more merit by suffering than by great action. You
have always acted well. Now try to suffer well."

When she had answered his letter she was practically in a state
of physical helplessness.

Now I am incapable of doing anything, Reverend Father, except
prepare myself for my approaching end. Alas, the nearer death approaches the less prepared I am to meet my Divine Spouse, in Whom,
nevertheless, I place all my confidence.

You spoke to me, Reverend Father, of the prayer of Saint Ignatius,
"Take and receive, O Lord" to which your superior general has added
a particular line for the hour of death. If you have this prayer close
at hand I would be happy to have a copy. What helped the saints to
gain entrance into eternity may be a means for me also.

With the turn of the year her sufferings intensified. Sleepless
nights, pain-filled days left visible scars on the sufferer's face. Although the brain tumor had twisted her face with excruciating
pain, there remained a remarkable tranquillity in her eyes.

On the eighth of January the sisters gathered around her bed
as Bishop Edward O'Dea gave Mother Joseph the Last Sacraments. Shakily, but firmly, she, Esther Pariseau, in religion Sister
Joseph of the Sacred Heart, renewed her vows, and then looking
at the kneeling sisters, spoke words of pardon and of being par-

doned for her many faults. "Sisters, I ask your pardon for all the grief I have caused you. On my part I forgive with all my heart whatever sorrow you may think you have caused me. . . . I recommend myself to your prayers. I am happy to die in the community.... I have always loved my community. Tell my higher superiors that I do not regret having spent my strength in the works of the Institute. . . ."

The legacy which the pioneer nun then left to her community was an elaboration of the virtue half-uttered by Mother Gamelin as she died fifty-one years before. "My dear sisters, allow me to recommend to you the care of the poor in our houses, as well as those without. Yes, take care of them. Do not be afraid of so doing. Help them . . . and I assure you that you will have no regrets. Never say that such does not concern you, or let others see to them. *Sisters, whatever concerns the poor is always our affair . . .*"

Friends constantly came to the door inquiring about Mother Joseph's condition, or asking if they might have a last glimpse of her. For eleven days she remained in a dying condition. Occasionally she would rally and ask the sisters to come and sing *O Douce Providence.* Then sinking back into great pain, she would whisper, "My God, may Your Holy Will be done. I accept and submit to all Your fatherly hand gives me. I would not exchange my sufferings, nor lessen them. I desire whatever is your good pleasure, my Jesus, for the salvation of my soul . . ."

On January eighteenth she grew worse. Interrupting a pastoral visitation, Bishop O'Dea hastened -to the bedside of the dying nun. When Mr. J. B. Blanchet, her co-builder, came for a last word, Mother Joseph recognized him. "Come in . . . come in, my friend, Blanchet."

On the feast of the Holy Name of Jesus, at the end of the Benediction services in the chapel, Mother Joseph of the Sacred Heart died. It was January 19, 1902. She was in her seventy-ninth year of life.

The clear-toned bell in the cupola of the House of Providence rang out in honor of her passage to Life, as the special funeral service began in the chapel on January 22. Its reverberations were caught up in the Cathedral's somber knells on January 23, as hundreds gathered with Bishop O'Dea to pay their respects to the life and death of Mother Joseph of the Sacred Heart.

. . . .

Mother Mary Antoinette's letter to the Community expressed the grief of all the sisters. It had a sincerity and insight which could come only from a woman who had probably been one of the most understanding friends that Mother Joseph ever had in the Community.

A life precious to us all has just dosed. The death of Mother Joseph of the Sacred Heart has cast a shadow of mourning over all the Institute; and with the feelings of regret that rise in our hearts are mingled sentiments of a just and profound admiration.

For had not that dear Mother been the valiant woman par excellence and the perfect model of a Sister of Charity, with her soul of flame, and her will of tempered steel! God had endowed her with varied talents rarely found in a woman. She excelled not only in feminine arts, from the most ordinary to the finest, but she was also skilled in works considered the domain of men.

She had the characteristics of genius: incessant works, immense sacrifices, great undertakings; and she never counted the cost to self. She exercised an extraordinary influence in the Church of the West. She supported and protected the priest and the missionary, and besides, had her own personal apostolate-an insatiable desire to spend and sacrifice herself for the salvation of souls. Hence her noble ambition for the continual extension of our field of action, and her ardor for the progress of the works. Mother Joseph was truly the instrument of Divine Providence for the accomplishment of great designs on our Institute. And these far-off missions benefited for close to fifty years by the skill and intelligence of this valiant missionary.

She never faltered in her blind submission to legitimate authority . . . Mother Joseph had the defects of her virtues; but these failings were a means of increasing her merit, when with childlike candor she humbled herself for her faults. And these latter were, after all, but the luxuriant outgrowth of the extraordinary aptitudes with which God had enriched her.

How consoling it would have been to be at her bedside, as you, dear sisters. You received her last words. Treasure them as the precious legacy of a dying mother, whose only disquietude was that you might lose the spirit of our works.

We shall often think of her virtues, and that thought will be a healing balm in our common sorrow. . . .

The first line of Canon Alfred Archambault's letter of condolence summed up the significance of Mother Joseph of the Sacred Heart:

In her the Western missions lose their foundress, their guide, their support. God alone knows what all those missions owe to Mother Joseph. By her indefatigable zeal in extending far and wide her field of action and influence, by her inviolable attachment to the Mother House, its spirit and its traditions, by her generosity in sacrifice, by her astonishing activity in the accomplishment of works of mercy, by her courage and energy in the face of difficulties and obstacles; finally, by her resignation to the Holy Will of God in her hour of trial, especially in the intense sufferings of the last months of her life, Mother Joseph will remain in the history of the Institute as one of its most remarkable members.

. . . Let us continue the works she has begun. . . .

Thousands of years before, David the Psalmist had cried out . . .

> *Like a tree growing by the rivers of*
> *water . . . his leaf shall not wither*
> *and whatsoever he doeth shall prosper.*

The Bell and the River

Errata

Re: Steamer Brother Jonathan…Page 100:

The author states that the sisters traveled from San Francisco to Vancouver, Washington Territory in December 1856 aboard the steamer Brother Jonathan but with further research we believe it was more likely the steamer Columbia.

The error occurs from a conflict in sources. The original journal kept by the five foundress sisters at the time of their journey to Vancouver states that they traveled on the Columbia. "We resumed our voyage [taking] the last steamer, called Columbia, that was going to Portland, a city ten leagues from Vancouver, where our residence is." The Brother Jonathan is first mentioned in the Providence Academy, Vancouver chronicles that were actually written in 1884, 28 years after the sisters' arrival. "A few years later [after the sisters' arrival in Vancouver], our steamer, Brother Jonathan, perished there* with all of its passengers." [*Even here the historical context is not correct because the previous sentence in the chronicles refers to the bar of the Columbia River. Neither ship sank on the bar: the Brother Jonathan sank off the coast of California.]

Research of coastal steamers shows that the Columbia was a regularly scheduled liner between California and Oregon from 1851-1862. The Brother Jonathan ran between New York and Chagres (later Aspinwall) from 1851-1852 and from 1852-1856 between San Francisco and San Juan del Sur, Nicaragua. In 1857 it was renamed Commodore and then served west coast routes. Later, the Commodore reverted to its original name, Brother Jonathan, until its sinking in 1865. When the chronicles were written in 1884 the name Columbia could have been confused with Commodore and the sister annalist recorded the name by which it was known at its sinking, Brother Jonathan.

Re: American Institute of Architects award…Page 258:

It has been published in many books and articles that the American Institute of Architects (AIA) declared Mother Joseph the first architect in the Northwest in 1953. This is incorrect.

The AIA did hold its 1953 national convention in Seattle, Washington. During the meeting newspaper articles in Seattle and Yakima, Washington alluded to the opinions of individual architects which were later misread as an official action of the American Institute of Architects. In fact, a thorough search of records and minutes in the AIA Archives reveals that there was no official discussion of Mother Joseph nor a formal declaration of her status as the region's first architect. This is not to say Mother Joseph should not be honored for her role in designing and supervising construction of hospitals and schools. Her skills and activities in the field are well documented through chronicles, correspondence, oral history, and newspaper reports of the time, and have been acknowledged by architectural historians. So, while it is not correct to say that she was acclaimed by the AIA as the first architect in the Northwest, it is definitely appropriate to state that Mother Joseph "is recognized as one of the first architects of the Northwest."

Loretta Zwolak Greene
Archivist, Mother Joseph Province
November 2005

The BELL
and the RIVER

By Sister Mary of the
Blessed Sacrament McCrosson

Mother Joseph yearned for a beautiful, cleartoned bell—a bell for the frontier villagers to set their clocks by, a retiring bell with quiet tones to announce bedtime to the village children. And through her life flowed the mighty Columbia River, her "highway" for trips to far-flung missions.

This is the biography of a great and unusual woman who made outstanding contributions to the winning of the West. Mother Joseph and four other young Sisters of Providence arrived at Vancouver in the Territory of Washington at the height of the gold rush days in 1856. They came to minister to the needy, but found not even a cabin to accommodate them. Not daunted, Mother Joseph, with hammer and saw, set up planks for beds and made straw mattresses in an unused attic. From this humble beginning was to spring a fourstory brick building covering two acres of ground.

Mother Joseph and the Sisters dedicated themselves to the task of establishing schools, missions, homes for the aged, hospitals for the unfortunate, and orphanages. In her role of leadership Mother Joseph faced suffering, hardship, and a continual struggle for financing. But her work forged ahead steadily and the institutions she founded became an enduring heritage for ensuing generations of followers.

A constant need for funds forced the Sisters to travel afar on begging tours into the mining areas of Idaho and Montana and even to South America. Sometimes they could secure only a few hundred dollars, but once returned with a princely $10,000, a tribute to their persuasiveness. From these unflagging efforts spread works of mercy and hope which now reach from Alaska to Lower California and across Idaho and Montana.

Mother Joseph is now recognized by the West Coast Lumberman's Association as the first Northwestern artist to work in the medium of wood. In 1953, fifty-one years after her death, the American Institute of Architects acclaimed her as the Pacific Northwest's first architect. Trained in the art of design and work in wood by her carriage-maker father in Quebec, she gave to the young country architectural designs far ahead of anything else of that time in the West.